STUDIES IN THE ATONEMENT

Dr. Robert A. Morey

Christian Scholars Press
1350 E. Flamingo Rd. Suite 97
Las Vegas, NV. 88119

Printed in the United States of America

Dedicated to

ANNE

Who is not only my beloved wife,

but my best friend.

About the Author

Dr. Morey is the Executive Director of the Research and Education Foundation and the author of over forty books, some of which have been translated into French, German, Italian, Polish, Finnish, Dutch, Spanish, Norwegian, Swedish, and Chinese. He is an internationally recognized scholar in the fields of philosophy, theology, comparative religion, the cults and the occult. For more information on his books, audiotapes, and videotapes, write to: The Research and Education Foundation, P.O. Box 7447 Orange, CA 92863 (1-800-41-Truth). He has also written:

The Trinity
Fearing God
Satan's Devices
The Islamic Invasion
The Truth About Masons
Death and the Afterlife
Battle of the Gods
How to Keep Your Faith While in College
The New Atheism and the Erosion of Freedom
An Introduction to Defending the Faith
An Analysis of the Hadith
When Is It Right to Fight?
How to Answer a Jehovah's Witness
How to Answer a Mormon
Reincarnation and Christianity
Horoscopes and the Christian
Worship Is All of Life
How to Keep Your Kids Drug-Free
An Examination of Exclusive Psalmody
Is Allah Just Another Name for God?
Here Is Your God
The Reformation View of Roman Catholicism
Is the Sabbath for Today?
The Dooyeweerdian Concept of the Word of God
The New Life Notebook, Vol. I
The New Life Notebook, Vol. II
The Mood-god Allah in the Archeology of the Middle East

Preface

With his usual reliable research, Dr. Morey expertly unfolds the drama of the Cross in a very comprehensive manner. As a result, we are enabled theologically and practically to better understand Calvary with apostolic vision.

Morey's treatment of the doctrine of justification is much needed today. He demonstrates the forensic or judicial nature of justification with clear scriptural proof, listing over twenty references illustrating the forensic nature of justification. Dr. Morey is absolutely right when he says, "If we are going to witness a true Reformation or revival in our day, we must preach the biblical doctrine of justification. The great themes of salvation must be thundered once again."

This book reveals *why* the human race needs to be justified and *how* justification is the backbone of the Gospel. *Studies in the Atonement* shows how a Holy God is able to be just and yet justify sinners at the same time. The biblical meaning of the word "justification" is demonstrated step-by-step: its ground, its means and its effect.

There are many helpful charts found in the book which clarify and illustrate different aspects of the atonement. They are great teaching aids which any pastor or Sunday School teacher can use to great effect. The inclusion of prayers and hymns makes reading this book an exercise in worship. It touches the heart as well as exercises the mind.

The Trinitarian emphasis of this book is refreshing. Salvation is presented as something planned by God the Father, accomplished by God the Son, and applied by God the Holy Spirit, Blessed God Three in One.

Studies in the Atonement will pave the way for personal and church renewal if we only believe and then act upon the glorious Gospel truths presented within its pages. GRACE ALONE, CHRIST ALONE, FAITH ALONE is our firm foundation. I give this book my highest recommendation.

Prof. Colin P. Akridge
West Angeles Bible College

Introduction

It is popular in our day to state that the Bible is the inspired record of the unfolding drama of the history of redemption. And if we take the Bible seriously, this description of the Holy Scriptures is true. The Scriptures record the history of God's mighty acts and words. They also record the various responses of saints and sinners to this manifold revelation of God. But we must not be content with a mere assertion of the historical character of the Word of God. We must seek to understand the nature and purpose of the history of redemption.

Upon contemplation, it is obvious that the history of redemption was not spun out of chance. Neither did it unfold according to the dictates of blind fate. Instead, it is clear that the history of redemption has a definite theme and message. This central theme concerns the person and work of the Lord Jesus Christ for the history of redemption is actually the history of the Redeemer. In the Lord Jesus Christ the history of redemption finds its meaning, unity, power and climax "for from Him and through Him and to Him are all things" (Rom. 11:36).

The Old Testament is the record of the history of redemption in that it records all the various ways in which God prepared His people for the coming of Christ. The types, shadows, symbols and ceremonies of the Old Testament were all prophetic in character and were fulfilled in the person and work of the Lord Jesus. For "was it not necessary for the Christ to suffer these things and to enter into His glory? And beginning with Moses and all the prophets, he explained to them the things concerning Himself in all the scriptures" (Luke 24:26-27). Regardless if one reads the Law (John 5:46) or the Prophets (Acts 8:32-35), the central theme and message of the Old Testament is the person and work of the Lord Jesus Christ.

The New Testament also concerns the history of redemption. But in contrast to the Old Testament, the New Testament deals with the manifestation and explanation of the person and work of the Redeemer. It records in detail the birth, life, death, resurrection, ascension and session of Christ. It explains the nature of the salvation which Jesus Christ accomplished. Thus the entire New Testament finds its central meaning and theme in the person and work of Christ. The principle writer of the New Testament "determined to know nothing among you except Jesus Christ, and him crucified" (I Cor. 2:2).

Once we have seen that both the history of redemption and the Scriptures (which alone record that history) have the person and work of Christ as their central theme, we are warranted to ask, "What was the central concern of Jesus Christ in His work?"

The Scriptures reveal that the central concern and mission of Christ was to accomplish the work of atonement. "For thou shalt call His name Jesus, for He shall save His people from their sins. For the Son of Man has come to seek and to save that which was lost. It is a worthy statement, deserving full acceptance, that Christ Jesus came into the world to save sinners" (Matt. 1:21; Luke 19:10; I Tim. 1:15). Jesus Christ did not come as a Marxist revolutionist or as a humanistic moralist. He came to accomplish a saving work for sinners.

This line of thought brings us to the following conclusions:

1. To the degree we understand the atonement is to the degree we understand the person and work of Christ.
2. To the degree we understand the person and work of Christ is to the degree we understand the Scriptures.
3. To the degree we understand the Scriptures is to the degree we understand the history of redemption.
4. Therefore, ignorance of the Biblical doctrine of the atonement means ignorance of the work of Christ, the Scriptures and the history of redemption.

These conclusions force upon us the importance and necessity of studying the Biblical doctrine of the atonement. The atonement should be the constant object of study, worship and praise by all the people of God and not just by professional theologians. To a great degree, the low level of sanctification in the 20th Century Church is due to the appalling ignorance concerning the saving work of Jesus Christ. May God use this study to cause the light of the person and work of Christ to shine into the hearts of the people of God. To Him be the glory forever and forever.

We would like to acknowledge from the outset that we have freely built upon the classic works on the atonement from past and present authors. Since our studies on the atonement were developed over many years in the context of preaching and teaching in a local church, it is impossible to give individual credit for the many insights gained from different authors. Also since these studies were delivered in the context of a local church, no apology is given for the deliberate homiletical and experiential thrust of these studies.

Contents

Part I

Part II

Part III

Appendix

CHAPTER 1

Guiding Principles

Having established the importance and necessity of studying the saving work of Christ, it would be helpful to lay down several guiding principles. These principles will help us to derive greater benefit from our study.

   I. The doctrine of the atonement is exclusively a subject of special revelation and thus we are entirely dependent upon the Scriptures.

Christianity is unique and singular in its concept of the atonement. We will search history in vain to find another religion which developed the concept of God becoming man to die as the sinner's substitute. False religion always views man as seeking God and providing for his own salvation while Christianity views God as seeking man and providing salvation for him. The Scriptures view men as guilty rebellious sinners who are running from God as fast as they can (Rom. 1:18).

Thus we cannot look to man's reason, feelings or experiences to tell us the truth about salvation. We will trust only in the infallible Written Word of God for "all Scripture is inspired of God and is profitable for doctrine, reproof, correction, for instruction in righteousness" (II Tim. 3:16). "To the law and to the testimony, if they speak not according to the word it is because there is no light in them" (Isa. 8:20).

   II. Approach the doctrine of the atonement as the solution to your problems and not as the problem itself.

1

The saving work of Christ is God's answer to man's greatest questions. How can a man be just before God? How can sins be forgiven? How can spiritually dead sinners be made alive? How can we escape the just punishment of eternal perdition? Who takes the initiative in salvation? Is salvation all of God or does it involve the works of man? The answers to such questions are found in the Biblical doctrine of the atonement.

Perhaps a word could be said here to theological students. Beware of being "problem-centered." Too often theological studies are designed to give as many problems to the student as possible. He is taught "the problem of the existence of God," "the problem of the inspiration and text of the Bible," "the problem of preaching," "the problem of evil," etc. It is apparent that some seminary and Bible college professors are excellent in presenting problems but weak in giving solutions! This results in weak, undecided ministers who can't say anything dogmatically to their people. The people in turn are not doctrinally strong and are soon "tossed here and there by waves, and carried about by every wind of doctrine, by the trickery of men, by craftiness in deceitful scheming" (Eph. 4:14).

Don't be sold short in your theological education by being problem-centered. Seek the Biblical solution to each issue. Study until you are convinced that you know what the Word of God teaches. Then preach and teach it with the boldness of the Holy Spirit. Never rest until you have an answer to your questions.

III.   Approach the doctrine of the atonement in an experimental manner.

We must not be content with a mere intellectual grasp of the atonement. If our study of this precious truth of God's Word does not spiritually profit us in terms of salvation or sanctification, we have missed the underlying purpose of the study. We are dealing with the suffering and death of the Son of God. We should visualize afresh the bleeding sacrifice made on our behalf.

The test of our understanding is to measure our love to Christ. Experimentally we should grow in our devotion and love to Christ as a result of this study.

IV.   To see the true nature of sin, look to the cross of Christ.

To see sin as it really is, contemplate what it cost to remove it. If we had fallen into a deep pit, we could tell how deep we had fallen by the length of the rope let down to save us. In the same way, we can only understand the depths of depravity into which sin has brought us by the lengths to which God must go to redeem us.

God Himself had to die a bloody death at the hands of wicked sinners. To see the awful suffering and to hear the awful cry, "My God, my God, why have Thou forsaken Me?" reveals how awful sin must be in the sight of God. Don't look at sin to see sin's true nature. Look at what it did to Christ on the cross. Experimentally, we should grow in our hatred of sin as a result of the study.

> Ye who think of sin but lightly,
> Nor suppose the evil great
> Here may view its nature rightly,
> Here its guilt may estimate.
>
> Mark the sacrifice appointed
> See who bears the awful loss;
> Tis the Word, the Lord's anointed,
> Son of Man and Son of God.*

V.   Take the simple step of faith with each new understanding of the atonement.

True Biblical faith involves assent and trust as well as knowledge. It is not enough to know *about* the atonement, you must assent *to* and trust *in* the saving work of Christ. A new or deepened understanding of every aspect of the atonement should be followed by the affirmation of the heart, "Lord, I believe." The doctrine of the atonement should provide much fuel for praise and many arguments to be used in prayer. Seek to appropriate and to use your Biblical knowledge in your life everyday.

With these basic principles in mind, we can now begin our study of the saving work of Christ.

---

*"Stricken, Smitten, and Afflicted" by Thomas Kelly, 1804.

CHAPTER 2

The Necessity of the Atonement

I. Its Legitimacy.

Was the saving work of Christ necessary for man's salvation? Can God merely forgive and forget? Did God have at His disposal an infinite number of ways to save sinners? Or was the work of Christ the only possible way of salvation?

Such questions as these are often dismissed by modern humanistic theologians as being irrelevant and highly speculative. The necessity of the atonement was an important issue in the Middle Ages and during the Scholastic Protestant period following the Reformation. But today the issue is ignored.

We would agree that it is time to throw out speculative theological topics which are irrelevant. But before we act, we should search the Scriptures to see if our forefathers had Biblical grounds for their concern.

When we turn to the Scriptures, we soon discover that *the question of the necessity of the atonement arises out of a concrete exposure to the Word of God.*

> O my Father; *if it be possible, let this cup pass from me:* nevertheless, not as I will, but as thou wilt (Matt. 26:39).

> The Son of Man *must* suffer . . . and be rejected . . . and killed, and after three days rise again (Mark 8:31, cf. Luke 9:22; 24:7).

5

But first he *must* suffer many things and be rejected of this generation (Luke 17:25).

As Moses lifted up the serpent in the wilderness, even so *must* the Son of Man be lifted up (John 3:14).

The Son of Man *must* be lifted up (John 12:34).

For as yet they knew not the Scripture, that he *must* rise again (John 20:9).

Neither is there salvation in any other: for there is *none other name* under heaven given among men whereby we *must* be saved (Acts 4:12).

Opening and alleging, that Christ *must needs* have suffered, and risen again from the dead (Acts 17:3).

For where a testament is, there *must* also of *necessity* be the death of the testator (Heb. 9:16).

Without shedding of blood is *no* remission. *It was therefore necessary* . . . the heavenly things themselves (purified) with better sacrifices than these (Heb. 9:22-23).

It is obvious even to the casual reader that there is some kind of necessity attributed to the saving work of Christ. Regardless if you read the Gospels, the Acts or the Epistles, you will find necessity attributed to the atonement. *To ask, therefore, what kind of necessity must be attributed to the atoning work of Christ is to ask a Biblical question.* In that it is Biblical it is a legitimate, relevant and important question to ask for "all of scripture is inspired and is profitable" (II Tim. 3:16).

II. Its Definition.

Much carefulness needs to be observed when defining the nature of the "necessity" of the atonement.

There are two distinct aspects of the atonement which have been called "necessary." Some apply "necessity" to the *motive* behind the atonement, while others apply it to the *means* employed to bring it about. The failure to distinguish between motive and means has led to much confusion.

The motive of the atonement deals with the question as to whether or not it was necessary for God to save man. Was God bound by His own qualities of love, mercy and pity to save sinners? Did man's significance as image-bearer or his helpless state make it necessary for God to save man? Or, could God have left all sinners to judgment and eternal perdition? Was salvation a free choice of God?

The means of the atonement deals with the question of *how* God saves sinners. Once God decided to save sinners, was there an infinite number of ways and means by which He could do this? Was the work of Christ just one possible means among many? Or did the work of Christ constitute the only possible way to save sinners?

The following diagram illustrates all the possible positions on the necessity of the motives and means of salvation.

Position one states that there was nothing in God that made it necessary for Him to save man and that Christ's death was not necessary because God could save sinners in an infinite number of ways.

Position two states that while it was not necessary for God to save anyone, Christ's death was the only possible way to bring about man's salvation.

Position three states that God had to save man and that Christ had to die to bring about man's salvation.

Position four states that God had to save man but Christ's death was just one option among an infinite number of different ways of salvation.

The Atonement

Motive	Means
1. Not necessary	Not necessary
2. Not necessary	Necessary
3. Necessary	Necessary
4. Necessary	Not necessary

It is our conviction that the Bible teaches position number 2. It was not necessary for God to save sinners but it was necessary for Christ to accomplish atonement if sinners were to be saved.

When we turn to the Scriptures, we find that salvation is due to the free choice of God. He was not bound by any kind of necessity to save sinners. That this is the teaching of Scripture is based on the following lines of thought.

First, there are the clear explicit statements of Scripture which attribute sovereign freeness to God's decision to save sinners. Every part of God's plan of salvation is said to arise out of God's free choice. Did not the Apostle Paul trace election and predestination to "the good pleasure of His will" in Ephesians 1:5? Is not the work of Christ described as a "free gift" in Romans 5:15-16, 18?

Salvation is not a "free gift" in the sense that it costs nothing. Salvation cost the infinite value of the blood of Christ. But whenever the Biblical authors used the words "free gift," they were referring to God's freedom in giving salvation to whomever and whenever He pleases (Rom. 9:15-18). Salvation is a "free gift" because God gives it freely (not of necessity).

When we turn to the application of redemption, God's saving work is said to be freely done. Are not we "justified *freely* by His grace" (Rom. 3:24)? Is it not the case that the ministry of the Spirit helps us to "know the things that are *freely* given us of God" (I Cor. 2:12)? Thus we conclude with the Apostle Paul in Romans 8:32, where he says God will *"freely* give us all things."

Second, God is a self-sufficient Trinity. From all eternity the Father, Son and Holy Spirit had fellowship, communication and love with one another. On this basis it is clear that man was not created because God was lonely and needed someone for fellowship. There is no defect in God's being that makes man necessary.

Third, God is sovereignly free. He is free to do His will on earth as well as in heaven (Dan. 4:33-37). God could have let everyone go to hell. His justice and holiness would have been glorified by this righteous act (Rom. 9:22).

Fourth, sin causes demerit. Man does not deserve anything but hell. Man's rebellion and sin demand judgment, not mercy.

Fifth, the Biblical authors view God's freeness as an essential part of their concept of grace. This is the heart of Paul's argument in Romans 4:1-5. Salvation should never be looked upon as something God owes us by way of debt. God doesn't owe anyone anything. Rather, salvation is given freely by God to sinners.

The sovereign freeness of God's grace in salvation should produce in us wonder, awe and praise. Since salvation was not something that God had to do, how much more should we praise Him. He could have left us in our sins for we deserve nothing but wrath and judgment. But in love and mercy, He decided to save sinners. Oh, the richness of God's free grace! Stop and thank Him right now for freely deciding to save sinners.

Now that we have examined the motive behind the atonement, let us examine the means of redemption. Having decided out of free sovereign love to save sinners, could God use many different means to accomplish salvation? Was the work of Christ necessary? Or did God have at His disposal an infinite number of ways of saving sinners?

It is our conviction that the work of Christ was the necessary means of salvation. There was no other way to save sinners than through the work of Christ.

The following definition of the necessity of the atonement will serve to clarify the position and to set forth its Biblical foundations.

> Once God freely decided out of His sovereign electing love to save sinners, there was but one way of bringing about this desired salvation which would be in harmony with God's character, the law of God, the nature of sin and the needs of man. This one way was by the substitutionary blood atonement of the incarnate Son of God.

We will now deal with each of the Biblical foundations upon which the necessity of the atonement rests.

III.   Biblical Foundation No. 1: The Character of God

The nature and character of God necessitate a certain kind of salvation: one which will be in harmony with God's moral character.

If you were asked "Can God do anything?" how would you answer? It would seem that the only pious answer is that God can do anything. Yet upon closer examination, it is clear that *God cannot do everything for He cannot do anything which contradicts His character or nature.* All things are possible for God as long as they do not contradict His character or nature for "He cannot deny Himself" (II Tim. 2:13).

Thus the only salvation which God can provide for man must be a salvation which is in harmony with the moral character of God. Several illustrations from Scripture of this basic principle will demonstrate its valildity.

A.   The Justice and Righteousness of God

God's justice and righteousness are both attributes of God's moral character. Because God *is* just and righteous, His works are described as being just and righteous. We should not make the mistake of thinking that God's justice is only a description of His works and not reflective of His being. God *is* just and therefore *acts* justly.

God's justice and righteousness are consistently joined together in Scripture as being descriptive of God's very being and character. Moses declared that God is "just and right" (Deut. 32:4). The Psalmist declared that "Justice and righteousness are the foundation of (God's) throne" (Psa. 89:14). Zephaniah 3:5 states, "The just LORD is in the midst thereof, He will not do iniquity." The Apostle John tells us to confess our sins to God "for He is just and righteous" (I John 1:9).

Because God is just and righteous, He will never do anything which would contradict these attributes. This is the underlying assumption behind Abraham's famous statement, "Shall not the Judge of all the earth do right?" (Gen. 18:25). The Apostle Paul asks the same type of question in Romans 9:14, "Is there unrighteousness with God?" (KJV) or, "There is no injustice with God, is there?" (NAS). The Judge of all the earth cannot do anything unless it is in conformity to His own righteousness. It is blasphemy to attribute injustice to God. His ways are always just and right.

The Scriptures also teach us that God cannot simply forgive sinners and let their sins go unpunished because God's justice is displayed by the vindication of His righteousness in the punishment of sin. Did not God declare to Moses, "I will not acquit the guilty" (Ex. 23:7)? Or again, "He will by no means leave the guilty unpunished" (Ex. 34:7)? Does not the Psalmist state, "For thou art a God who takes no pleasure in wickedness; no evil dwells with thee. The boastful shall not stand before thine eyes; thou dost hate all who do iniquity. Thou dost destroy those who speak falsehood; the Lord abhors the man of bloodshed and deceit" (Psa. 5:4-6)?: Is not this same principle found in Romans 2:5-6, "But because of your stubbornness and unrepentant heart you are storing up wrath for yourself in the day of wrath and revelation of the righteous judgment of God who will render to every man according to his deeds?"

The justice and righteousness of God demand that sin be punished. And the penalty for sin is death for "the person who sins will die; for the wages of sin is death" (Ex. 18:20; Rom. 6:23; Jas. 1:15). *Either the sinner himself must be punished unto death or a suitable substitute must be found who will be able to bear the full punishment of sin.*

It is necessary, therefore, if God is "to be just and the justifier" of sinners (Rom. 3:26), that a perfect and proper substitute be found, who having no sin of his own, may be able to bear the full punishment of sin in the place of those to whom the punishment is due.

It was only God Himself who could be the exact, perfect and proper substitute to atone for the sins of His people, and completely satisfy the vindication of His justice and righteousness, and thus render man acceptable in His sight.

The substitute could not be an animal "for it is impossible for the blood of bulls and goats to take away sins" (Heb. 10:4).

Neither could an angel be the substitute, for the substitute must take upon himself human nature (Heb. 2:14).

No sinner could atone for his fellow sinners for "no man can by any means redeem his brother, or give to God a ransom for him — for the redemption of his soul is costly, and he should cease trying forever" (Psa. 49:7-8).

The Scriptures point out the necessity of Christ's assuming a human nature in order to atone for sin.

> Since then the children share in flesh and blood, He, Himself, likewise partook of the same, that through death he might render powerless him who had the power of death, that is, the devil . . . therefore, *he had to be made like his brethren in all things, that he might become a merciful and faithful high priest* in things pertaining to God, *to make propitiation for* the sins of the people (Heb. 2:14-17).

Jesus Christ alone could be the fitting or proper high priest for He only was "holy, innocent, undefiled, separated from sinners and exalted above the heavens" (Heb. 7:26).

The sinlessness of the substitute is necessary for "He made Him *who knew no sin* to be sin on our behalf, that we might become the righteousness of God in him" (II Cor. 5:21).

Thus we find the Apostle Paul arguing that the death of Christ was necessary because it alone could satisfy the demands of God's righteousness.

> Being justified as a gift by his grace through the redemption which is in Christ Jesus; whom God displayed publicly as a propitiation in his blood through faith. *This was to demonstrate his righteousness,* because in the forebearance of God He passed over the sins previously committed; *for the demonstration, I say, of His righteousness at this present time, that He might be just and the justifier of the one who has faith in Jesus* (Rom. 3:24-26).

In order to be just and at the same time justify sinners, God had to vindicate His righteousness by the death of the sinner's substitute. Jesus Christ was the only perfect and proper substitute who could die in our place. When He prayed, *"If it is possible,* let this cup pass from me" (Matt. 26:39), the Father heard Him. If there were any other way of bringing about redemption, the Father would have delivered His Son. "But the LORD was pleased to crush Him, putting Him to grief; surely our griefs He Himself bore, and our sorrows He carried; yet we ourselves esteemed Him stricken, smitten of God and afflicted" (Isa. 53:10, 4).

The story is told of an oriental judge who had gained a great reputation for his absolute righteousness and severity in passing judgment on criminals. He would not show partiality nor accept any bribes. Because of a famine, he ordered that the water be rationed and anyone caught stealing water should be punished by thirty lashes.

That evening cries rang out as a thief was caught stealing water. The judge had the criminal brought before him only to discover it was his aged mother. He was in a dilemma. To let her go unpunished would undermine his reputation of being a just judge. But to punish her would no doubt kill such an aged one as she. What would he do?

He called for his mother. He stated the charges and found her guilty and called for the men to bring the whip. He ordered her to kneel down. Then he took off his royal robes and approached his mother and laid upon her and commanded that the punishment be given. He took the thirty lashes which his mother deserved. In this way justice was vindicated for he bore her punishment.

How much more do we owe to the Judge of all the earth, who stripped Himself of His heavenly glories and bore our sins upon the cross.

> For you know the grace of our Lord Jesus Christ, that though He was rich, yet *for our sake He became poor,* that you through His poverty might become rich (II Cor. 9:8).

> Who, although He existed in the form of God, did not regard equality with God a thing to be grasped, but emptied Himself, taking the form of a servant, and was made in the likeness of men. And being found in appearance as a man, He humbled Himself by becoming obedient to the point of death, even death on a cross (Phil. 2:6-8).

How can we help but fall at the feet of Him who completely satisfied the justice and righteousness of God in our behalf for our sin? Pause right now and praise the Savior for all you owe Him.

> O for a thousand tongues to sing
> my great Redeemer's praise,
> the glories of my God and King,
> the triumphs of His grace.

> My gracious Master and my God,
> assist me to proclaim,
> To spread through all the earth abroad,
> the honors of Thy name.
> Jesus, the name that charms our fears,
> that bids our sorrows cease;
> tis music in the sinner's ears,
> 'tis life, and health, and peace.

> He breaks the power of cancelled sin,
> He sets the prisoner free;
> His blood can make the foulest clean;
> His blood availed for me.

> Hear Him, ye deaf! His praise, ye dumb,
> Your loosened tongues employ;
> Ye blind, behold your Savior come;
> and leap, ye lame, for joy.*

B. The Holiness of God

God's holiness necessitates a salvation in which man's sinfulness is removed and a perfect holiness is given to him.

The holiness of God has central place in the Old Testament concept of a character of God. Jehovah is distinguished from the pagan gods on the basis of His holiness for "who is like thee among the gods, O LORD? Who is like thee, majestic in holiness?" (Ex. 15:11). God's veracity is based upon His holiness because God swore "by my holiness; I will not lie to David" (Psa. 89:34). Thus the Law (Ex. 15:11), the Writings (Psa. 89:34) and the Prophets (Amos 4:2) all point to the centrality of God's holiness.

In the New Testament, the seraphim's cry of "Holy, Holy, Holy, is the LORD of Hosts" (Isa. 6:3), is seen as trinitarian in form for Holy is the Father (John 17:11), Holy is the Son (Acts 3:14) and Holy is the

*"O For a Thousand Tongues"

Spirit (Matt. 1:18). Blessed God three in One!

Because God is Holy, His "eyes are too pure to approve [look upon] evil, and Thou canst not look on wickedness with favor" (Hab. 1:13). Or, again in Psalm 5:4-6, we find:

> For thou art not a God who takes pleasure in wickedness; no evil dwells with thee. The boastful shall not stand before thine eyes; thou dost hate all who do iniquity, thou dost destroy those who speak falsehood; the LORD abhors the man of bloodshed and deceit.

Man was created to bear God's image and thus it is not surprising that man was created with original holiness (Gen. 1:26-27). But man fell into sin and lost that holiness (Gen. 3). When God looked upon man after the fall, instead of holiness, He "saw that the wickedness of man was great on the earth, and that every intent of the thoughts of his heart was only evil continually" (Gen. 6:5).

God's holiness demands judgment against sin and thus we find that the history of redemption is filled with awesome displays of God's holy anger. We could examine man's expulsion from the garden, the flood, the tower of Babel, the judgments of Egypt and on the Jews in the wilderness, the destruction of the Canaanites, the Assyrian and the Babylonian Captivities, etc. All of these judgments arose because God is Holy and man unholy.

Man's unholiness must be removed for his sin has separated him from God.

> Behold, the LORD's hand is not so short that it cannot save; neither is His ear so dull that it cannot hear. *But your iniquities have made a separation between you and your God, and your sins have hid His face from you, so that He does not hear* (Isa. 59:1-2).

Man must be given holiness in order to stand before God. Was not Isaiah cleansed of his sin before God spoke to him (Isa. 6:7)? Did not Joshua the high priest have his filthy clothes removed in order to be dressed in white robes before he would intercede for God's people (Zech. 3:1-5)? Did not both the Old Testament and the New Testament state that we must be holy because God is Holy (Lev. 11:44; I Pet. 1:15)? Is not our salvation described in Ephesians 4:24 as being recreated in "righteousness and holiness"?

The only way to remove our unholiness is by way of the death of a substitute sacrifice. No other sacrifice than the death of Christ could have removed our sin.

The only way to obtain holiness is by way of imputation on the basis of our substitute's obedience and righteousness. Jesus Christ alone could establish this holiness for us.

C. God's Hatred of Sin

God's consuming hatred of sin necessitates a salvation in which the execution of His hatred of sin is completely carried out in the full punishment of sin.

Moses warned the people that God would judge them if they disobeyed His commandments because "our God is a consuming fire" (Deut. 4:23, 27). The people were assured that the wicked Canaanites would be destroyed because "our God is a consuming fire" (Deut. 9:3). The writer of the book of Hebrews warns that apostasy results in God's judgment because "our God is a consuming fire" (Heb. 12:29).

Because of God's moral character, He hates sin and is provoked by it to consume it in judgment. Simply to dismiss the death sentence for sin is impossible for "He cannot deny Himself" (II Tim. 2:13).

Thus the only kind of salvation possible is one in which God's hatred of sin is satisfied by the death of a sinner's substitute. And who but Christ could have smothered the consuming fire of God's hatred of sin by having it fall on Himself as the sinner's substitute?

The character of God necessitates the saving work of the Son of God. Meditate on the following hymn to impress this truth on your heart.

> Not what my hands have done
> Can save my guilty soul;
> Not what my toiling flesh has borne
> Can make my spirit whole.
>
> Thy work *alone*, O Christ,
> Can ease this weight of sin;
> *Thy blood alone*, O Lamb of God,
> Can give me peace within.
>
> Thy love to me, O God,
> Not mine, O Lord, to thee,
> Can rid me of this dark unrest,
> And set my spirit free.

Thy Grace alone, O God,
To me can pardon speak;
Thy power alone, O Son of God,
Can this sore bondage break.

No other work, save thine,
No other blood will do;
No strength, save that which is divine,
Can bear me safely through. *

Biblical Foundation No. 2: The Law of God

The nature of the demands of the Law of God necessitates a certain kind
of salvation which shall fully satisfy all the Law's requirements for blessing
and endure all its penalties for disobedience.

The Law of God is commonly divided into two parts: moral and
positive or moral and ceremonial.

The moral Law of God is that part of the divine commandments
which reflects the character of God. Because we were created to bear
God's image in this world, God tells us by the moral Law in what ways
we are to reflect His person and work. Thus the moral Law is binding
upon all men because all are image-bearers. It is binding in all generations and will be binding even in the future state. The moral Law
cannot change because God does not change and neither does the
image-bearing purpose of man.

We are commanded by the moral Law, "Be holy" (Lev. 11:44; I Pet.
1:15). Why should we be holy? We are pointed to God's holy character
as the basis of God's command. "Be holy, *for I am holy*" (Lev. 11:44); "You
shall be holy, *for I am holy*" (I Pet. 1:16). Or again, "Be ye therefore perfect, *even as your heavenly Father which is in heaven is perfect*" (Matt. 5:48).

The moral Law tells us "you shall not bear false witness against your
neighbor" (Deut. 5:20). Why is lying forbidden? We are told "God is
not a man that He should lie" (Num. 23:19) and "it is impossible for
God to lie" (Heb. 6:18). If a man is to reflect God's moral character,
then he must not lie for God does not lie.

One of the reasons for the present rise of situation ethics is that the
moral Law of God has been cut off from its true foundation in the character of God and man's unique function as image-bearer.

The ceremonial law does not reflect God's moral character and
neither does it primarily show us how to bear God's image. The cere-

*Hymn: "Not What My Hands Have Done"

monial law was only temporary and binding upon one nation. It passed away under the New Covenant because its purpose had been accomplished. The ceremonial law was primarily prophetic in character and function. It prepared God's people for the coming of the Christ and His church. This is why the ceremonies of the Old Testament are said to be "only a shadow of good things to come and not the very form itself" (Heb. 10:1). The ceremonial law was "imposed until a time of reformation" (Heb. 9:10).

The prophetic and didactic function of the ceremonial law is particularly singled out by the Apostle Paul in Galatians 3:23-25:

> But before faith came, we were kept in custody under the law, *being shut up to the faith which was later revealed. Therefore the law has become our tutor to lead us to Christ,* that we might be justified by faith. But now that faith has come, we are no longer under a *tutor.*

The Mosaic Law has been fulfilled, thus done away with for Christ came and fulfilled the Law for us (Matt. 5:17-18).

On the basis of our understanding of the nature of God's Law, we can conclude that since salvation primarily consists of recreating man in the image of God (Eph. 4:24), this salvation must be in harmony with the moral Law of God.

Having seen the nature of God's Law, we can now consider the demands of the Law of God. When we turn to the Scriptures to see what the Law demands, we soon discover the twofold division of Promise and Penalty or Blessing and Cursing.

> See, I am setting before you today *a blessing* and *a curse:* the *blessing,* if you listen to the commandment of the LORD your God, which I am commanding you this day: and the *curse,* if you do not listen to the commandments of the LORD your God (Deut. 11:26-27).

> See, I have set before you today *life* and *prosperity,* and *death* and *adversity;* in that I command you today to love the LORD your God, to walk in His ways and to keep His judgments, that you may live and multiply, and that *the LORD God may bless you* in the land where you are entering to possess it. But if your heart turns away and you will not obey, but are drawn away and worship other gods and serve them, I declare to you today that *you shall surely perish* (Deut. 30:15-18).

The Promise of the Law is the reward of the blessing of God gained through absolute obedience. In order to gain the blessing of God your obedience must be: (1) *personal*: "If *you* listen to the commandment" (Deut. 11:26); (2) *perfect*: "what does the LORD your God require from you but to fear the LORD your God, to walk in *all* His ways and love Him, and to serve the LORD your God with *all* your heart and with *all* your soul" (Deut. 10:12); (3) *perpetual*: "Oh, that they had such a heart in them, that they would fear me, and keep *all* my command-ments *always*" (Deut. 5:29).

The only obedience acceptable before God is one in which 100% of you keeps 100% of the Law 100% of the time. "For whoever keeps the whole law and yet stumbles in one point, he has become guilty of all" (Jas. 2:10).

Dear Reader, has your obedience come up to the perfect standard of the Law? Or must you confess that you have not kept the Law per-sonally, perfectly or perpetually? "For all have sinned and fallen short of the glory of God" (Rom. 3:23).

If you have not perfectly obeyed God's Law, then you have not se-cured the blessing of God. Instead, you have secured for yourself the Penalty of the Law for disobedience.

The Penalty of the Law is the reward of the curse of God obtained through disobedience. Was it not the Apostle Paul who said, *"Cursed is every one who does not abide by all things written in the book of the law, to perform them"* (Gal. 3:10)? Do we not find God giving ex-plicit warnings of cursing for disobedience in Deuteronomy 27:15-26; 28:15-69?

The curse of God for man's disobedience is *death* in contrast to God's blessing of *life*. In the garden, did not God warn Adam and Eve that disobedience will lead to death "for in the day that you eat from it you shall surely die" (Gen. 2:17)? Did not Moses sternly warn the people "you shall surely perish" if they disobeyed God's Law (Deut. 30:18)? Does not the New Testament teach that disobedience results in death for, "The wages of sin is death; and sin when it is accomplished, it brings forth death" (Rom. 6:23; Jas. 1:15)?

The execution of the Promise of Penalty aspect of the Law rests upon God's covenantal faithfulness.

"Know therefore that the LORD your God, He is God, the faithful God, *who keeps His covenant* and His loving kindness to a thousandth generation of those who love Him and keep His commandments; but *repays those who hate Him to their faces, to destroy them"* (Deut. 7:9-10).

God cannot merely sweep aside the requirement of obedience to the Law. Why not? Because His character is unchanging (Mal. 3:6) and man is still God's image-bearer (Jas. 3:9).

Therefore, the Law of God necessitates a certain kind of salvation in which:

1. A personal, perfect and perpetual obedience must be executed by the person or his substitute in order to gain the reward of eternal life and thus satisfy the just demands of God's Law.
2. The full curse of God must be endured unto death either by the person or by his substitute in order to satisfy fully the just penalty of the Law of God for disobedience.

Who else but the Son of God could live the life we should have lived and die the death we should have died? Neither angels nor sinners could fulfill the demands and penalty of God's Law! Someone had to live a perfect life of obedience to obtain eternal life for us. Someone had to die under the curse of God that we might be delivered.

The Lord Jesus Christ alone could gain eternal life for us through perfect obedience. This is why the obedience of Christ is viewed as *necessary* for our salvation. Was He not "born of a woman, *born under the law*" (Gal. 4:4)? Did not John baptize Christ *"to fulfill all righteousness"* (Matt. 3:15)? Did not Jesus say, "Do not think that I came to abolish the law or the prophets; I did not come to abolish, but *to fulfill*" (Matt. 5:17)? Does not the Apostle Paul sum up the saving work of Christ in terms of Christ's obedience gaining eternal life for us in Romans 5:19? Finally is it not true that the Father exalted Christ and gave Him a name above every name because Christ was obedient for "He humbled Himself and became obedient . . . therefore hath God highly exalted Him" (Phil. 2:5-11)?

The obedience of Christ not only points to His perfect life but it also points to His death because He "became *obedient to the point of death*, even the death of the cross" (Phil. 2:8). He endured the curse of God and thus satisfied the just penalty for our disobedience to God's law. "Christ redeemed us from *the curse of the law, having become a curse for us* — for it is written, Cursed is everyone who hangs on a tree" (Gal. 3:13). *"He made Him* who knew no sin *to be sin on our behalf* that we become the righteousness of God in Him" (II Cor. 5:21).

The nature and demands of the Law of God must be satisfied before we can come into God's presence. Only Jesus Christ could obtain the blessing and endure the curse on our behalf. There was no other way.

Our salvation rests upon Christ's thirty-three and one-half years of maintaining perfect obedience to God's Law as much as His obedience unto death on the cross. We often forget the years of obedience which Christ performed for us. Have you ever stopped to consider what Christ's obedience to God's Law means to you? How it relates to your salvation? Set apart some time to meditate on the obedience of Christ and then sing an appropriate hymn of thanksgiving and praise to God.

> Not the labors of my hands
> Can fulfill thy law's demand;
> Could my zeal no respite know,
> Could my tears forever flow;
> Thou must save and thou alone.
>
> Thy pains, not mine, O Christ
> Upon the shameful tree,
> Have paid the law's full price
> and purchased peace for me.
>
> To whom, save thee,
> Who canst alone
> For sin atone
> Lord, shall I flee?
>
> Thy cross, not mine, O Christ,
> Has borne the awful load.
> Of sins that none in heaven
> Or earth could bear but God.*

Biblical Foundation No. 3: The Nature of Sin

The nature of sin demands a salvation in which sin must be completely removed before men can come before God.

We must confess "that all have sinned and fallen short of the glory of God" (Rom. 3:23). "Indeed, there is not a righteous man on earth who continually does good and who never sins" (Eccles. 7:20).

By nature, sin renders us guilty before the Law in the sight of God. This is why Ezra confesses sin in terms of being guilty before God in Ezra 9:6-13. God rebuked the people in Ezekiel 22:4 by saying, "You have become *guilty* by the blood which you have shed." Thus we find James saying, "whoever keeps the whole law and yet stumbles in one point,

*Hymn: "Rock of Ages"

has become *guilty* of all" (Jas. 2:10).

Sin is a real criminal offense against God. We should not confuse guilt feelings with real guilt. All men are guilty before God (Rom. 3:19). Yet, most men do not know it or feel it. Modern psychology and psychiatry attempt to remove guilt feelings. But no one can remove our real guilt but God Himself.

The fact that our sin has made us guilty before God demands that expiation and justification take place in order that our guilt be removed.

By nature, sin provokes God's anger and creates emnity between the sinner and God. "O LORD God of Israel, Thou art righteous: for we remain yet escaped, as it is this day: Behold, we are before thee in our trespasses: for we cannot stand before thee because of this" (Ezra 9:15). "For Thou art not a God that hath pleasure in wickedness: neither shall evil dwell with thee. The foolish shall not stand in thy sight; Thou hatest all workers of iniquity. Thou shalt destroy them that speak leasing; The LORD will abhor the bloody and deceitful man" (Psa. 5:4-6). "The LORD is in His holy temple, the LORD's throne is in heaven: His eyes behold, His eyelids try, the children of men. The LORD trieth the righteous: but the wicked and him that loveth violence his soul hateth. Upon the wicked he shall rain snares, fire and brimstone, and an horrible tempest: this shall be the portion of their cup. For the righteous LORD loveth righteousness; his countenance doth behold the upright" (Psa. 11:4-7). "For if, when we were enemies, we were reconciled to God by the death of his Son, much more, being reconciled, we shall be saved by his life" (Rom. 5:10).

Thus sin demands propitiation and reconciliation for its removal.

By nature, sin makes us liable to the penal or death punishment of the Law of God, "But of the tree of the knowledge of good and evil, thou shalt not eat of it: for in the day that thou eatest thereof thou shalt surely *die*" (Gen. 2:17). "Behold, all souls are mine; as the soul of the father, so also the soul of the son is mine: the soul that sinneth, it shall *die*" (Eze. 18:4). "For the wages of sin is *death*; but the gift of God is eternal life through Jesus Christ our Lord" (Rom. 6:23).

Thus sin demands the death of either the sinner or the sinner's substitute. A substitutionary blood atonement is necessary to remove the penal consequence of sin.

The present rejection of capital punishment can be traced back to the denial of the penal aspect of the Law of God. Liberal theologians taught that God dealt with sin in a corrective way; not in a punitive way. The death of Christ was not necessary because sin does not demand death.

Capital punishment was instituted by God in the garden before man fell into sin (Gen. 2:17). Then, after the fall, we read concerning Adam, "and he died" (Gen. 5:5). The Apostle reminds us, "Through one man sin entered into the world, and *death through sin* and so death spread to all men, because all sinned [in Adam]" (Rom. 5:12).

After the flood, God again instituted capital punishment in Genesis 9:6:

> Whoever shed man's blood,
> by man his blood shall be shed.

During the Mosaic economy, capital punishment was viewed as a Divine punishment for sin (Lev. 19:1-21). Even the destruction of the Canaanites should be viewed as capital punishment because it was on account of their sin that God ordered them killed (Lev. 18:24-25).

The Apostle Paul urged the death penalty for certain sins in Romans 1:32: *"Those who practice such things are worthy of death."* And in Romans 13:1-4, he established the principle that the state is to punish wrongdoers with the sword.

If we only *correct* sin and never *punish* sin, we are denying the penal consequence of sin. In so doing, we are making the death of Christ foolishness.

In summary, sinful man cannot deny, ignore or remove his real guilt, the enmity between God and himself or his liability to the penal punishment of the Law of God.

This truth is particularly clear in such a passage as Hebrews 9:22: "Without the shedding of blood there is no forgiveness." When we examine this verse in its context, we come to several important conclusions.

1. This verse does not merely describe an Old Testament practice but it sets forth a fundamental principle that the nature of sin demands a blood atonement for its forgiveness. That this is the case can be demonstrated from the fact that the author draws in verse 23 a necessary deduction from verse 22: "Therefore it was necessary for. . . ." This shows us that the author viewed verse 22 as a foundational principle from which he could rightly draw certain conclusions.

2. The conclusion drawn from verse 22 is that it was necessary that Jesus shed His blood if man's sin was to be forgiven (vs. 23-28). This necessity is elsewhere supported by the writer of Hebrews from the observation that no animal, human or angelic sacrifice

could atone for sin because of their inadequacy to satisfy the character of God, the Law of God or the nature of sin (Heb. 2:14; 7:26-28; 9:11-15; 10:1-4; 10:14). Only through the person and work of Christ could expiation, justification, reconciliation, propitiation and atonement be provided.

In order to seal truth to your heart, meditate on the following hymn.

What can wash away my sin?
Nothing but the blood of Jesus.
What can make me whole again?
Nothing but the blood of Jesus.

Nothing can for sin atone —
Nothing but the blood of Jesus.
Naught of good that I have done —
Nothing but the blood of Jesus.

O precious is the flow
That makes me white as snow;
No other fount I know
Nothing but the blood of Jesus.

He died that we might be forgiven
He died to make us good.
That we might go at last to heav'n,
Saved by His precious blood.

There was no other good enough
To pay the price of sin;
He *only* could unlock the gate
Of heav'n, and let us in.*

Biblical Foundation No. 4: The Needs of Man

The needs of man which sin created necessite a certain kind of salvation which will satisfy those needs.

Man as sinner has certain needs in his person. Since we are spiritually dead (Eph. 2:1), we need regeneration (Jn. 3:3). since we are defiled (Eze. 22:11), we need sanctification. Because we are slaves of sin (Jn. 8:34), we need glorification.

Man as sinner has certain needs concerning his position or stand-

---

*Hymn: "Nothing But the Blood"

ing before God and the law. Because of the nature of our sin, we need justification, forgiveness, propitiation, reconciliation, redemption, expiation, and atonement.

Man as sinner needs a prophet, i.e., one who will tell him the truth as God's representative to man. Our minds have been darkened by the sin and Satan (II Cor. 4:3-4) and are devoid of true understanding (Rom. 3:11). Thus we need a prophet to teach us the truth (Acts 8:31).

Man as sinner needs a priest, i.e., one who can represent him before God. Because of our sin, we cannot come before God (Psa. 5:5). Therefore, we need a mediator.

This mediator must be both God and man. A mediator not quite God or not quite man is like a bridge broken at either end. Our mediator must be a man to represent us before God (I Tim. 2:5). He must also be God to present fully the Father to us (John 1:10).

Man as sinner needs a king, i.e., one who will guide, protect and provide for his life. We are like sheep who need a shepherd (Luke 15:4-7).

The entire complex of the needs of man which sin created point to the necessity of various ingredients of the atonement as well as the necessity of Jesus Christ being the agent. What Jesus accomplished was necessary for man's salvation. Thus the necessity of the atonement involves the work of Christ as well as His person.

Given all our needs, who but the mighty Son of God could meet all of them? There was no other way of meeting our needs than through the saving work of Christ.

> O Thou th' Eternal Son of God
> None tread with thee the holy place;
> Thou sufferest alone;
> Thine is the perfect sacrifice
> Which only can atone.
>
> Nor silver nor gold,
> Nor silver nor gold hath obtained my redemption,
> The guilt on my conscience too heavy had grown;
> The blood on the cross is my only foundation,
> The death of my Saviour could only atone.*

The necessity of Christ's atonement magnifies the wonder and freeness of God's grace. The following story may be helpful to illustrate this truth.

*Hymn: "O Thou the Eternal Son of God"

One day a guard who was in charge of the raising and lowering of a drawbridge which spanned a large river decided to take his only son with him to work in order to spend the day together.

Even though the job of raising and lowering a bridge may not seem very difficult, it does require precision timing. At 4:00 p.m. the bridge had to be raised to allow a ferry boat to proceed down river. But at 4:15 p.m. the bridge had to be lowered to allow a regularly scheduled passenger train to cross the river.

On this fateful day, after the bridge had been raised, the guard allowed his son to venture out on the bridge to get a better view of the ferry boat as it passed beneath the bridge. To his horror, he saw his son slip and fall into the gears of the drawbridge. The boy was so entangled in the gears that without help and unlimited time the father could not possibly rescue his son. The father tried everything he could think of but all attempts were of no avail.

It was at this point that the father was shocked back to reality when he heard the whistle of the approaching train. A look at his watch revealed that he had only five minutes to lower the bridge.

Two choices faced the guard. On one hand, he could save his son by not lowering the bridge. But this meant that the train with all of its passengers would crash into the river. No doubt many lives would be lost. On the other hand, he could lower the bridge and save the train. But when the bridge was lowered it would crush his son.

The guard did not owe the passengers on this train anything. Thus if he decided to save them, it would be his free act of love and mercy. But once he decided to save the train, the death of his son was an absolute necessity. There was no other way.

The guard made his decision and quickly lowered the bridge, saving the train but killing his own son.

In the same way, God the Father gave up His only Son to die for our eternal salvation. God did not owe us anything but freely out of His matchless grace and mercy delivered up His Son for us. O dear child of God, what grace! What mercy! What compassion! What pity! O, the depths of the love of God!

In Summary

We have briefly examined some of the Biblical foundations for the necessity of the atonement. Indeed, there are many other arguments for is it not true that the work of Christ gives God the most glory by being the highest and most perfect expression of God's love and mercy (Rom.

5:8)?

We must also emphasize that the necessity of Christ's person and work magnifies God's free choice to save sinners. Faced with the necessary agonies of Christ on one hand and the eternal agonies of sinners on the other, God freely delivered up His Son for us. It would have been an easier choice for God if there were an infinite number of ways of saving sinners. But the Father sent the Son as the sinner's substitute to satisfy fully all the demands of His own character, the Law of God, the nature of sin and the needs of man.

Reader, do you love Jesus Christ? Do you appreciate all that He has done for you? Then give Him your heart. Give Him your praise and your obedience. He died the just for the unjust that you might no longer live for yourself, but live for Him instead (II Cor. 5:15). O, live for Him, dear Christian! Will anything else matter when you stand before Him on that great day?

CHAPTER 3

The Nature of the Atonement

Our first task in approaching the nature of the atonement is to establish the relationship between the necessity of the atonement and its nature.

The nature of the atonement arises out of the same considerations from which we derived the necessity of the atonement, i.e., the character of God, the Law of God, the nature of sin and the needs of man.

While the doctrine of the necessity of the atonement answers the question "*Why* did Jesus die?" the doctrine of the nature of the atonement answers the question, "*What* did Christ accomplish by His death?"

We will find that propitiation and reconciliation have as their central concern the character of God. Redemption answers the problems connected with our relationship to the Law, sin and Satan. Expiation relates to the needs of man which sin created.

I. Propitiation

Definition: *Propitiation is that priestly work of Christ wherein He removed God's anger and wrath by the covering over of our sins through the substitutionary sacrifice of Himself to God, thus securing our acceptance before God.*

In seeking to understand a Biblical word, we must examine the way it is used in the Scripture for our definitions of Biblical words should reflect the understanding of the authors of Scripture.

Our first step in defining "propitiation" is to examine how this word is used in non-theological or everyday language. What this world meant in common speech should form our basic understanding of its meaning when used in reference to the work of Christ.

In the Greek version of the Old Testament we find the same word which is translated "propitiation" in the New Testament.

Our first example is found in Genesis 32:20:

> And say ye moreover, "Behold, thy servant Jacob is behind us." For he said, "I will *appease* [propitiate] him with the present that goeth before me, and afterward I will see his face; per-adventure he will accept me."

The story of Jacob meeting Esau is meaningful as well as touching. Jacob had offended Esau by stealing his birthright (Gen. 25:27-34) and blessing (Gen. 27:1-29). Esau was justly angered and would have killed Jacob if Jacob had not run away (Gen. 27:41-43).

After many years Jacob returned to the land of his father. This meant he must encounter Esau. He knew that his brother would kill him unless he could appease, placate, pacify or propitiate him. In order to remove Esau's anger and wrath, Jacob sent several flocks as rich gifts to his brother. Even though Esau started out with 400 men to destroy Jacob and his family, these rich gifts appeased him to such a degree that he met Jacob with a kiss instead of a sword (Gen. 33:4). Reconciliation was only possible because Jacob propitiated Esau's anger.

We also find the word "propitiation" in Proverbs 16:14. "The wrath of a Kind is as messengers of death: but a wise man will *pacify* [propitiate] it." Solomon saw the wise man as seeking to remove, pacify, placate, appease or propitiate the anger of the king. Unless propitiation took place, the King's wrath would be satisfied by the death of the offender.

From these two sample passages, it is clear that our definition of propitiation must include the following points:

1. Two or more parties are involved.
2. One person has been offended and is angry at the offender.
3. The offender seeks to appease, pacify, placate or remove the anger of the offended one in order that he may come before his presence with acceptance. Reconciliation is only possible because of appeasement, i.e., propitiation.

The Old Testament also uses the word propitiation in a theological or religious context.

In Leviticus 4:35 we read:

> And he shall take away all the fat thereof, as the fat of the lamb is taken away from the sacrifice of the peace offerings;

and the priest shall burn them upon the altar, according to the offerings made by fire unto the LORD; and the priest shall make an *atonement* [propitiation] for his sin that he hath committed, and it shall be forgiven him.

We find the same word in Leviticus 16:30:

For on that day shall the priest make an *atonement* [propitiation] for you, to cleanse you, that ye may be clean from all your sins before the LORD.

From these two passages and the other places where propitiation is found in the Old Testament, it is clear that propitiation involves the following points.

1. It is in reference to sin that propitiation takes place.
2. It is "before" the LORD and "to" the LORD that propitiation takes place. God is the one who is propitiated.
3. The purpose and effect of propitiation is to cover over the sin and to bring forgiveness, reconciliation and acceptance with God.
4. The propitiation finds acceptance with God because of its substitutionary character in which the sacrifice, instead of the sinner, is consumed by the fire of God's wrath. When we turn to the New Testament, we find the fulfillment of the Old Testament concept of propitiation in the work of Christ.

The Apostle John tells us that the Father "sent His Son to be the propitiation for our sins" (I John 4:10).

The writer of Hebrews also views the work of propitiation as being part of the central purpose of Christ's incarnation and priestly office.

Wherefore in all things it behoved him to be made like unto his brethren, that he might be a merciful and faithful high priest in things pertaining to God, *to make propitiation for the sins of the people* (Heb. 2:17).

In the above passage, the Old Testament background is self-evident. Any definition of propitiation which seeks to cast off the Old Testament concept of the word is hopelessly deficient. The writer of Hebrews is obviously portraying Christ as the fulfillment of the Old Testament ceremony of the Day of Atonement (Lev. 16:30).

As the high priest, Christ removed God's wrath by becoming the propitiatory sacrifice Himself for *"He is the propitiation for our sins"*

(I John 2:2).

Christ accomplished His work of propitiation when He was consumed by God's wrath and anger as He was lifted up on the cross as the substitutionary sacrifice for the people of God. The Apostle Paul viewed the propitiatory character of Christ's death as being necessitated by the justice and righteousness of God.

> Whom God hath set forth to be a propitiation through faith in his blood, *to declare his righteousness* for the remission of sins that are part, through the forbearance of God; *To declare*, I say, *at this time his righteousness*: that he might be just, and the justifier of him which believeth in Jesus (Rom. 3:25-26).

In summary, Christ Jesus removed God's wrath by covering over our sins by the sacrifice of Himself in our place. But someone will object. "God doesn't really get angry at sinners. God loves sinners but hates their sin. Therefore, propitiation cannot refer to removing God's wrath and anger."

This objection is based upon ignorance of the Word of God. It is clear from the Old and New Testaments, from the mouth of prophets, Apostles and Jesus Christ Himself, that God is angry at *sinners* because of their sin. God's anger, hatred and wrath are said to be directed toward the sinner as well as towards sin: "He that sitteth in the heavens shall laugh: The LORD shall have them in derision" (Psa. 2:4); "The foolish shall not stand in thy sight: thou *hatest* all workers of iniquity. Thou shalt destroy them that speak leasing: the LORD will *abhor* the bloody and deceitful man" (Psa. 5:5-6); "God judgeth the righteous, and God is *angry* with the wicked every day" (Psa. 7:11); "The LORD trieth the righteous; but the wicked and him that loveth violence his soul *hateth*" (Psa. 11:5); "For the *wrath* of God is revealed from heaven against all ungodliness and unrighteousness of men; who hold the truth in unrighteousness" (Rom. 1:18); "But after thy hardness and impenitent heart treasurest up unto thyself *wrath* against the day of wrath and revelation of the righteous judgment of God; Who will render to every man according to his deeds. To them who by patient continuance in well doing seek for glory and honour and immortality, eternal life. But unto them that are contentious, and do not obey the truth, but obey unrighteousness, *indignation* and *wrath*" (Rom. 2:5-8); "For if, when we were *enemies*, we were reconciled to God by the death of His Son, much more, being reconciled, we shall be saved by His life" (Rom. 5:10); "As it is written, Jacob have I loved, but Esau have I *hated*" (Rom. 9:13); "Among whom also we all had our conversation in times past in the lusts of our flesh, fulfilling the desires of the flesh and of the mind; and were by nature the children of *wrath*, even as others" (Eph. 2:3); "And the kings of the earth, and the great men, and the chief captains, and the mighty men, and every bondman, and every free man hid themselves in the dens and in the rocks of the mountains. And said to the mountains and rocks, fall on us, and hide us from the face of him that sitteth on the throne, and from *the wrath of the lamb*: For the great day of his *wrath* is come; and *who shall be able to stand*"; (Rev. 6:15-17).

If God only hates sin and not the sinners who committed the sins, why does He throw *sinners* into hell? Why did God punish Christ as the sinner's substitute and not just punish sin?

To be sure, the Biblical doctrine of the propitiation does not picture Christ as overcoming the reluctance of the Father to save sinners. Instead, propitiation is supplied by the Father so that we can come before Him with acceptance. Propitiation is the love gift from God to remove His just and righteous anger and wrath.

To jettison the concept of the wrath of God toward sinners from the definition of propitiation, is to destroy its central and essential meaning. It is to do violence to the Holy Scriptures.

"*The wrath of God* is revealed from heaven" (Rom. 1:18). With this statement, the Apostle Paul begins his exposition of the Gospel. The only way to escape the coming wrath of God is to flee to the Lord Jesus Christ as your only hope in life and in death.

"He that believeth on the Son hath everlasting life; and he that believeth not the Son shall not see life; but *the wrath of God abideth upon him*" (John 3:36).

The Thessalonians testified in I Thessalonians 1:10 to the fact that Jesus "delivered us from *the wrath* to come."

Dear Reader, are you safe in the arms of Jesus? Are you ready for the Judgment Day? Have you passed over from being under God's wrath to being under His grace and mercy? You should pray to God that you will know His wrath only as a doctrine and never by experience.

II. Reconciliation

Definition: *Reconciliation is that sovereign work of God the Father in which His alienation from sinners is removed through the propitiatory sacrifice of Jesus Christ. Reconciliation flows out of and is based upon propitiation.*

Before man's fall into sin, God and man walked together in harmony. They had a beautiful relationship in which they considered each other friends. But man's sin destroyed this beautiful harmony.

God was alienated from man at the Fall because of man's sin and rebellion. God now views rebel sinners as His enemies. A proper interpretation of Romans 5:10: "while we were enemies," will clearly show that in this passage, sinners are viewed as the enemies of God. As propitiation deals with the wrath of God, so reconciliation deals with the alienation of God.

There is a paradox and mystery with reconciliation as with propitiation. God is the One who initiates the reconciliation between rebellious sinners (whom He views as His enemies) and Himself. Reconciliation comes from God Himself as a gift of sovereign love and grace.

In contrast to propitiation being a work of Christ, reconciliation is a work of God the Father.

> But *God* demonstrates His love toward us, in that while we were yet sinners, Christ died for us. For if while we were enemies, we were reconciled to God through the death of His Son, much more, having been reconciled, we shall be saved by His life (Rom. 5:8, 10).

> Now all these things are from *God*, who reconciled us to Himself through Christ . . . *God* was in Christ reconciling the world to Himself (II Cor. 5:18-19).

In the work of reconciliation, man is reconciled to God, i.e., God's alienation is removed so that God and man can once again enter into a harmonious relationship. God and man can once again walk and talk together as friends. *Thus reconciliation does not primarily refer to a change in man's attitude toward God but, rather, in God's attitude toward man.* Reconciliation provides the forensic or legal basis upon which God can turn to save sinners.

This understanding of reconciliation is much denied today. Some protest and state that reconciliation refers to a change in *man's* attitude, not God's.

The only way we can decide the meaning of reconciliation is to turn to the Scriptures, for the Word of God is sufficient for all matters of doctrine and life.

We have already stressed the fact that the primary meaning of a word is based upon its usage in everyday speech. With this in mind, we turn to the Old Testament.

In I Samuel 29:4, the Philistines did not want David in their army "lest in the battle he be an adversary to us: for wherewith should he *reconcile* himself unto his master? Should it not be with the heads of these men?"

It is clear from other passages that Saul was angry at and alienated from David. He viewed David as his enemy because David was a threat to his throne (I Sam. 18).

There is no evidence that David had this same attitude toward Saul. In fact, David viewed Saul as the Lord's anointed and would not kill him even when he had the chance (I Sam. 26:8-9).

David's reconciliation to Saul consisted of a change in *Saul's* attitude toward David in which Saul would no longer be angry at David.

When we turn to the New Testament, we find the word "reconciliation" used in exactly the same way as in the Old Testament. Our Lord Himself used the word "reconciled" in Matthew 5:23-24:

> If therefore you are presenting your offering at the altar, and there remember that *your brother has something against you*, leave your offering there before the altar, and go your way; first *be reconciled to your brother*, and then come and present your offering.

It is obvious that our LORD has in mind a situation in which you have offended someone and he is angry with you. He has something against you. There is no indication that you have any negative feelings toward the one you have offended. You must be reconciled to the offended one. *This reconciliation consists of a change in his attitude toward you and not primarily in your attitude toward him.*

From both the Old Testament and New Testament, to be reconciled to someone means that *they have a change of attitude toward you.* Thus, when we read of man being reconciled to God, it refers to a change in God's attitude toward man.

God's alienation arises out of His just wrath over man's sin and rebellion. By reconciliation, God's alienation is removed because His wrath is appeased through the propitiatory sacrifice of Christ.

> We were *reconciled to God through the death of His Son* (Rom. 5:10).

> God, who *reconciled us to Himself through Christ* (II Cor. 5:18).

> God was *in Christ* reconciling the world to Himself (II Cor. 5:19).

> *Through Him to reconcile* all things to Himself, having made
> peace *through the blood of His cross* . . . yet he has not *reconciled*
> you *in his fleshly body through* death (Col. 1:19-22).

Since reconciliation is tied to the propitiatory sacrifice of Christ,
it is obvious that it is an accomplished fact of history. The work of reconciliation does not carry on into the present century. It took place
on Mount Calvary nearly 2,000 years ago. Thus the writers of the New
Testament consistently place reconciliation in the completed past tense
(Rom. 5:10-11; Rom. 11:15; Eph. 2:16; Col. 1:20-22). The tense of the
word in the New Testament is sufficient to show that reconciliation
does not consist of man's conversion.

But someone may protest, "How do you interpret II Corinthians
5:20, 'Be ye reconciled to God'? Doesn't this verse point to man's conversion?"

The answer to this question is found in the context and in a general principle of interpretation.

In the context, Paul has already clearly stated that the work of reconciliation is an accomplished fact of history in that he ties it to the
death of Christ in verses 14-15. The Gospel is the good news that reconciliation has been accomplished by Christ. Hence it is called "the
Word of Reconciliation" (v. 19). In the light of the context, verse 20
cannot contradict the historicity of the reconciliation described in verses
14-19.

Second, there is a general rule of interpretation which also applies
in this situation. *Always interpret the unclear in the light of the clear.* It
is clear from *every* other place in the New Testament where reconciliation is mentioned, that it is an accomplished work tied to the once-
for-all-time propitiatory sacrifice of Christ. Therefore, verse 20 must
conform to this understanding.

When Paul said, "Be ye reconciled to God," he was saying "enter
into the benefits of the reconciliation which God accomplished through
Jesus Christ." He was referring to *the application* of the reconciliation
which was accomplished by Jesus Christ.

How thankful we must be to God the Father. He took the initiative
and sought us when we were yet helpless, ungodly, sinners and enemies (Rom. 5:6-10). Was it not God who first sought out fallen Adam
and Eve (Gen. 3:8-9)? Although God was alienated from us because
of His anger over our sins, He loved us so much that He sent His Son
to be our Savior. Let us praise the Father for His work of reconciliation.

Lord, with glowing heart I'd praise thee
For the bliss thy love bestows,
For the pard'ning grace that saves me,
And the peace that from it flows:
Help, O God, my weak endeavors;
This dull soul to rapture raise:
Thou must light the flame, or never
Can my love be warmed to praise.

Praise, my soul, the God that sought thee,
Wretched wand'rer far astray;
Found thee lost, and kindly brought thee,
From the paths of death away:
Praise, with Love's devoutest feeling,
Him who saw thy guilt-born fear,
And, the light of hope revealing,
Bade the blood-stain'd cross appear.*

III. Redemption

Definition: *Redemption is that priestly work of Christ wherein He delivered us from our bondage to the Law, Sin and Satan through purchase by the ransom of His substitutionary obedience in life and in death.*

In the New Testament we find twenty clear references to redemption as being a saving work of Jesus Christ. We are told that the mission and purpose of Christ in coming to this earth was to accomplish the work of redemption.

> The Son of man did not come to be served, but to serve, and *to give his life a ransom for many* (Matt. 20:28).

> But when the fullness of the time came, God sent forth His Son, born of a woman, born under the Law, *to redeem* those under the Law, that we might receive the adoption of sons (Gal. 4:4-5).

> Who gave Himself for us, *that He might redeem* us from every lawless deed (Tit. 2:14).

We are told that redemption has been accomplished *by* Christ and thus it is to be secured *in* Christ. "Being justified freely by His grace through the redemption that is *in* Christ Jesus" (Rom. 3:24). "But of

*Hymn: "Lord, With Glowing Heart I'd Praise Thee"

him are ye in Christ Jesus, who of God is made unto us wisdom, and righteousness, and sanctification, and redemption" (I Cor. 1:30). *"In whom we have redemption through His blood, the forgiveness of sins, according to the riches of His grace"* (Eph. 1:7). *"In whom we have redemption through His blood, even the forgiveness of sins"* (Col. 1:14).

The basic meaning of the word redemption is deliverance through purchase, i.e., the payment of a price. The word redemption or redeem is used over 160 times in the Bible. Therefore, it is not difficult to discover its primary meaning.

We find the word "redemption" used in several non-theological or common-speech passages in the Old Testament.

Our first passage is found in Exodus 21:28-32: "If an ox gore a man or a woman, that they shall die: then the ox shall be surely stoned, and his flesh shall not be eaten; the owner of the ox shall be quit. But if the ox were wont to push with his horn in time past, and it hath been testified to his owner, and he hath not kept him in, but that he hath killed a man or a woman; the ox shall be stoned and his owner also shall be put to death. If there be laid on him *a sum of money*, then he shall give for *the ransom* of his life whatsoever is laid upon him. Whether he have gored a son, or have gored a daughter, according to his judgment shall it be done unto him. If the ox shall push a manservant or a maidservant; he shall give unto their master thirty shekels of silver and the ox shall be stoned."

In this passage, Moses says that if a man owned an ox which he knew was dangerous and he had been warned that it might gore people to death, and if this ox did kill someone, then the ox and its owner should be put to death except "if a *ransom* is demanded of him, then he shall give for the *redemption* of his life whatever is demanded of him."

The owner could be delivered from death through purchase, i.e., the payment of a price.

Our second passage is found in Leviticus 25:23-33: "The land shall not be sold forever; for the land is mine; for ye are strangers and sojourners with me. And in all the land of your possession ye shall grant a *redemption* for the land. If thy brother be waxen poor, and hath sold away some of his possession, and if any of his kin come to *redeem* it, then shall he *redeem* that which his brother sold. And if the man have none to *redeem* it, and himself be able to *redeem* it; then let him count the years of the sale thereof, and restore the overplus unto the man to whom he sold it; that he may return unto his possession. But if he be not able to restore it to him, then that which is sold shall remain in the hand of him that hath bought it until the year of jubilee; and in the jubilee it shall go out, and he shall return unto his possession. And if a man sell a dwelling house in a walled city, then he may *redeem* it within a whole year after it is sold; within a full year may he *redeem* it. And if it be not *redeemed* within the space of a full year, then the house that is in the walled city shall be established for ever to him that bought it throughout his generations: it shall not go out in the jubilee. But the houses of the villages which have no wall round about them shall be counted as the fields of the country: they may be *redeemed,* and they shall go out in the jubilee. Notwithstanding the cities of the Levites, and the houses of the cities of their possession, may the Levites *redeem* at any time. And if a man purchase of the Levites, then the house that was sold, and the city of his possession, shall go out in the year of jubilee: for the houses of the cities of the Levites are their possession among the children of Israel."

In this passage Moses instructs the people that the way to *redeem* the land is to *purchase* back the land *by the payment of an acceptable price.*

These are but two examples of the general way in which the word redemption is used in the Bible. Redemption refers to deliverance through payment of a price.

In the New Testament, the work of Christ is described as being the purchase price through which we have gained deliverance. Is not the church of God *"purchased* with His own blood" (Acts 20:28)? Doesn't the Apostle Paul exhort the Corinthians to "glorify God in your body" because they "have been *bought* with a price" (I Cor. 6:20)? Is not *the price* of redemption "the precious blood of a lamb unblemished and spotless, the blood of Christ" (I Pet. 1:18-19)? What will the elect in heaven sing?

> Worthy art thou to take the Book, and to break its seals; for
> thou wast slain and *didst purchase for God with thy blood* men
> from every tribe and tongue and people and nation (Rev. 5:9,
> cf. also Rev. 14:3).

Christ's work of redemption cannot therefore be reduced to simply deliverance. *It is deliverance through ransom, i.e., the payment of a price.* This ransom aspect of Christ's redemptive work is clearly taught in Matthew 20:28 and in I Timothy 2:6 where we read,

> To give His life *as a ransom.*

But what is the focus of redemption? From what did He deliver us? How did He accomplish our deliverance? These questions should now be answered.

The focus of redemption has in view our bondage to the Law, sin and Satan.

1. Christ came to deliver us from our bondage to the Law (Gal. 4:4-5). We are not saying that Christ delivered us from our responsibility to obey the moral Law. Indeed, Christ came to mold us in conformity to that Law. But Christ did come to deliver us from the *curse of the Law*. The law demanded our death. Someone had to die. Either the sinner must die under the curse or the sinner's substitute. Thus we read in Galatians 3:13:

> Christ redeemed us from the curse of the law, having become
> a curse for us.

The purchase price for our deliverance from the curse of the Law entailed the curse-bearing of our substitute saviour.

We were also in bondage to *the ceremonial Law*. And Christ came to deliver us from this bondage through His substitutionary perfect obedience to that Law. He did away with the ceremonial Law by fulfilling it perfectly (Matt. 5:17). This is why the Apostle Paul could sum up the redemptive work of Christ as "the obedience of the One" in Romans 5:19.

The purchase price of our deliverance from the ceremonial law centered in our substitute's perfect obedience to that law (Gal. 4:4-5).

> Nor silver nor gold hath obtained my Redemption,
> The holy commandment forbade me draw near;
> The blood of the cross is my only Foundation,
> The death of my Savior removeth my fear.*

2. By nature we are in bondage to sin for both Jesus (John 8:34) and Paul (Rom. 5:20) called us "slaves of sin."

We are in bondage to the *penalty* of sin (Rom. 6:23). Christ delivered us by bearing the penalty in our place. Thus justification and forgiveness are said to flow directly out of Christ's redemptive death.

> Being *justified* freely as a gift by His grace *through the redemption* which is in Christ Jesus (Rom. 3:24).

> *In him* we have *redemption through His blood, the forgiveness of our trespasses* (Eph. 1:7).

*Hymn: "Nor Silver Nor Gold Hath Obtained My Redemption"

In whom we have *redemption, the forgiveness of sins* (Col. 1:14).

We are also in bondage to the *power* of sin. Sin is a cruel master and we need deliverance. Christ delivered us through the price of His own death (I Cor. 6:20).

> For ye are *bought with a price:* therefore glorify God in your body, and in your spirit, which are God's: Forasmuch as ye know that ye were not *redeemed* with corruptible things, as silver and gold, from your vain conversation received by tradition from your fathers; But *with the precious blood of Christ,* as of a lamb without blemish and without spot (I Pet. 1:18-19).

> Who gave Himself for our sins, that He might *deliver us out of this present evil age* (Gal. 1:4).

> Who gave Himself for us, that he might *redeem us from every lawless deed and purify for Himself* a people for His own possession, zealous of good works (Tit. 2:14).

Well did the hymn writer say, "He breaks the power of reigning sin, and sets the prisoner free."

Christ has delivered us from the penalty and the power of sin. And one day He will deliver us from the very *presence* of sin by virtue of His redemptive work. Thus the second coming of Christ is called "the day of redemption" in Ephesians 4:30, and the resurrection of the Christian is called "the redemption of our body" in Romans 8:23.

By the ransom of His own substitutionary death, Christ has secured our deliverance from the penalty, power and presence of sin.

> Ye slaves of sin and hell,
> Your liberty receive;
> Redemption through His blood
> Throughout the world proclaim.
> O perfect redemption, the purchase of blood!
> To every believer the promise of God;
> The vilest offender who truly believes,
> That moment from Jesus forgiveness receives.*

3. Lastly, *we are in bondage to Satan* for he is the father of all unregenerate sinners (John 8:44). And they are under his control (Eph. 2:2). Thus they are said "to be held captive by him" (I Tim. 2:26).

*Hymn: "Blow Ye the Trumpet, Blow!"

Christ did not pay a ransom to Satan as some medieval theologians thought. But, rather, Christ's ransom was paid to God to remove sin for it is by sin that Satan holds us captive. By removing our sins through the death of Christ, God "delivered us from the power of darkness" (Col. 1:13, cf. Acts 25:18).

Christ has bound Satan because the Kingdom of God had come (Matt. 12:28-29). He can no longer deceive the nations (Rev. 20:1-3). Christ has taken away Satan's power of death (Heb. 2:14-15, cf. Rev. 1:18). Christ now sits exalted over all demonic forces (Eph. 1:20-22). Those who are in union with Christ are also seated in the heavenlies far above all spiritual rulers (Eph. 2:6). They join with Christ in crushing the head of the Serpent (Rom. 16:20) for Christ has triumphed over Satan (Col. 2:15).

We are delivered from Satan's power and Kingdom through the redemption which is in Christ Jesus. This truth should be most comforting and encouraging in an age when Satanism and demon worship is growing. "Greater is He who is in us, than he that is in the world" (I John 4:4).

Stop for a moment and ask yourself, "Am I still in bondage to the Law, sin or Satan? Have I found the price of my deliverance in the bloody death of the Son of God? Am I in Christ and He in me?" If you are still a captive of Satan, cry out to King Jesus. He is mighty to save.

IV.   Sacrifice (Expiation)

Definition: *Sacrifice (expiation) is that priestly work of Christ wherein He removed our sin and its guilt by offering up Himself to God in our place.*

Upon reading the New Testament, it is not long before one recognizes the fact that the person and work of Christ Jesus are described in terms of a sacrifice offered to God on behalf of the people of God. One such example is found in I Corinthians 5:7: "Christ our Passover has been *sacrificed.*" And throughout the New Testament sacrificial language is applied to the person and work of Christ. "The next day John seeth Jesus coming unto him and saith, Behold *the Lamb of God*, which taketh away the sin of the world" (John 1:29); "And walk in love, as Christ also hath loved us, and hath given Himself for us an *offering* and a *sacrifice* to God for a sweet-smelling savour" (Eph. 5:2); "For he hath made him to be sin for us, who knew no sin; that we might be made the righteousness of God in him" (II Cor. 5:21); "But with the precious blood of Christ, as of a *lamb* without blemish and without spot" (I Pet. 1:19).

We not only find that sacrificial language is applied to Christ in the New Testament, but we also find an explanation behind such a sacrificial description.

Did not our Lord explicitly state that the Old Testament in its entirety spoke concerning Him and that the Old Testament in its unexplained ceremonies, unfulfilled prophecies and unsatisfied longings is fulfilled in His own person and work? "Think not that I am come to destroy the law, or the prophets: I am not come to destroy, but to fulfill. For verily I say unto you, Till heaven and earth pass, one jot or one tittle shall in no wise pass from the law till all be fulfilled" (Matt. 5:17-18); "Ought not Christ to have suffered these things, and to enter into His glory? And beginning at Moses and all the prophets, He expounded unto them, These are the words which I spake unto you while I was yet with you, that all things must be fulfilled, which were written in the law of Moses, and in the prophets, and in the psalms, concerning me" (Luke 24:26-27, 44); "Search the scriptures; for in them ye think ye have eternal life; and they are they which testify of me" (John 5:39).

Did not the Apostles teach that the Old Testament sacrificial system was fulfilled in the person and work of Christ? Did they not call Him a High Priest? Did they not designate His death as a sacrifice? "Philip findeth Nathanael, and saith unto him, We have found Him, of whom Moses in the law, and the prophets, did write, Jesus of Nazareth, the son of Joseph" (John 1:45); "Purge out therefore the old leaven, that ye may be a new lump, as ye are unleavened. For even Christ our passover is sacrificed for us" (I Cor. 5:7); "For I delivered unto you first of all that which I also received, how that Christ died for our sins according to the Scriptures; And that he was buried, and that he rose again the third day according to the Scriptures" (I Cor. 15:3-4); "Which are a shadow of things to come; but the body is of Christ" (Col. 2:17); "It was therefore necessary that the patterns of things in the heavens should be purified with these; but the heavenly things themselves with better sacrifices than these. For Christ is not entered into the holy places made with hands, which are the figures of the true; but into heaven itself, now to appear in the presence of God for us" (Heb. 9:23-24); "For the law having a shadow of good things to come, and not the very image of the things can never with those sacrifices which they offered year by year continually make the comers thereunto perfect" (Heb. 10:1).

With this understanding, we can come to this conclusion:

We must investigate the Old Testament concept of sacrifice if we are to understand the New Testament use of sacrifice in reference to the person and work of Christ. Let us turn to the book of Leviticus where we will find the fullest expression of the Old Testament sacrificial system: Leviticus 1-5.

Now it would not be to our purpose to begin a detailed exposition of each of these different sacrifices. *What we want to discover are the common elements in the sacrificial system which are taken up by the New Testament writers and applied to the person and work of Christ.* Thus we will be concerned with animal sacrifices where blood was shed.

Leviticus 3:1-2: "And if his oblation be a sacrifice of peace offering, if he offer it of the herd; whether it be a male or female, he shall offer it without blemish before the Lord. And he shall lay his head upon the head of his offering, and kill it at the door of the tabernacle of the congregation: and Aaron's sons the priests shall sprinkle the blood upon the altar round about."

There are four distinct elements in this sacrifice which are shared by other sacrifices.

A. **The presentation of a perfect victim "without blemish."** This perfection points to the necessity for an innocent and blameless substitute. As there could not be any physical defect in the animal in the Old Testament, so we learn in the New Testament that there could not be any moral defect in Christ Jesus (Heb. 9:13-14; I Pet. 1:19). The Lord Jesus Christ was the sinless, blameless and spotless Lamb of God.

B. **The imputation of sin.** This is found in the reference to the laying of the hands on the animal (v. 2). That this is what it meant is clear from Leviticus 16:21: "And Aaron shall lay both his hands upon the head of the live goat, and confess over him all the iniquities of the children of Israel, and all their transgressions in all their sins, putting them upon the head of the goat, and shall send him away by the hand of a fit man into the wilderness."

At the point of the laying on of hands, the sinner's guilt and liability to punishment are transferred to the sacrificial victim. Thus the victim takes the sinner's place as his substitute.

In the Holy Scriptures, we find that all the sins of the elect were imputed to Christ and He became a sinner in their place. That this is true is seen from several lines of argument.

1. There are explicit statements: "Surely he hath borne our griefs,

and carried our sorrows. Yet we did esteem him stricken, smitten of God, and afflicted. But he was wounded for our transgressions, he was bruised for our iniquities: the chastisement of our peace was upon him; and with his stripes we are healed. All we like sheep have gone astray; we have turned every one to his own way, and the Lord hath laid on him the iniquity of us all" (Isa. 53:4-6); "The next day John seeth Jesus coming unto him, and saith, Behold the Lamb of God, which taketh away the sin of the world" (John 1:29); "For he hath made him to be sin for us, who knew no sin; that we might be made the righteousness of God in him" (II Cor. 5:21); "Who his own self bare our sins in his own body on the tree, that we, being dead to sins, should live unto righteousness by whose stripes ye were healed" (I Pet. 2:24).

2. Christ is said to die in our place *for* our sins: "For I delivered unto you first of all that which I also received, how that Christ died for our sins according to the Scriptures" (I Cor. 15:3); "Who gave himself for our sins, that he might deliver us from this present evil world, according to the will of God and our Father" (Gal. 1:4).

C. **The slaying of the victim.** The victim must die; for death was the just punishment for the sinner whose place the victim took (Ezek. 18:20; Rom. 6:23). The victim's blood had to be shed (Lev. 17:11; Heb. 9:22). No atonement was possible without the shedding of blood. Thus we find in the New Testament that Christ Jesus as the Lamb of God had to die in such a way that His blood was shed.

The New Testament is filled with references to the blood of Christ (Rom. 3:25; 5:9; I Cor. 10:16; Eph. 1:7; 2:13; Col. 1:20; Heb. 9:12, 18, 21; 12:24; I Pet. 1:2, 19; I John 1:7; 5:6, 8; Rev. 1:5, etc.). In the light of the Old Testament background, the blood of Jesus Christ must be understood as sacrificial blood.

D. **The sprinkling of the blood on the altar,** v. 2. It is at this point that expiation takes place. It is the blood upon the altar that atones (Lev. 17:11). Why? The altar was the place of the presence of God. No sinner could come into the presence of God without being destroyed. Therefore, God's holiness and righteousness must be satisfied by the death of the sinner or his substitute sacrifice before He could be approached. The blood signified that (1) the sinner had died, (2) God was now satisfied. With the blood of sprinkling, the priest atoned for the sins of the sinner.

In the New Testament, Christ's blood is not only said to have been shed but we are told that it was sprinkled. (Hebrews 12:22-24: "But ye are come unto Mount Zion, and unto the city of the living God, the heavenly Jerusalem, and to an innumerable company of angels, to the general assembly and church of the firstborn, which are written in heaven, and to God the Judge of all, and to the spirits of just men made perfect. And to Jesus the mediator of the new covenant, and to *the blood of sprinkling,* that speaketh better things than that of Abel." I Peter 1:2: "Elect according to the foreknowledge of God the Father, through sanctification of the Spirit, unto obedience and *sprinkling of the blood of Jesus Christ;* Grace unto you, and peace, be multiplied.") The sprinkling of the blood of Jesus is mentioned that we might know for sure that God accepted the sacrifice and that we can now come before God's presence without fear (Heb. 10; 19:22: "Having therefore, brethren, boldness to enter into the holiest by the blood of Jesus, By a new and living way, which he hath consecrated for us, through the veil, that is to say, his flesh; and having a high priest over the house of God; Let us draw near with a true heart in full assurance of faith, having our hearts sprinkled from an evil conscience, and our bodies washed with pure water.")

With this basic background of the Old Testament view of sacrifice and a presentation of the ways in which Christ fulfilled the common elements of the Old Testament sacrificial system, we can now ask *What is the exact focus of the sacrifice of Christ?* i.e., as:

> Propitiation has in focus God's wrath.
> Reconciliation has in focus God's alienation.
> Redemption has in focus our bondage to the Law, sin and Satan.

So, sacrifice has a certain object in focus. What is it?

Sacrifice or expiation has in view the removal of our sin and guilt and our accountability to God (Rom. 3:14). We are guilty sinners before God and this guilt must be removed. This is the basic meaning of the word expiation: *to remove sin and its guilt by covering it over with the blood of a substitutionary sacrifice. Therefore, expiation is that priestly work of Christ wherein He removed our sin and guilt through covering them over by the bloody substitutionary sacrifice of Himself to God.*

But we must ask, *"What flows from Christ's work of expiation or sacrifice? What did this expiation bring about or cause?* The answer to this question reveals that expiation or sacrifice is a summary term which catches up the other elements of the atonement. It is by expiation that propitiation, reconciliation and redemption take place. Once our sin and guilt is removed, God's wrath and alienation, and our bondage to the law, sin and Satan are also removed.

Dear Reader, have you been stirred to praise the Savior yet? Do you appreciate all that He has done for you? One test of your salvation is whether or not you are truly thankful for the work of Christ.

Upon contemplating the nature of the atonement, Bliss wrote:

> Man of sorrows! What a name
> For the Son of God who came
> Ruined sinners to reclaim:
> Hallelujah! What a Saviour!
>
> Bearing shame and scoffing rude,
> In my place condemned He stood,
> Sealed my pardon with His blood:
> Hallelujah! What a Saviour!
>
> Guilty, vile and helpless, we;
> Spotless Lamb of God was He;
> Full atonement! Can it be?
> Hallelujah! What a Saviour!
>
> Lifted up was He to die,
> "It is finished!" was His cry.
> Now in heav'n exalted high;
> Hallelujah! What a Saviour!
>
> When He comes our glorious King,
> All His ransomed home to bring,
> Then anew this song we'll sing:
> Hallelujah! What a Saviour!*

*Hymn: "Man of Sorrows!"

CHAPTER 4

The Perfection of the Atonement

The perfection of the atonement is a complex doctrine and special care must be taken to gather and balance all the different aspects of it. It cannot be reduced to one simple idea or concept. Therefore, to omit or over-emphasize any of the aspects of the perfection of the atonement can lead to a distortion or destruction of the doctrine itself.

Our first task is to define carefully the key terms used in reference to this doctrine.

1. **Unique:** used in reference to the *singularity* of the work.
2. **Final:** used in reference to *time* of the work.
3. **Satisfying:** used in reference to the *character and laws* of God.
4. **Sufficient:** used in reference to *the demands of sin.*
5. **Efficient:** used in reference to *the needs of man.*
6. **Complete:** used in reference to any supposed *additions* to the atonement.

A. **Was the atonement UNIQUE?** Is there or could there be a comparable or similar work? Is the atonement something so different that it stands alone or are there other works which equal it?

The saving work of Christ can never be equaled to or compared with any other work. It is the only one of its kind. It is singular in its author, agent, nature and perfection.

The uniqueness of the atonement rests upon the uniqueness of the person who accomplished it. As the unique God-Man, Jesus Christ is "the *only* mediator between God and Man" (I Timothy 2:15). He stated that He was *"The* Way" (John 14:6). The writer to the Hebrews es-

47

tablishes the uniqueness of Christ's work upon the superiority of the person of Christ and His work (Heb. 1-3). It cannot be equaled by angels, men or animals.

The necessity of the atonement also points to its uniqueness. Only the saving work of the incarnate Son of God could release us from our sins. If the atonement is not necessary, but other works by other agents could save sinners as well, then Christ's work is only one among many and thus not unique.

B. **Was the atonement FINAL?** Was it finished at a definite point in time? Was it something repeatedly done in history? Can it be repeated today? When did it take place in history?

The atonement was completely finished by Jesus Christ during His earthly existence and it will never be repeated. The work of atonement is not being accomplished by the priests of Rome in the mass and neither did it await the visions of Ellen G. White. By His life, death, resurrection and ascension, Christ accomplished eternal salvation for He is "the author of eternal salvation" (Heb. 5:9).

When we turn to the Scriptures, we find direct statements which stress that fact of the finality of the atonement.

> Knowing that Christ, having been raised from the dead, is *never to die again*, death no longer is master over him. For the death that he died, he died to sin *once for all time*; but the life that he lives, he lives to God (Rom. 6:9-10).

> For it was fitting that we should have such a high priest, holy, innocent, undefiled, separated from sinners and exalted above the heavens; Who does not need daily, like those to offer up sacrifices, first for his own sins, and then for the sins of the people, because this he did *once for all time* when he offered up himself (Heb. 8:26-27).

> By this will we have been sanctified through the offering of the body of Jesus Christ *once for all time* (Heb. 10:10).

> Now at the consummation he has been manifested to put away sin by the sacrifice of himself. And inasmuch as it is appointed for men to die *once*, and after this comes judgment; so Christ also, having been offered *once for all time* to bear the sins of man, shall appear a second time, *not to bear sin*, to those who eagerly await him (Heb. 9:27-28).

> And every priest stands daily ministering and offering time after time the same sacrifice, which can never take away sins; but he, having offered *one* sacrifice for sins *for all time*, sat down at the right hand of God (Heb. 10:11-12).

> For Christ also died for sins *once for all time*, the just for the unjust, in order that he might bring us to God, having been put to death in the flesh, but made alive by the Spirit (I Pet. 3:18).

In the above passages, various versions of the New Testament only say "once for all." Some have misunderstood this expression to refer to Christ's dying for all people. But this is not at all what the authors of Scripture were trying to communicate. An examination of the usage of the Greek word in I Corinthians 15:6 and II Corinthians 11:25 will show that "once for all" meant "once for all *time.*"

Several other facts from Scripture also reveal the finality of the atonement.

1. The fact that the New Testament uses the past tense in its description of the nature of the atonement reveals that the authors of the New Testament viewed it as a finished work. Propitiation, Reconciliation, Redemption and Expiation were all perfectly accomplished by Christ.

2. The fact that Christ has sat down at the right hand of the Father reveals that His work was finished. "Who being the brightness of his glory, and the express image of his person, and upholding all things by the word of his power, when he had by himself purged our sins, sat down on the right hand of the Majesty on high" (Heb. 1:3); "Now of the things which we have spoken this is the sum: We have such an high priest, who is set on the right hand of the throne of the Majesty in the heavens" (Heb. 8:1); "From henceforth expecting 'till his enemies be made his footstool" (Heb. 10:13).

3. The fact that the Father gave the gift of the Holy Spirit to the Son and that He has poured out this gift upon the church reveals that the atonement is finished. "This Jesus hath God raised up, whereof we all are witness. Therefore, being by the right hand of God exalted, and having received of the Father the promise of the Holy Ghost, he hath shed forth this, which ye now see and hear" (Acts 2:32-33).

4. The fact that Christ has now been glorified reveals that His

work is finished. "Therefore, being by the right hand of God exalted, and having received of the Father the promise of the Holy Ghost, he hath shed forth this, which ye now see and hear. Therefore let all the house of Israel know assuredly, that God hath made the same Jesus, whom ye have crucified, both Lord and Christ" (Acts 2:33, 36). "Wherefore God also hath highly exalted him, and given him a name which is above every name; that at the name of Jesus every knee should bow, of things in heaven and things in earth, and things under the earth; And that every tongue should confess that Jesus Christ is Lord, to the glory of God the Father" (Phil. 2:9-11).

5.   The fact that Christ has begun His intercessory ministry reveals that His work of oblation or sacrifice has been finished. "Who is he that condemneth? It is Christ that died, yea rather, that is risen again, who is even at the right hand of God, who also maketh intercession for us" (Rom. 8:34). "Wherefore he is able also to save them to the uttermost that come unto God by him, seeing he ever liveth to make intercession for them" (Heb. 9:24). "If any man sin, we have an advocate before the Father, Jesus Christ the righteous" (I John 2:1).

The work of Christ is clearly described in terms of the work of the Old Testament high priest (Heb. 2:17). And the high priest could not intercede for the people until the sacrifice was finished.

In conclusion, did not our Lord plainly state on the cross that His work of atonement was "finished" (John 19:30). By "finished" He meant "paid in full."

> Hark! the voice of love and mercy sounds aloud from Calvary
> See, it rends the rocks asunder, shakes the earth, and veils the sky:
> "It is finished!" "It is finished!" "It is finished!"
> Hear the dying Saviour cry; Hear the dying Saviour cry.
>
> "It is finished!" O what pleasure do these precious words afford;
> Heav'n-ly blessings, without measure, flow to us from Christ the
>   Lord:
> "It is finished!" "It is finished!" "It is finished!"
> Saints the dying words record; Saints the dying words record.
> Finished all the types and shadows of the ceremonial law;
> Finished all that God has promised; Death and hell no more
>   shall awe:
> "It is finished!" "It is finished!" "It is finished!"

Saints, from hence your comfort draw; Saints, from hence your
comfort draw.

Tune your harps anew, ye seraphs, Join to sing the glorious
theme;
All in earth, and all in heaven, Join to praise Emmanuel's Name:
Alleluia! Alleluia! Alleluia!
Glory to the bleeding Lamb! Glory to the bleeding Lamb!*

C. **Was the atonement SATISFYING?** Did it satisfy the character
and Law of God so that man can once again come into His presence with
God's favor?

The saving work of Christ was designed by God to satisfy perfectly
all the demands of His character and Law. We have already examined
what those demands are and how Christ satisfied each one.

The perfect satisfaction of Christ's work is built on two foundational
principles from the Word of God.

1. Foundational principle #1: *The indivisible union between the char-
    acter and Law of God.*

    God's character and the Law of God are placed together be-
    cause the moral law is a manifestation of God's moral character.
    Man was created to be the image-bearer of God, and the Law
    of God serves as a standard by which man can see in what ways
    he is to be likened unto God. Example: God does not lie (Tit.
    1:2). Therefore, the Law teaches us that we should not lie (Ex.
    20:16). God is perfect and holy: Therefore, man must be perfect
    and holy if he is to be the image-bearer of God (Lev. 19:2; Matt.
    5:48; I Pet. 1:16).

2. Foundational principle #2: *Satisfaction of the one means satisfac-
    tion of the other.*

    Because of the union between the character and Law of God,
    to demonstrate the satisfaction of either one proves the satisfac-
    tion of the other, for if God's character is satisfied by the work
    of Christ, then His law must also be satisfied because it is a mani-
    festation of that character.

The prophet Isaiah tells us in Isaiah 53:11 that God the Son is satisfied by His work. Could He be satisfied if He had failed to satisfy all
the demands of God's character and Law?

*Hymn: "Hark! The Voice of Love and Mercy"

God the Father is satisfied by the work of Christ. This is seen from several lines of evidence.

1. The fact that God raised Christ from the dead reveals that He was satisfied. If God was not satisfied, Christ would still be in the grave today (Rom. 6:9-10).
2. The ascension and glorification of Christ reveals that God was satisfied (Acts 2:32-36; Phil. 2:9-11).
3. The concrete results of the atonement show that it has satisfied God for it brought about propitiation and reconciliation (Rom. 3:24-25; 5:10).

The Law of God is satisfied by the work of Christ. Is it not the case that Christ came to satisfy the just demands of the Law of God by way of fulfillment and curse-bearing (Matt. 5:17; Gal. 3:13; 4:4-5; Isa. 53:4-6)? Is not God's moral character satisfied by Christ's work? Do we not have free access to God because we are now under grace instead of being under the curse of God (Rom. 6:14; Heb. 4:14-16; 10:19-22)?

D. Was the atonement SUFFICIENT? Did it perfectly satisfy all the demands of sin? Did it perfectly provide for its forgiveness and cleansing?

We have already seen from our study of the necessity of the atonement what the nature of sin is and what is necessary to remove it. Then we examined the nature of the atonement and saw that Christ had perfectly dealt with the demands of sin. His work is perfectly sufficient.

E. Was the atonement EFFICIENT? Did it perfectly satisfy the needs of man which sin created?

We have already seen from our study of the necessity and nature of the atonement that Christ's work is perfectly efficient in satisfying all the needs of man in his person and position. Thus the Apostle Paul states "in *Him* you have been made *complete*" in Colossians 2:10. The efficiency of the atonement is based upon the deity of Christ "for in Him all the fulness of deity dwells in bodily form" (Colossians 2:9).

F. Was the atonement COMPLETE? Did Christ leave anything undone? Did He fail to accomplish a full and complete redemption? Is man the sinner to contribute anything to Christ's work or has Christ done it all? Did Christ infallibly secure the eventual salvation of all those for whom He died?

Two distinct questions are asked in this doctrine:

1. Was the atonement complete in respect of its fully satisfying the character of God, the Law of God, sin and the needs of man which it created? We have already proven that the atonement is complete in this sense.

2. Was the atonement complete in respect to its *actually securing the salvation of all the objects of the work?* No work can be considered *complete, perfect,* or *finished* if it fails to accomplish the stated goal or purpose.

Imagine if you sent your child to the store to get some bread. Would you consider his mission complete if he merely offered to pay for it and then left the store without it? No. Not until the bread is secured is the mission complete.

In the same way, *Christ did not come merely to make salvation possible.* He was sent by the Father to *save sinners.* Did not the angels promise us that "he *shall save* his people from their sins" (Matt. 1:21). Or again, I Timothy 1:15 states:

Christ Jesus came into the world *to save sinners.*

Christ came and actually secured the eternal salvation of all those for whom He died (John 6:37-39; 10:10-11, 16-17, 27-30; 17:2, 4, 9, 20; Col. 2:10, cf. Heb. 9:12).

False religion always has the sinner adding something to his own salvation. Regardless if this "something" is called works, merit, indulgence, faith or repentance, the sinner is viewed as "doing his part" for his salvation.

But in contrast to this, the Word of God teaches us that Christ's atonement provides the gifts of faith and repentance and even includes works. "Him hath God exalted with his right hand to be a Prince and a Saviour, for *to give repentance* to Israel, for forgiveness of sins" (Acts 5:31); "When they heard these things, they held their peace, and glorified God, saying, Then hath God also to the Gentiles *granted repentance unto life*" (Acts 11:18); "And a certain woman named Lydia a seller of purple, of the city of Thyatira, which worshipped God, heard us: *whose heart the Lord opened,* that she attended unto the things which were spoken of Paul" (Acts 16:14); "And when he was disposed to pass into Achaia, the brethren wrote, exhorting the disciples to receive him: who, when he was come, helped them much which had *believed through grace*" (Acts 18:27); "In meekness instructing those that oppose themselves; if God peradventure will *give them repentance* to the acknowledging of the truth" (II Tim. 2:25); "For by grace are ye saved through *faith, and that not of yourselves: it is the gift of God:* Not of works, lest any man should boast. For we are his workmanship created in Christ Jesus unto good works, which God hath before ordained that we should walk in them" (Eph. 2:8-10); "For *unto you it is given* in the behalf of Christ, not only *to believe on him,* but also to suffer for his sake" (Phil. 1:29); "For it is *God* which worketh in you *to will* and *to do* of his good pleasure" (Phil. 2:13).

Christ's work is viewed as being complete because it even provides the means by which it is received. This provision is absolutely necessary if man is to receive any benefit from Christ's work. By nature we are in bondage to sin (John 8:34) and lack any ability to seek God and Christ or to repent of sin and believe the Gospel (John 6:44; Rom. 3:11; 8:7; I Cor. 2:14; 12:3). Unless we are regenerated "from above" we will never see or enter the kingdom of God (John 3:3-5). Christ must by necessity make a complete salvation in which He undertakes to secure our acceptance of it through grace. It is by grace that we believe (Acts 18:27). Sovereign grace opens our hearts (Acts 16:14).

Any position which ignores or rejects the completeness of the atonement rejects the perfection of the atonement. In so doing, it accuses our Saviour of failing to accomplish a full salvation.

In conclusion, the perfection of the atonement is a great foundation upon which to establish the assurance of salvation. We trust in Him for eternal salvation.

"He is able to keep you from falling and to present you faultless before the presence of His glory with exceeding joy" (Jude 24). God "*will equip* you in every good thing to do his will, *working in you* that which is pleasing in his sight" (Heb. 13:21). Our complete sanctification is guaranteed because "faithful is he who calls you, and *he also will bring it to pass*" (I Thess. 5:23-24). God "*is at work* in you, both to will and to work for his good pleasure" (Phil. 2:13).

Child of God, when you get to heaven, it is all due to Christ! You cannot take any credit. When you are on your knees praying or on your feet praising, you know that you contributed *nothing* to your salvation. All glory, praise, and honor to God for He has done everything!

> How vast the benefits divine
> Which we in Christ possess!
> We are redeemed from guilt and shame
> And called to holiness.
>
> But not for works which we have done,
> or shall hereafter do,
> Hath God decreed on sinful man
> Salvation to bestow.

The glory, Lord, from first to last,
Is due to thee above;
Ought to ourselves we dare not take,
Or rob thee of thy crown.

Our glorious Surety undertook
To satisfy for man;
And grace was given us in him
Before the world began.*

*Hymn: "How Vast the Benefits Divine"

CHAPTER 5

The Extent of the Atonement

I t is a shame that the issue of the extent of the atonement is such an emotionally charged topic. The heat of controversy always obscures the light of reason. Many Christians do not approach this doctrine with an open mind or a humble heart. They are all too quick to decide this issue before studying the Biblical evidence involved. May God grant us a humble heart and mind as we search the Scriptures to discern the mind of God on this subject.

In order to avoid confusion, it would be helpful to set down several foundational principles of approach.

I. The extent of the atonement must be viewed as a part of God's plan of salvation. We must not isolate it or deal with it in abstraction from the other aspects of God's plan. The confusion surrounding this doctrine often results from the failure to view it in the light of the whole plan of salvation. Therefore, the parts should be interpreted or understood in the light of the whole.

What are the parts of God's plan of salvation? The Scriptures reveal at least four distinct parts of God's plan: 1. motive; 2. purpose; 3. means; 4. objects.

We must discover from Scripture God's motive which was behind salvation; His purpose or goal which He planned to accomplish; the means which He chose to bring it about; the object or persons for whom salvation was planned, accomplished and executed.

II. The extent of Christ's work can be discerned by viewing it in the light of its relationship to the distinctive works of the

other members of the Godhead. Certainly the work of the Father and the work of the Holy Spirit will tell us much concerning the work of the Son. Salvation is the work of the Triune God and this perspective must not be ignored or denied.

III. **The extent of the atonement is determined by the nature of the atonement.** We must *first* establish the purpose and nature of what Christ accomplished by His work before we can establish for whom He died. For example, once we have determined the meaning of the word "propitiation" in I John 2:2, then we can attempt to understand the words "whole world."

IV. **The extent of the atonement is admittedly a very controversial doctrine. Special care must be taken to maintain brotherly love and fellowship when disagreement arises.** A person's doctrinal position on the extent of the atonement will not determine his salvation or sanctification. Great and notable men of God have stood on opposite sides throughout church history. It is unlikely that this issue will be settled once and for all in this century. Past generations have come and gone and yet this issue remains. It is our task to agree to disagree with our fellow saints and to await that day when we all will no longer see through a glass darkly but then face to face (I Cor. 13:12).

Having established our basic principles of approach, we can now turn to the doctrine itself.

When you begin to study the extent of the atonement, it is not long before you discover entire volumes written on the subject. Because so much has been written on this topic and these works are still in print, it would be unprofitable for us to treat this subject in great detail. Therefore, we will briefly survey all the arguments which are put forth to establish the Biblical truth of Particular Redemption.

Particular Redemption is the doctrine which states that *the extent of the atonement must be limited to the elect of God.* When Christ died, He had certain particular people in mind as the only ones for whom He accomplished salvation. The atonement was particular or limited and not universal or general.

On the other hand, the doctrine of Universal Redemption states that when Christ died, He died for all men everywhere in all generations past, present and future including those already in hell or heaven. By His death Christ only made salvation *possible* for all. It was definite for none. Christ did not secure the salvation of any one person in particular. Whereas Particular Redemption views Christ's work as being limited to definite and particular sinners, Universal Redemption views Christ's work as indefinite and general.

The following is a summarization of the arguments for Particular Redemption:

I. The Plan of Salvation

What was the motive of the Triune God in planning salvation? The Father, Son and Holy Spirit had only one motive: LOVE (John 3:16; 13:1). They all agree as to the *motive* behind the plan of salvation.

What was the *purpose* of the Triune God in this plan? The Father, Son and Holy Spirit planned *to redeem and save sinners* (Matt. 1:21; Luke 9:10; Gal. 1:4; Eph. 5:25-27; I Tim. 1:15; Tit. 2:14). Not once are we told that God only wanted to make salvation *possible*. All the members of the Godhead agree as to the purpose of the plan of salvation.

What *means* did God choose to accomplish His purpose? The Father, Son and Holy Spirit all agreed to a division of labor in which the Father did the planning, the Son did the accomplishing and the Spirit did the applying. They all agree to the means of redemption.

Who are the *objects* or *persons* of God's plan of salvation? The Father, Son and Holy Spirit all agree as to the objects of salvation. Those whom the Father chooses, the Son redeems and the Spirit seals. There is no disagreement as to the objects of God's plan of salvation.

The plan of salvation from beginning to end concerned the actual salvation of particular sinners. *To teach that the Triune God is in agreement when it comes to the motive, purpose and means of redemption but disagree when it comes to the objects of salvation is to destroy the harmony and unity of the entire plan of salvation.*

When you view the extent of the atonement in the light of God's entire plan of salvation, it is clear that Particular Redemption is the only possible position which does justice to the unity and continuity of the plan of salvation. Universal Redemption usually pictures the Father choosing only some and the Spirit saving only some but the Son dying for all. Thus there is disagreement as to the objects of the plan of salvation. This disagreement destroys the unity and harmony of the plan of redemption. But God's plan is one harmonious whole and this truth points us to Particular Redemption.

II. The Doctrine of the Trinity

We have already stated that the plan of God is one. This is true simply because God is one. The Father, Son and Holy Spirit are one in nature, glory and purpose. They never disagree with each other. They work in harmony with each other.

Is it not true that the Father chose, elected, predestinated and ordained unto salvation *only a portion of mankind?* And that He did *not* elect all mankind to eternal life? That this is true is seen from the following references.

1. Chose: Matt. 21:16; Mark 13:20; I Cor. 1:27-28; Eph. 1:4; II Thess. 2:13; I Pet. 2:9; Rev. 17:14.
2. Elected: Matt. 24:24, 31; Luke 18:7; Rom. 8:33; Col. 3:12; Tit. 1:1; I Pet. 1:2; Rom. 9:11; 11:5, 7, 28; I Thess. 1:4; II Pet. 1:10.
3. Predestinated: Rom. 8:29-30; Eph. 1:5, 11.
4. Ordained: Acts 13:48.

Is it not also true that the Holy Spirit only saves *a portion of mankind?* He was sent to save those chosen by the Father and purchased by the Son (Rom. 5:5; 8:9, 11, 14-16; Gal. 4:5-6). He does not save all mankind.

To interject universalism into the work of Christ when it is not a part of the Father's or Spirit's work, not only destroys the unity of the plan of salvation but it also threatens the unity within the Godhead itself. Universalism is actually anti-trinitarian in its foundation. This is true not only on theoretical grounds but also as a fact of church history. Did not Arminius derive much of his teaching from the anti-trinitarian Servetus? Is it not a fact that Unitarianism arose out of Arminian circles? Even among Baptists, was it not the General Baptists who first went into Unitarianism?

On this basis, we are led to the following conclusions:

Conclusion #1: The Father, Son and Holy Spirit all agree as to the motive, means, purpose and objects of the plan of redemption. The elect are chosen by the Father, purchased by the Son and sealed by the Spirit.

Conclusion #2: Any view which interjects universalism into the plan of redemption at any point destroys the harmony within the Godhead, i.e., is actually anti-trinitarian.

III. **The Harmony Within the Work of Christ**

All of the redemptive works of Christ had the *same* motive, purpose, means and objects. The work of Christ is one harmonious whole.

The New Testament points to the work of the Old Testament High Priest as a prophetic pre-picture of the work of Christ. Thus Christ's redemptive work is divided into sacrifice and intercession (Rom. 8:34; Heb. 7:25-27).

In order to retain the unity and harmony within Christ's work, we must say that *the objects of His sacrifice are the objects of His intercession.* Or, to put it in other words, *the ones for whom He intercedes must be the same ones for whom He died.*

When we turn to Scripture, we find that *Christ only intercedes for the elect of God.* This is so clear that none can deny this truth (Isa. 53:11-12; John 17:2, 6, 9, 11, 15, 17, 20, 24; Rom. 8:31-34; Heb. 7:25; 9:24; I John 2:1-2).

The particular and definite character of Christ's intercession necessitates a particular and definite atonement. He intercedes for those for whom He died. He intercedes only for the elect. Therefore, He died only for the elect. Any view which interjects universalism into the work of Christ destroys the harmony within Christ's work.

IV. **The Efficacy of Christ's Intercession**

The Father always hears and answers the prayers of His Son for His Son only asks what is God's will (John 11:41-42). And when we ask about the nature of Christ's intercession, we find that the intercession of Christ is Christ's earnest prayer to the Father that He would save and sanctify all of the ones for whom He died (Isa. 53; John 17; Rom. 8; Heb. 7 & 9).

Given the two facts above, is it not obvious that all of the ones for whom He intercedes will be saved and sanctified because the Father hears His Son (John 6:37-39)? Therefore we come to the following conclusions:

Conclusion #1: The objects of Christ's intercession are the objects of His death: the elect of God.

Conclusion #2: To teach that Christ died and intercedes for all but the Father only saves some is to destroy the efficacy of Christ's intercession.

V. **The Definite Character of the Atonement**

Was the coming of the Son of God to earth an incident of pure chance? No, the Son of God came according to the plan and will of God (John 6:38; Gal. 4:14; Heb. 10:5-7).

What was the purpose, goal or end of God's plan? God's plan was to redeem and save sinners (Luke 19:10; I Tim. 1:15).

Did Christ accomplish the plan of God in actually *securing* the salvation of sinners? Yes, He accomplished the work which God sent Him to do (John 4:34; 17:4; cf. John 6:37-39; Heb. 9:12; Heb. 1:3).

Could Christ have failed to carry out the plan of God? No, for He is sinless (I Pet. 2:22).

With these basic facts before us, we can see that if God planned for all to be saved, then all will be saved because Christ Jesus cannot fail to carry out God's plan. But the Word of God does not teach universalism. Rather, Christ had particular elect sinners in mind when He accomplished redemption. They will all be saved because "Jesus never fails."

VI. **The Reality and Efficacy of Christ's Death Which Flows From the Nature of His Redemptive Work**

We have already shown that Christ actually accomplished propitiation, reconciliation, redemption and expiation. Thus the ones for whom He accomplished salvation are the ones who will be infallibly saved.

Since Christ's work is efficacious, there are only two possible views which would be in harmony with this efficacy.

a. All will be saved.
b. The elect will be saved.

The New Testament does not teach universalism but it does teach Particular Redemption. Christ's death secured eternal salvation for His people.

VII. **The Old Testament Prophecies and Ceremonies**

The Old Testament prophecies concerning the suffering of the Messiah clearly limit it to the same people for whom He intercedes, and to the ones He will justify (Isa. 53:8-12).

The Old Testament sacrificial system is the shadow of the sacrifice of Christ (Heb. 10:1). It pre-pictured Christ's sacrifice on the cross. Since the Old Testament sacrifices were explicitly limited only to the people of God, therefore, *Christ's death must be limited to the people of God or it does not fulfill the Old Testament types or prophecies.* "Wherefore in all things it behoved Him to be made like unto His brethren, that He might be a merciful and faithful high priest in things pertaining to God, *to make reconciliation for the sins of the people (of God)*" (Heb. 2:17).

VIII. **The New Covenant**

Just as Moses and his work must be understood in terms of the Old Covenant, the person and work of Christ must be understood in terms of the New Covenant. Did not the writer to the Hebrews demonstrate the superiority of Christ over the Old Covenant by proving that Christ in His person was "better" sacrifice offered through a "better" priesthood? (Heb. 8-10). Did not Jesus make the Lord's Supper a ceremony of the New Covenant when He designated the communion cup as "the cup of the New Covenant"? (Matt. 26:28). Are not New Testament pastors "ministers of the New Covenant"? (II Cor. 3:6). Is not the blood of Jesus "the blood of the covenant"? (Heb. 13:20).

The significance of the covenant aspect of Christ's death is that in the economy of God *salvation was accomplished by Christ only for those in that covenant.* Thus the salvation promises of the New Covenant are not given to all mankind, but only to the elect of God called "Israel" in the Old Testament and the "church" in the New Testament (Jer. 31:31-34; 32:37-40; Ezek. 37:26-27; Heb. 8:8-12; 10:15-18). The particular and limited character of the New Covenant corresponds to the Abrahamic and Mosaic covenants which likewise did not include all mankind.

Since the New Covenant concerns only the elect of God whose salvation is therein infallibly promised and secured, the covenantal death of Christ must be viewed as limited and particular.

IX. **The Lord's Supper**

Biblically speaking, the Lord's Supper must be viewed as a covenantal ceremony because during it we remember the death of our covenant Head who secured for us the salvation promised in the New Covenant (Matt. 26:28; Luke 22:20; I Cor. 11:25).

If Christ died for all without exception then all without exception should be invited to partake of the Lord's Supper which celebrates Christ's death for them. Thus the unbeliever as well as the believer should be allowed the Supper. Historically, universalism has always led to such a view of the Lord's Supper.

But since Christ died only for *His* people, then only *His* people should be allowed to partake of the Lord's Supper. *Thus, whenever the Lord's Supper is restricted to believers only, limited atonement is publically proclaimed.*

The New Testament is clear that just as the Passover feast was restricted to the Old Testament covenant community even so the Lord's Supper should be restricted to the New Testament covenant community — the Church which Christ purchased with His own blood (Eph. 5:25).

X. The Life-Union Between Christ and the Ones for Whom He Died

When Christ lived, died, was buried, arose, ascended, and sat down at the right hand of the Majesty on high, we are told that the ones for whom He did these things are to be viewed as being in such a life-union with Him as their covenant head and representative that it is said that they lived, died, were buried, arose, ascended and sat down at the Father's side "in Christ" (Rom. 6:1-11; Gal. 2:20; 6:14; Eph. 2:5-6).

To say that Christ died for all is to say that all died in Christ. It means that unbelievers are to be told that they have been crucified with Christ, been buried with Christ, have been resurrected with Christ and have ascended and sat down with Christ. This position is so manifestly false that it should grieve the child of God even to consider it. But to speak of the elect being "in" and "with" Christ in His redemptive work is Scriptural. Therefore the Biblical doctrine of union with Christ points us to Particular Redemption.

XI. Election and Reprobation

Mankind is divided into two groups or classes. One is either elect or reprobate. Reprobation involves two things:

1. A "passing over" in that God allows certain sinners to remain under condemnation. He does not elect them to salvation. This can be called "passive reprobation."
2. A divine decree that certain sinners shall go to hell because of their sin and for the glory of God's justice. This can be called "positive reprobation."

That both passive and positive reprobations are explicit teaching of Scripture is clear from the following passages.

At that time Jesus answered and said, I thank thee, O Father, Lord of heaven and earth, because thou hast *hid* these things from the wise and prudent, and hast *revealed* them unto babes. Even so, Father: for so it seemed good in thy sight. All things are delivered unto me of my Father: and no man knoweth the Son, but the Father; neither knoweth any man the Father, save the Son, and he *to whomsoever the Son will reveal him* (Matt. 11:25-27).

And he shall set the sheep on his right hand, but the goats on the left. Then shall the King say unto them on the right hand, Come, ye blessed of my Father, inherit the kingdom *prepared for you from the foundation of the world:* Then shall he say also unto them on the left hand, Depart from me, ye cursed, into everlasting fire, prepared for the devil and his angels (Matt. 25:33-34, 41).

And he said unto them, Unto you *it is given to know* the mystery of the kingdom of God: but unto *them that are without,* all these things are done in parables: That seeing they may see, and *not* perceive; and hearing they may hear, and *not* understand, *lest at any time they should be converted, and their sins should be forgiven them* (Mark 4:11-12).

I am the good shepherd: the good shepherd giveth his life *for the sheep.* But he that is an hireling, and not the shepherd, whose own the sheep are not, seeth the wolf coming, and leaveth the sheep, and fleeth: and the wolf catcheth them, and scattereth the sheep. The hireling fleeth, because he is an hireling, and careth not for sheep. I am the good shepherd, and know *my sheep,* and am known of mine. As the Father knoweth me, even so know I the Father: and I lay down my life *for the sheep.* And other sheep I have, which are not of this fold: them also I must bring, and they shall hear my voice; and there shall be one fold, and one shepherd. *But ye believe not, because ye are not of my sheep,* as I said unto you (John 10:11-16, 26).

Therefore they could not believe, because that Esaias said again, He hath *blinded* their eyes, and *hardened* their heart; that they should *not* see with their eyes, nor understand with their heart, and *be converted,* and I should heal them (John 12:39-40).

And when the Gentiles heard this, they were glad, and glorified the word of the Lord: and *as many as were ordained to eternal life believed* (Acts 13:48).

For there are certain men crept in unawares, *who were before of old ordained to this condemnation,* ungodly men, turning the grace of our God into lasciviousness, and denying the only Lord God, and our Lord Jesus Christ (Jude 4).

Not as though the word of God hath taken none effect. For they are not all Israel, which are of Israel: Neither, because they are the seed of Abraham, are they all children: but, In Isaac shall thy seed be called. That is, they which are the children of the flesh, these are not the children of God. But the children of the promise are counted for the seed. For this is the Word of Promise, At this time will I come, and Sarah shall have a son. And not only this; but when Rebecca also had conceived by one, even by our father Isaac; (For the children being not yet born, neither having done any good or evil, that *the purpose of God according to election might stand, not of works, but of him that calleth;)* It was said unto her, the elder shall serve the younger. As it is written, *Jacob have I loved, but Esau have I hated.* What shall we say then? Is there unrighteousness with God? God forbid. For he saith to Moses, I will have mercy on whom I will have mercy, and I will have compassion on whom I will have compassion. *So then it is not of him that willeth, nor of him that runneth, but of God that sheweth mercy.* For the scripture saith unto Pharaoh, Even for this same purpose have I *raised thee up, that I might shew my power in thee, and that my name might be declared throughout all the earth.* Therefore hath he *mercy* on whom he will have mercy, and *whom he will he hardeneth.* Thou wilt say then unto me, Why doth he yet find fault? For who hath resisted his will? Nay but, O man, who art thou that repliest against God? Shall the thing formed say to him that formed it, Why hast thou made me thus? Hath not the potter power over the clay, of the same lump to make *one vessel unto honour, and another unto dishonour?* What if God, willing to shew his wrath, and to make his power known, endured with much long-suffering *the vessels of wrath fitted to destruction:* And that he might make known the riches of his glory on *the vessels of mercy,* which he had afore prepared unto glory (Rom. 9:6-23).

And for this cause *God shall send them strong delusion, that they should believe a lie: That they all might be damned who believed not the truth, but had pleasure in unrighteousness* (II Thess. 2:11-12).

And a stone of stumbling, and a rock of offence, even to *them which stumble at the word*, being disobedient: *whereunto also they were appointed.* But ye are a *chosen* generation, a royal priesthood, an holy nation, a peculiar people; that ye should shew forth the praises of him who hath called you out of darkness into his marvellous light (I Pet. 2:8-9).

For God hath put in their hearts to fulfil his will, and to agree, and give their kingdom unto the beast, until the words of God shall be fulfilled (Rev. 17:17).

God's plan for the elect is their salvation by His grace.

But we are bound to give thanks alway to God for you, brethren beloved of the Lord, because *God hath from the beginning chosen you to salvation* (II Thess. 2:13).

God's plan and will for the reprobate is their eternal condemnation.

And the Lord said unto Moses, When thou goest to return into Egypt, see that thou do all those wonders before Pharaoh, which I have put in thine hand: but *I will harden his heart*, that he shall not let the people go (Ex. 4:21).

And *I will harden Pharaoh's heart*, and multiply my signs and my wonders in the land of Egypt (Ex. 7:3).

And *the Lord hardened the heart of Pharaoh*, and he harkened not unto them; as the Lord had spoken unto Moses (Ex. 9:12).

And the Lord said unto Moses, Go in unto Pharaoh: for *I have hardened his heart*, and *the heart of his servants*, that I might shew these my signs before him. But the *Lord hardened Pharaoh's heart*, so that he would not let the children of Israel go. But *the Lord hardened Pharaoh's heart*, and he would not let them go (Ex. 10:1, 20, 27).

And *I will harden Pharaoh's heart*, that he shall follow after them; and I will be honoured upon Pharaoh, and upon all his host; that the Egyptians may know that I am the Lord. And they did so (Ex. 14:4).

But Sihon King of Heshbon would not let us pass by him. For *the Lord thy God hardened his spirit*, and *made his heart obstinate*, that he might deliver him into thy hand, as appeareth this day (Deut. 2:30).

There was not a city that made peace with the children of Israel, save the Hivites the inhabitants of Gibeon: all other they took in battle. For *it was of the Lord to harden their hearts*, that they should come against Israel in battle, *that he might destroy them utterly*, and *that they might have no favour, but that he might destroy them*, as the Lord commanded Moses (Josh. 11:19-20).

The Lord hath made all things for himself: yea, *even the wicked for the day of evil* (Prov. 16:4).

I pray not for the world, but for them which thou hast given me; for they are thine (John 17:9).

For God hath not appointed us to wrath, but *to obtain salvation by our Lord Jesus Christ* (I Thess. 5:9).

Since salvation was planned only for the elect and we know that Christ came to execute this plan, we come to the conclusion that Christ died only for the elect.

XII.   The Explicit Statements of Scripture

At His birth, the angel proclaimed that Christ's name, "Jesus," referred to His future saving work which was limited to "His people" (Matt. 1:21).

In agreement with this, we find that Christ clearly stated that He had come to save all those whom the Father had given Him (John 6:37-39; 10:10-11; 17:2).

Thus we find definite statements in Scripture which limit the work of Christ to the elect. We are told that Christ died for:

1.   "The Many" (Isa. 53:11-12; Matt. 20:28; 26:28; John 17:2; Rom. 5:15, 19).
2.   "His people" (Matt. 1:21).
3.   "The children of God" (John 11:52).
4.   Those "given Him" by the Father (John 6:37-39; 17:2, 6, 9, 19, 24).
5.   "The Church" (Eph. 5:25).

6. "Many sons" (Heb. 2:10).
7. "His brethren" (Heb. 2:11-12, 17).
8. "The children" (Heb. 2:13-14).
9. "The seed of Abraham" (Heb. 2:16).
10. "The people" of God (Heb. 2:17).

If the Biblical authors believed in Universal Redemption, they would never have spoken of Christ's death in such terms.

XIII. The Spread of the Gospel

If Christ died for all mankind, why has the Gospel gone only to some and not to all? The gospel is sent to the elect for they are the ones for whom Christ died (II Tim. 2:10; Acts 11:4-18).

Only the doctrines of election and Particular Redemption can explain why Western Europe was sent the Gospel instead of Asia. Paul was directed to Europe simply because the elect were there (Acts 16:6-10, cf. 18:9-10).

XIV. The Intercessory Work of the Holy Spirit

The intercession of the Spirit is limited to the people of God (Rom. 8:26-27). He intercedes for the ones purchased by Christ. Therefore, Christ died only for the elect.

The harmony between the work of Christ and the work of the Holy Spirit is destroyed by universalism.

XV. The Glory of the Triune God

Particular Redemption ascribes all the glory of salvation to the Triune God. Salvation is totally the work of God. We are chosen by the Father not for any good in us but on the basis of His good pleasure (Eph. 1:5). Christ Jesus came and actually secured the eternal salvation of all the ones whom the Father gave Him (John 17:2). The Holy Spirit was sent by the Father and the Son to apply to the elect what Christ accomplished according to the plan of the Father. For all eternity we will praise our Great God who sovereignly saved us by His grace.

On the other hand, if God planned for all to be saved and Christ died for all and the Spirit is sent to all then we are presented with a very unglorious God. The Father is *disappointed* because His plan failed. The Son is *dissatisfied* because His blood was shed in vain for the majority of mankind. The Spirit is *defeated* by the majority of mankind. Thus for all eternity, we are faced with a disappointed, dissatisfied and defeated God who could not accomplish what He set out to do. But is this the Biblical picture of God? No! Our God is in heaven and He has done whatever He wanted to do. No one can resist Him or make His plans fail. "I know that Thou canst do all things, And that *no purpose of Thine can be thwarted*" (Job 42:2). "But our God is in the heavens. *He does whatever He pleases*" (Ps. 115:3). *"Whatever the Lord pleases, He does,* (Ps. 115:3). *"Whatever the Lord pleases, He does,* In heaven and in earth, in the seas and in all deeps" (Ps. 135:6). "But at the end of that period I, Nebuchadnezzar, raised my eyes toward heaven, and my reason returned to me and I blessed the Most High and praised and honored Him who lives forever.

> For His dominion is an everlasting dominion.
> And His kingdom endures from generation to generation.
> And all the inhabitants of the earth are accounted as nothing.
> But *He does according to His will in the host of heaven*
> And *among the inhabitants of earth;*
> And no one can ward off His hand
> Or say to Him, What hast Thou done? (Dan. 4:34-36).

"You will say to me then, 'Why does He still find fault? For *who resists His will?' On the contrary, who are you, O man, who answers back to God? The thing molded will not say to the molder, 'Why did you make* me like this' will it? Or does the potter have a right over the clay, to make from the same lump one vessel for honorable use, and another for common use? What if God, although willing to demonstrate His wrath and to make His power known, endured with much patience vessels of wrath prepared for destruction? And He did so in order that He might make known the riches of His glory upon vessels of mercy, which He prepared beforehand for glory" (Rom. 9:19-24). "For from Him and through Him and to Him are *all* things. To Him be the glory forever. Amen." (Rom. 11:36). "Also we have obtained an inheritance, having been predestined according to *His purpose who works all things after the counsel of His will*" (Eph. 1:11).

XVI. **The Bankruptcy of Universal Redemption**

The Bible nowhere teaches that Christ died for every single human being who has, is or will live. Universalism produces so many absurdities and contradictions that it refutes itself. The consistent universalist is trapped into one of two courses.

  A. If he accepts the Biblical teaching on the nature of the atonement, he must see all men ultimately saved.

B. Thus he must either weaken the word "ALL" or weaken the nature of the atonement.

C. Because of his dogmatism on the word "all," he generally weakens the nature of the atonement by saying that:

    (1)   The Father's election has nothing to do with salvation but concerns only service. Or, it is based on foreseen faith and repentance which are the contributions made by the sinner through the power of his own Freewill.

    (2)   Christ did not come actually to save the elect or anyone. He came to satisfy the Father in order to make salvation merely possible for all men. He did not actually accomplish anything on the cross.

    (3)   The Holy Spirit only seeks to persuade men and He never tampers with their nature or will. The ultimate choice concerning the salvation or damnation of a sinner rests in the sinner and not in God.

Universalism makes man the captain of his own soul and the one who determines his own fate. It is thoroughly man-centered instead of being God-centered because it teaches that salvation depends on sinners saving themselves. God is said to be helpless and impotent to save sinners. Thus Universalism is actually a religious form of humanism. Man is on the throne and God is his puppet. God cannot move until man pulls the strings!

How different is the Biblical picture of God's relationship to man. God is the potter and man the clay. And God molds the clay anyway He pleases (Rom. 9:19-23). Some clay is molded into vessels of honor for they reveal God's grace and kindness (Eph. 2:7). Other vessels are formed which will glorify God's just and holy wrath against sin (Rom. 9:22-23).

If you are uneasy with the doctrine that God is the potter and that you are the clay and that He molds vessels of honor and dishonor, you reveal unbelief in the Word of God. No one can read Rom. 9 or Isa. 29:16; 45:9; 64:8; Jer. 18:6 and not fail to see that God is on the throne and not man. *God saves sinners all by Himself.* Any doctrine which adds human works to the saving work of Christ is humanistic at its very foundation.

Problem Texts

While the above arguments are compelling for some, they are not conclusive to all. The main reason that some people do not accept Particular Redemption is the presence of verses in the Bible which seem to contradict it.

We freely admit that there are verses which are difficult to interpret. But we do not admit that these verses teach Universal Redemption.

There are several important principles which must be observed when approaching problem texts. If we fail to follow these principles, we open up ourselves to much confusion.

I. **Every Bible doctrine has its problem passages.**

The presence of such cults as the Jehovah Witnesses should remind us that there are problem texts which can be seized upon to "refute" the Trinity, the deity of Christ, the immortality of the soul and hell. To refute the deity of Christ they point to John 14:28: "The Father is greater than I."

Thus it is not surprising or disturbing in the least to the Christian that there are problem passages which seemingly contradict Particular Redemption. Every other Bible doctrine has problem passages.

II. **Always interpret the unclear in the light of the clear.**

When we interpret John 14:28 in the light of John 1:1, 18; 5:18, 23; 20:28, it is clear from these passages that Christ is God. Therefore we approach John 14:28 with this clear doctrine.

In the same way, it is clear that God's plan of salvation is one: that the Father chose only some and the Spirit saves only some; that Christ came and accomplished a real atonement so that all the ones for whom He died will be saved, etc. With these clear truths we approach all problem passages.

III. **We can sometimes be more sure and certain about what a verse cannot say, than what it does, in fact, say.**

Whatever John 14:28 says, it *cannot* mean that Christ is a creature and not God for that would contradict what the rest of the Bible teaches and we know that the Bible does not contradict itself.

So, whatever a problem text on Christ's death may say, it *cannot* mean that Christ died for every sinner who will ever live for that would contradict the rest of Scripture. The Bible is clear on the nature of the atonement. Thus we approach each problem passage in this light. If we run across a verse which we do not know how to interpret, at least we know what it cannot mean.

IV. **Don't read your own meaning into Bible words. Rather, let Scripture interpret Scripture.**

John 14:28 is a good example of this principle. Christ said "The Father is greater than I." The Jehovah Witness points to the word "greater" and says that Christ is a creature and not equal to God in any sense. They pour their own meaning into the word "greater."

But if we study the word "greater" as it is used in the Bible, we find that the word is used in terms of *office and work* and *not in reference to being or nature.* As the obedient servant of God, Christ was under the Father's authority and therefore the Father by virtue of His office in redemption is said to be greater. John 14:28 refers to the economical Trinity and not to the ontological Trinity.

The word "better" is used in the Bible to contrast *superior and inferior beings.* Christ is "better" than the angels (Heb. 7:19; 8:6). His death was a "better" sacrifice (Heb. 9:23). His blood spoke "better" things than Abel's (Heb. 12:24). Throughout Hebrews, Christ is pictured as *better* than angels, Moses, Aaron, the High Priest, sacrifices and temple. Christ is superior in His *nature* to all of these for He is *God* (Heb. 1:3, 8, 10).

In the same way, the universalist pours his own meaning into the Biblical words "world" and "all." Wherever the Bible says that Christ died for "All" or for "the world," the universalist will insist that these verses teach that Christ died for every sinner everywhere in all generations including those in hell at the time Christ died. But to decide what these words mean without checking Scripture is to pour your own meaning into them.

When we examine how the Bible uses the words "all" and "world," we find that these words hardly ever and maybe never refer to every sinner who will ever live. There are many places where the words *cannot* mean this by any stretch of the imagination. In the following verses, wherever the words "all" and "world" appear, substitute them with this universalistic definition: "All sinners everywhere in all generations, past, present and future including those in heaven and hell at the time Christ died."

A. "world": "And it came to pass in those days, that there went out a decree from Caesar Augustus, that *all the world* should be taxed" (Luke 2:1). "He was in *the world*, and *the world* was made by Him, and *the world* knew Him not" (John 1:10). "For there is no man that doeth any thing in secret, and he himself seeketh to be known openly. If thou do these things, shew thyself to *the world"* (John 7:4). "If *the world* hate you, you know that it hated me before it hated you" (John 15:18). "I pray for them: *I pray not for the world*, but for them which thou hast given me; for they are thine" (John 17:9). "Love not *the world*, neither the things that are in the world. If any man love the world, the love of the Father is not in him" (I John 2:15). "And we know that we are of God, and *the whole world* lieth in wickedness" (I John 5:19).

B. "all": "Then went out to him Jerusalem, and *all* Judaea, and *all* the region round about Jordan, And were baptized of him in Jordan, confessing their sins" (Matt. 3:5-6). "And ye shall be hated of *all* men for my name's sake: but he that endureth to the end shall be saved" (Matt. 10:22). "And there went out unto him *all* the land of Judaea, and they of Jerusalem, and were *all* baptized of him in the river of Jordan, confessing their sins" (Mark 1:5). "And they came unto John, and said unto him, Rabbi, he that was with thee beyond Jordan, to whom thou barest witness, behold, the same baptizeth, and *all* men come to him" (John 3:26).

The above verses should prove beyond any doubt that no one has the right to assume that such words as "all" or "world" mean every sinner who ever lived. The doctrine of the extent of the atonement can not be settled just by quoting John 3:16. We must use Scripture to interpret John 3:16 in order to discover its Biblical meaning. Indeed, all the various texts which have been used in the past to refute Particular Redemption or to establish universalism have been ably dealt with by great men of God. If one is deeply concerned and exercised over certain verses, he should obtain and read the following works:*

A. *The Cause of God and Truth*, by Dr. John Gill.
B. *The Death of Death in the Death of Christ*, by Dr. John Owen.
C. *The Reformed Doctrine of Predestination*, by L. Boettner.
D. *The Atonement*, by A.W. Pink.
E. *The Atonement*, by A.A. Hodge.
F. *The Atonement of Christ*, by Turrettin.
G. *The Atonement According to Christ and the Apostles*, by Smeaton.

*See also our discussion on the Love of God in Part III where John 3:16 is exegeted.

CHAPTER 6

The Application of Salvation

We have completed our examination of what Christ Jesus accomplished by His person and work. Yet, we shall see that unless God *applies* what Christ accomplished no one would ever reap the benefits of eternal life. No sinner would or could worship the true God in spirit or in truth. We must learn at the very beginning of our study to thank God that application follows accomplishments.

Our first task is to define what we mean when we speak of the *Application* of salvation:

> Salvation is applied when the benefits of the atoning work
> of Jesus Christ are put to the account of the made effectual
> in the elect of God.

We have seen that the work of Christ was accomplished in such a way that it removes our guilty standing before God and cleanses our depraved natures. Thus while justification is a benefit of Christ's work which is *put to our account* by the work of application, regeneration is a benefit of Christ's work which is *made effectual in us* by the work of application. Thus we can approach God through Christ's work because our position and person are made acceptable before Him by the work of application.

Secondly, we need to understand the relationship between accomplishment and application. The following observations are given to clarify this relationship.

I.   The Plan of Salvation

The following diagram will give us a bird's eye view of the whole plan of salvation and how application relates to the rest of the plan.

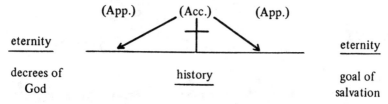

In eternity past, God decreed the salvation of the elect through the application (app.) of what Christ accomplished (acc.) in order that the elect of God might be with Christ in eternity future.

II.   Two Different Questions

While the doctrine of the accomplishments of salvation answers the question: "*Objectively* speaking, what did Christ Jesus do *for me* nearly 2,000 years ago?", the doctrine of the application of salvation answers the question: "*Subjectively* speaking, what had Christ Jesus done *in* and to *me* in my own life time?"

III.   Organic Relationship

We speak of things being in an organic relationship when life flows from one part to the other. The roots and fruit of a tree are in an organic relationship because they are members of the same living organism and the fruit derives its existence from the roots. In the same way, accomplishment and application are parts of the same plan of salvation and application flows out of and is secured by accomplishment. The accomplishment of redemption is the root while application is the fruit.

IV.   Structural Relationship

As well as using a tree to illustrate the relationship between accomplishment and application, we can illustrate this relationship by the parts of a building.

The accomplishment of salvation is the foundation of the building while application is the superstructure which rests upon that foundation. The following diagram pictures this relationship.

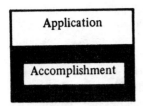

Application	<u>Superstructure</u>
Accomplishment	<u>Foundation</u>

V. Trinitarian Relationship

Biblical Christianity is trinitarian to is very core. Unless the deity of the Son and the Spirit are upheld, Christianity is reduced to a man-centered religion.

The plan of salvation must be understood as being the work of the Triune God.

We can generally say that the Father did the planning for salvation. This is His distinct work in the economy of redemption. The Son's unique work in salvation was to accomplish all that is needed to secure the Spirit's work is to apply to the elect what Christ accomplished according to the plan of the Father. The application of salvation must be viewed in the context of the economical Trinity.

Our third task is to examine why non-Reformed theologians omit any reference to the application of salvation. Is there a real difference between the terms application and appropriation?

It is our position that it is Biblically and theologically improper to substitute man's appropriation in the place of God's application. The following reasons reveal why we speak only of the application of salvation.

First, "application" is God-centered while "appropriation" is man-centered. Reformed theology stresses the fact that salvation is of the Lord 100%. *God* planned it. *God* accomplished it and *God* applies it. Non-Reformed systems stress that *man* must appropriate salvation. God offers it but *man* is the one who will decide whether or not salvation takes place.

Second, "application" views sinners as being actively hostile to God and entirely passive in seeking God. "Appropriation" views sinners as actively seeking and procuring salvation. "Application" is built upon the doctrine of man's total depravity while "appropriation" is built upon semi-pelagian views of man's nature (freewillism).

Third, "application" emphasizes the completeness of salvation for God *supplies the faith and repentance needed to receive it.* God opens the hearts of sinners and makes them willing to do His will (Acts 16;14; Phil. 2:13). On the other hand, "appropriation" views man's faith and repentance as his own additions to and completion of redemption. Without man's contribution, Christ's redemption is incomplete.

Fourth, "application" reveals the theistic unity in redemption. Salvation is totally the work of the Triune God. The Father planned it. The Son accomplished it and the Spirit applies it. Salvation is one. But "appropriation" brings in disunity. Salvation is divided between God and man. God is viewed as helpless and powerless to save sinners without the sinner's cooperation. "Appropriation" destroys the theistic unity in redemption.

There is an important principle of the Christian life which applies to this issue: *Defend God at all costs*. This principle is founded upon Rom. 3:4 where the Apostle Paul said, "Let God be true, though every man be found a liar."

We should be jealous of God's glory. We should allow no one to steal glory from God and give it to man. Too often we hear people defending the glory of man. Those who defend man at any cost would have us believe that man must be free even if it means God must be bound. Man's work must be ultimate even if it makes God's work conditional on man's help.

How different was Paul's attitude. God was true even if it meant that all men were liars. To question the sovereign freeness and justice of God was viewed as blasphemy by the apostle in Romans 9.

Reader, do you find yourself drawn to "application" or "appropriation?" If you are uneasy with the application of redemption, this reveals man-centered thinking. You need to be God-centered in your thinking. After all, why were you created? Was it not to glorify God? Are you jealous to defend man or God? Humble yourself and acknowledge that salvation is of the Lord. He saves sinners all by Himself. God does not need our help for He is the Lord of the universe.

CHAPTER 7

Foundational Principles

Having defined what we mean by the application of the atonement, we need to observe several important foundational principles. These principles will establish the proper context in which we can understand the application of redemption.

I. The application of redemption is a *process* which manifests unity, continuity and purpose. Thus, while we may examine any given part of the process in great detail, we must never forget that we are dealing with the process of the application of salvation.

II. The application of redemption is a result of the intercessory work of Christ as the High Priest of God's people.

The life, death, resurrection, ascension and session of Christ comprise the accomplishment of redemption. All these elements of redemption were completed in the past.

The intercession of Christ is a present and continuous work in which Christ prays to the Father that the benefits of His death might be applied to the elect of God.

The Old Testament prefigured this work of Christ by having the high priest intercede for the people of God after sacrifice has been made. It also prophesied that the Messiah would intercede for His people (Isa. 53:12).

When we turn to the New Testament, we find that Christ is the only mediator between God and man (I Tim. 2:5). His intercession guarantees that the elect will never be condemned (Rom. 8:34). It secures forgiveness of sins (Heb. 9:20-23). In John 17 we find that Christ's intercession secures eternal life (v. 2), saving knowledge (v. 3), preservation (v. 15), sanctification (v. 17), and spiritual unity (v. 22).

Dear child of God, Jesus Christ is praying for you 24 hours a day. He is praying for your eternal salvation. He is pleading for your complete sanctification. Learn to use Christ's intercession as a powerful argument in prayer and a powerful encouragement to grow in godliness.

III. Overall, we may say that the application of salvation is the particular work of the Holy Spirit. In Scripture He is expressly said to be the agent or author of most of the elements of the application of salvation. How thankful we should be to the third person of Trinity!

IV. The elements of salvation are everywhere in Scripture spoken of or described as being necessarily connected with each other. One element is never said to be in isolation from the other elements in the process of salvation. The Bible knows nothing of a piecemeal salvation. It is unscriptural to believe that someone can be regenerated in isolation from faith and repentance.

V. The application of redemption, while sovereign and free, is nevertheless always preceded by, and in the context of the Word of God. The Gospel must be communicated by a human instrumentally or salvation is not possible (Rom. 10:17). There must be light before life; knowledge before faith. The Spirit always works in conjunction with the Word of God.*

It is hoped that these foundational principles will help us to avoid false doctrine and to be balanced in our understanding of the application of salvation.

---

*See chapter on Heathen Question for a full exposition of this point.

CHAPTER 8

The Order of Application

Numerous elements of salvation are involved in the application of redemption such as calling, justification, adoption, forgiveness and glorification. Should we be concerned about arranging these elements in some kind of order? Is there a correct order versus a wrong order? Can we organize them?

When we turn to the Word of God, we discover that the Scriptures do place the elements of application in a certain order. There is thus a Biblical precedent and example which warrants our concern to arrange the elements of salvation in a proper order.

Did not our Lord say that regeneration takes place *before* one can see or enter the Kingdom of God? (Jn. 3:3, 6). Did not the Apostle Paul place justification *before* peace with God in Rom. 5:1? Did he not arrange calling, justification and glorification in their proper order in Rom. 8:29-30? Does not Eph. 1:13 state that sealing by the Spirit takes place after or in conjunction with believing the Gospel? Is it not the case that the Spirit give assurance of adoption after the act of adoption has taken place? (Gal. 4:6, 7).

In spite of such Biblical evidence, some modern theologians dismiss the issue of the order of application as being irrelevant. In so doing, they reveal their ignorance of Scripture. A pound of Puritan divinity often manifests more Scriptural knowledge than a ton of modern theology.

A proper ordering of the elements of the application of salvation is necessary not only because of Biblical precedent but also because very important doctrines depend on placing these elements in correct order.

One example of the importance of correct order can be illustrated by this question: Does regeneration precede or follow faith? The answer to this question reveals the importance of their respective order in the application of salvation.

Indeed, the order of regeneration and faith is the dividing line between Augustine and Pelagius; Luther and the Pope; Reformed and Arminian theology.

To say that regeneration follows faith is to say that man can believe without the inward regenerating work of the Spirit. It infers that sinners are not really dead in sins or totally depraved. It implies synergism, i.e., salvation is accomplished by man and God, each doing his own part. It implies free-willism, i.e., Adam's fall into sin and guilt did not bring man's will into bondage to sin.

On the other hand, if regeneration precedes faith, this implies monergesism, i.e., salvation is totally God's work from beginning to end. It implies that man is dead in sins and is incapable of spiritual good due to the effects of Adam's fall into sin. It means that faith is a gift of God and not the contributions of man.

The above observations reveal that very important issues arise when we begin to arrange the elements of application in their proper order.

But what is their proper order? Is it a matter of speculation and opinion? No! The Scriptures will supply us with enough material to place correctly most of the elements of salvation.

To answer the question as to whether regeneration comes before faith, we turn to a number of passages in the Bible which have direct bearing on the issue.

Our Lord's discourse on the new birth in John clearly reveals that God alone is the author and origin of regeneration for we must be born *"from above."* Thus the Apostle John draws the deduction that regeneration cannot be attributed to "the will of the flesh or the will of man" but to God alone (John 1:13).

Further, Christ places regeneration by the Spirit as a requirement before one can "see," i.e., believe or have faith in the Kingdom of God. He states quite emphatically that a sinner who is born of the flesh cannot believe the good news of the Kingdom until he is born by the Spirit. Thus according to the teaching of Christ, we believe *because* we are "born again." We are not "born again" because we believe!

Other passages in the Bible also teach the same truth that we believe because we have been regenerated by the Spirit of God. (See: John 6:44, 45; Acts 16:14; Eph. 2:1-10; Phil. 2:13, etc.).

Having seen that it is Biblical and important to arrange the elements of the application of redemption in their proper order, we are faced with the question of what *KIND* of order to use.

Some theologians are quick to reply that we must use a *logical* order and not a *chronological* order. Yet, we must confess that this distinction is not helpful but confusing. This arises from the fact that there are many conflicting "logical" orders. In fact there are almost as many "logical" orders as there are theologians!

This confusion over what constitutes a "logical" order results from a lack of understanding concerning the science of logic in general and the use of logic in argumentation in particular.

Logic has to do with the validity of the *form* of arguments. It declares whether or not the structure of the arguments is valid. It cannot say whether or not the premises or conclusion are true. Logic is not concerned with Truth *per se* but only *the validity of the method of argumentation.* Thus an argument can be logically valid and false at the same time.

This insight perhaps throws some light on the conflicting opinions of differing theologians who all claim to present that "logical" order of application. A theologian's order of application may be "logical" without being necessarily true. In fact, we can say that all the orders are "logical" and yet all are false at the same time.

What we will attempt to do is to examine the different "logical" orders of application which are possible on the basis of mere logic. Then we will present a different way of ordering the elements of application which will hopefully solve some of the problems involved with this doctrine.

First, what are the possible ways we can order the elements of salvation?

1. Chronological Order: We can say that element A happened in time before element B took place. A precedes B in respect of time.

2. Causal Order: We can say that A caused B. Thus A is prior to B. At times, John Murray used this kind of order.

3. Legal Order: We can say that A is the legal basis of B. Thus A must be prior to B. Kuyper and Commrie used this kind of order.

4. Presuppositional Order: A is presupposed by B. Thus A must be before B. John Murray also used this kind of order.

5. Pedagogical Order: A must be understood before you can understand B. Thus A is prior to B.

6. Teleological Order: The goal of the order is stated last and the

means arranged in an ascending order to reach this goal. For example, D is the goal. Therefore A-B-C-D is the proper arrangement.

7. Trinitarian Order: The elements of salvation are ordered according to which member of the Trinity applies them. The Father does the calling. The Son is the one with whom we come into saving union. The Spirit regenerates.

8. Harmotological Order: The elements are ordered according to whether they deal with the guilt, pollution, or misery of sin. For example, justification deals with the guilt of sin. Regeneration deals with the pollution of sin. And glorification deals with the misery of sin. Bavinck uses this kind of order.

It is our position that all the above kinds of orders are logical so far as *form* is concerned. Thus no one theologian can claim that his order is "logical" as opposed to the "illogical" arrangement of others.

It is also true that when we examine Scripture, we find that all of the above orders can be used in arranging some of the elements of salvation.

1. Justification is chronologically before glorification.
2. Regeneration causes faith.
3. Justification is the legal basis of adoption.
4. Justification is presupposed in sanctification.
5. Regeneration must be understood before you can understand progressive sanctification.
6. Teleogically, glorification is the goal and sanctification is a means unto this goal.
7. The elements of application can be divided between the Father, Son, and Holy Spirit.
8. The elements of application can be divided according to what aspect of sin they remove.

The main problem with the traditional approaches to the order of application is that each theologian usually picked only one kind of logical order. It was assumed that consistency demanded the use of only one kind of order. Then the theologian attempted to force *all* the elements of application into this one kind of order. The end result was that he soon discovered elements which did not fit into his arrangement. Insurmountable problems appeared which destroyed the "logical" ordering of the elements of application.

This type of reasoning is called theological reductionism. Reductionism takes place when you absolutize only one kind of logical order and then seek to reduce all the elements of salvation into this one order. This has been the main problem with the traditional approach to the order of application.

Perhaps there is a way out of this dilemma of reductionism by abandoning all together the linear approach to the problem. Instead of seeking only one "logical" key to help us properly order the elements of salvation, we should use a theological model or structure. Perhaps a model approach is better than the traditional linear approach.

The theological model of application could be constructed after the following pattern.

I. There is a nucleus or central point which stands for the one essential key element of application. Union with Christ is this one central essential key element. Indeed, the entire plan of salvation must be understood in the context of union with Christ. Did not the Father's decree of election take place "in Christ" (Eph. 1:4)? Did not the accomplishment of salvation take place in the context of union with Christ (Rom. 6; Eph. 2)? Is it not a fact that salvation is applied only in the context of union with Christ?

II. All the other elements of salvation are related to and dependent upon the nuclear element which is union with Christ. Each element flows out of union with Christ and is dependent upon union with Christ.

III. All the elements of salvation are interrelated and coordinated in many different ways. One element may be legally related to another element and, at the same time, be related chronologically to another. Or, two elements may be related to each other in several different ways. One element may be related chronologically, presuppositionally, legally and teleologically to another element.

IV. Thus any attempt to reduce the elements of application to a linear order 1-2-3-4-5 using only one kind of order is incorrect and hopelessly futile. A reductionistic linear method cannot do justice to the richness variety of Biblical material concerning the relationship between various elements.

The following diagram illustrates the different ways in which all the elements are related to each other. We will use justification as a sample element.

1. Notice that justification is connected to the nucleus as are all other elements. This is the solid line.

2. Notice that justification is related to all the other elements. This is represented by the broken lines. All the elements are connected with each other in one or more ways.

3. Notice that justification can be related to sanctification in several different ways. For example, they are related chronologically, legally and presuppositionally. At the same time, justification is related to glorification teleologically.

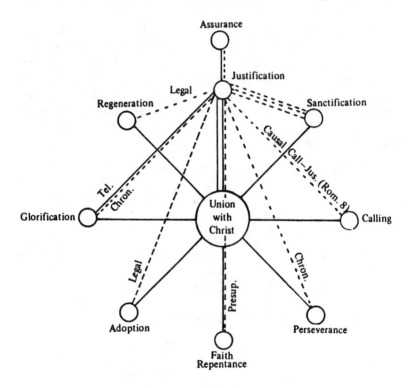

It is hoped that this approach will generate further research into the many different ways all the elements of the application of redemption relate to each other and to union with Christ. No longer will our concern be narrowed to the relationship between faith *and* regeneration. We must now investigate how regeneration relates to all the other elements as well.

On the basis of what has been established so far, we will now turn to an examination of the elements of application. While we will define from the Scriptures the exact nature of each element, we will generally refrain from relating them to the other elements because a detailed examination of all the ways each element relates to the other elements and to the nucleus really requires a full book. Perhaps one of our readers will produce such a volume.

CHAPTER **9**

Union With Christ

The Gospels record the historical *manifestation* of the person and work of Christ. Thus in our study of the principal concern of Jesus Christ in His mission on earth, we found that He was sent by the Father to "save His people from their sins" (Matt. 1:21).

While the Gospels are concerned with a historical narration of the person and work of Christ, we find that the Pauline Epistles are uniquely concerned with a theological *explanation* of Christ's person and work. The Pauline Epistles constitute the passage of full mention in the Word of God which deals with a thorough and detailed explanation for what Christ accomplished by His life and death.

When we turn to the Pauline Epistles themselves, we soon discover a constantly recurring theme or concept which is used by the apostle as a summary phrase of salvation. We are, of course, referring to what has been called Paul's motto: IN CHRIST.

To the Apostle Paul, union with Christ is the central or core doctrine in his whole understanding of salvation.

Some have mistakenly thought that Paul's eschatological views or his understanding of Christ's resurrection constituted a "Key" to unlock Pauline theology. But the resurrection of Christ viewed apart from the doctrine of union with Christ would be meaningless and reduced to an existential oddity. To view Pauline eschatology apart from union with Christ is impossible for even the coming resurrection is said to be "in Christ."

The face and importance of the doctrine of union with Christ is evidenced from every epistle the Apostle Paul ever wrote. "In Christ" was the apostle's favorite phrase and theme. If you are looking for a comprehensive doctrine which summarizes what the Bible teaches about salvation, you will find that union with Christ is such a doctrine.

Even more important, if you are seeking to understand your own salvation, study union with Christ. *To the degree you understand union with Christ, to that degree you will understand the Biblical concept of salvation.* Pause right now and ask God to make the doctrine of union with Christ a reality to your heart as well as to your mind.

Let us now set forth a general overall statement concerning union with Christ.

Every spiritual blessing which is necessary for our full salvation and which renders us complete in grace flows out of and is derived from our union with Christ.

That this general statement is Biblically correct can be seen from an examination of several passages in Scripture. First, did not the Apostle Paul state in Eph. 1:3 that the saints have every or all spiritual blessings "in Christ"? Did he not tell Timothy in II Tim. 2:10.

> I endure all things for the elect's sakes, that they may also obtain *the salvation which is in Christ Jesus* and with eternal glory.

Lastly, are not we told in Col. 2:10 that, "we are complete *in Him*"?

In just these three passages, union with Christ is the origin of: (1) every spiritual blessing; (2) salvation; (3) completeness in grace.

But what are these spiritual blessings which are ours by virtue of our union with Christ? In other words, what are the particular benefits of union with Christ according to Holy Scripture?

The particular benefits of union with Christ stretch from eternity to eternity. Thus in order to do justice to the benefits of union with Christ, we will arrange these benefits or blessings in four distinct groups or sections.

I. By virtue of our union with Christ, there are blessings which were ours before the world was created.

Having stated that believers have every spiritual blessing "in Christ" in Eph. 1:3, the Apostle begins to list some of these blessings which are ours. The first blessing he mentions is God's decree of election and predestination.

> Just as he *chose us in Him before the foundation of the world,* that we should be holy and without blame before Him; in love having *predestined* us to adoption as sons through Jesus Christ to Himself (vs. 4 & 5).

We are not "in Christ" because we were elected but our election took place in the context of our being "in Christ." This same teaching is found in II Tim. 1:9.

> Who has saved us, and called us with a holy calling, not according to our works, but according to His own purpose and grace *which was given us in Christ Jesus before the world began.*

Election and predestination must be viewed as spiritual blessings for this is how the Apostle viewed them. He even felt that election was a proper "grounds of thanksgiving" for having stated his thankfulness to God in verse 2 of I Thess. 1, the apostle gives election as one of the grounds of his thankfulness in verse 4!

> We give thanks to God. . . . Knowing, brethren beloved, your election of God.

Or again in II Thess. 2:13 he states,

> We are bound to give thanks alway to God for you, brethren beloved of the Lord, because God hath from the beginning chosen you unto salvation. . . .

It is a terrible thing to deal with election and predestination only in controversy and argument and never to use these blessings in worship and praise. Perhaps one of the greatest indictments against modern evangelical theology is that it cannot encourage Christians to give thanks for God's decree of election for this doctrine is denied by them. In so doing, are they not robbing themselves of the enjoyment of some of the blessings which are theirs by virtue of their union with Christ?

Because we are viewed as being "in Christ" before God spoke the world into being, the blessings of election and predestination are ours. How thankful we should be to God.

II. By virtue of our union with Christ there are blessings which were ours when Christ Jesus accomplished salvation upon the earth nearly 2,000 years ago.

Not only is union with Christ the context of the Father's plan in eternity, but it is also a core concept of the substitutionary life, death, resurrection, ascension and session of Christ. Christ's work of Redemption is said to be "in Christ" in Rom. 3:24; I Cor. 1:30; Eph. 1:17; Col. 1:14.

Even the work of reconciliation was accomplished in the context of union with Christ.

> God was *in Christ* reconciling the world to Himself, not count-
> ing their trespasses against them (II Cor. 5:19).

By the virtue of Christ's substitutionary and representative work,
the elect were "In Christ" when He died and was raised from the dead.
Thus the apostle could say,

> I have been crucified *with Christ*, and it is no longer I who live
> but Christ lives in me; and the life which I now live in the
> flesh I live by faith in the Son of God, Who loved me, and
> delivered Himself up for me (Gal. 2:20 cf. Rom. 6:4-8).

The work of Christ has direct bearing on our salvation essentially because of our union with His person. If we were not viewed as being
in union with Christ when He lived and died, then His life and death
could never save us. His death and resurrection if not viewed as being
vicarious and substitutionary by virtue of our union with Him would
be absolutely meaningless. As nothing took place in the eternal decrees of God but was decreed in the context of union with Christ, so
nothing in the accomplishment of salvation can be viewed apart from
union with Christ.

III. By virtue of our union with Christ there are many bless-ings which we receive when salvation is applied to us by the Spirit.

The work of the Spirit as well as the work of the Father and the
Son must be viewed in the context of union with Christ. This trinitarian understanding is emphasized by Paul in Eph. 1 where he enum-
erates what blessings are ours through union with Christ. The Father's
work is described in verses 3-6; the Son"s work vs. 7-12; and the Spirit's
work vs. 13-14. All the respective works of the Triune Jehovah are carried on and accomplished "in Christ" or "in Him."

IV. What are the blessings which are ours "in Christ"?

In short, everything which the true believer now enjoys through grace.
Because of the number of blessings which are explicitly said to be ours
by virtue of union with Christ (or "in Christ"), we can only present the
following list and encourage the reader to check the references.

1.   calling: I Cor. 1:2, 9; 7:22.
2.   regeneration: Rom. 6:3, 4; 8:10; II Cor. 5:17; Eph. 2:5, 6,

20; Col. 2:11-13.
3. justification: Rom. 3:24; 8:1, 2.
4. adoption: Rom. 8:16, 17; Eph. 2:4, 5.
5. sanctification: I Cor. 1:2, 30; Gal. 2:20; Col. 3:1.
6. forgiveness of sins: Eph. 1:7; Col. 1:14.
7. preservation: Rom. 8:35, 39; II Cor. 1:21.
8. righteousness: I Cor. 1:30; II Cor. 5:21.
9. boldness of access to God: Eph. 3:12.
10. all the treasures of wisdom and knowledge: Col. 2:10.
11. wisdom: I Cor. 1:30.
12. grace: II Tim. 2:1.
13. Christian liberty: Gal. 2:4.
14. spiritual maturity: Col. 1:28.
15. spiritual unity among believers: Rom. 13:5; Gal. 3:38; 6:15; Eph. 2:13, 21, 22.

V. By virtue of our union with Christ there are blessings which will be ours one day in the future.

The believer has blessings yet to be experienced due to his union with Christ.

While it is true that death is the last enemy to be destroyed, the Christian can look upon death as a door to spiritual blessings. Did not the Apostle say that death was "gain" to him (Phil. 1:21)? Are we not "absent from the Lord" while we are "present in the body" (II Cor. 5:6)? The believer is said to be "in Christ" when he dies as well as when he is alive. Do we not read in I Thess. 4:14 that believers are described as "those that slept in Jesus"? Thus the Apostle states in I Thess. 5;10,

> Who died for us, that whether we wake or sleep, we should live together *with Him.*

The bodies of the saints are still "in Christ" even though their souls are "with Christ" (Phil. 1:21-23; I Thess. 4:14). Death cannot separate us from the love of God which is "in Christ" (Rom. 8:38, 39). Thus we read in Rev. 14:13,

> *And I heard a voice from heaven saying unto me, Write, Blessed are the dead who die in the Lord* from henceforth: Yea, saith the Spirit, that they may rest from their labours; and their works do follow them.

The bodies rest "in Christ" while in the grave awaiting the resurrection. How shall they rise? I Cor. 15:22 says,

> For as in Adam all died, even so *in Christ* shall all be made alive.

Thus the coming resurrection must be viewed as another benefit of union with Christ. This is taught elsewhere in Rom. 6:5, 8 and Phil. 3:14, 21.

Glorification is the goal of the resurrection of the righteous. Indeed, it is the last link in the golden chain of Rom. 8:28-30. "And we know that all things work together for good to them that love God, to them who are the called according to His purpose. For whom He did foreknow, He also did predestinate to be conformed to the image of His Son, that He might be the firstborn among many brethren. Moreover whom He did predestinate, them He also called: and whom He called, them He also justified: and whom He justified, them He also glorified."

Thus glorification comes to us by virtue of our union with Christ (Col. 1:27; II Tim. 2:10).

Every spiritual blessing which is necessary for our salvation is ours by union with Christ. As we look to the future eternal state, we are told that it will mean eternal union with Christ for I Thess. 4:16-17 states.

> For the Lord Himself shall descend from Heaven with a shout, with the voice of the archangel, and the trump of God: and the dead in Christ shall rise first: Then we which are alive and remain shall be caught up together with them to meet the Lord in the air: and *so shall we ever be with the Lord.*

Having examined the importance and comprehensiveness of the Biblical doctrine of union with Christ, we now turn to study the nature of our union with Christ in order to answer the question, "How or in what way are we united to Christ?"

The first thing which must be established is the distinction between objective and subjective union with Christ. If at the outset of our study we fail to make this distinction, very little progress can be made in discerning the nature of union with Christ.

The terms "objective" and "subjective" are not intended as being exhaustively explanatory of every aspect of union with Christ. We are aware of the inadequacy of any present theological terminology. But it is hoped that this distinction will prove helpful in seeking to understand union with Christ.

When we speak of our *objective* union with Christ we are referring to our being "in Christ" in eternity and "in Christ" when He accomplished redemption in history. We are "His" and "in Him" in the eternal decree of salvation and during the life and death of Christ.

But in *subjective* union with Christ, He becomes "ours" and Christ is "in us" when the Holy Spirit begins the process of the application of redemption. We also enter into a new and living relationship to Christ in which we are "in Christ" in a new way.

While the elect sinner is "in Christ" objectively from eternity, Christ is not "in Him" subjectively until personal salvation. Thus the unregenerate elect sinner is both "in" and "out" of Christ at the same time!

If this sounds confusing, we do not intend to be so. But we must be true to Scripture. In Eph. 1:4 Paul states that these saints were "in Christ" from the eternal decree of election. In Eph. 2:1-10, he describes their transformation from dead, dominated and doomed sinners into saints. In his description of their lost estate he states that they were "without Christ" (2:12). Thus they are "in Him" (1:4) and "without Christ" at the same time!

Perhaps an illustration would be helpful at this point.

A very wealthy and wise man made a will which would take effect at his death in the future. He made this will with his children in mind. He included those present and any issue to come. Since the will was legal and binding the children could look at the riches and properties of their father and say that these things were theirs by will. Their father had them in mind when he made the will.

At the rich man's death, the will instructed that the lawyer set up trust funds for each child. All assets would be withheld from the children until they reached a certain age, then all would be theirs. Again the children could say, "All these riches are mine" even though *they did not actually possess, use or enjoy them.*

At the correct age, all the assets are given to each child for them to do with them as they please. Now they can say that the riches are theirs not only by will and trust but now by personal possession. Until now, they were "in the money" but at the same time "without money."

This illustration reveals a good parallel to a working concept of union with Christ.

In eternity past, the Father made a will respecting those who were viewed as being "in Christ." He elected them unto salvation. They were "in Christ" so far as God's plan was concerned though they did not yet exist.

In history, the Son came as the mediator of the Father's will or covenant. He accomplished redemption for those mentioned in God's plan. These elect sinners were "in Christ" when He lived and died.

When the fulness of time comes for each elect sinner, the Spirit is sent by the Father and the Son to give him all the assets of salvation which Christ accomplished according to the will of God. Thus the sinner is initially viewed as being objectively "in Christ" and subjectively or personally "without Christ." Only by personal salvation can a sinner say "I am His and *He is mine.*"

With this basic distinction between objective and subjective union with Christ established, we can now ask, "What is the nature of the relationship between Christ and His people?" We will find that the nature of objective union is different from the nature of subjective union with Christ.

I.   Objective Union With Christ

Our relationship to Christ is parallel to our relationship to Adam the first man.

> Wherefore, as by *one man* sin entered into the world, and death by sin; and so death passed upon all men, for that all have sinned: (For until the law sin was in the world: but sin is not imputed when there is no law. Nevertheless death reigned from Adam to Moses, even over them that had not sinned after the similitude of Adam's transgression, who is the figure of Him that was to come. But not as the offense, so also is the free gift. For if through *the offense of one* many be dead, much more the grace of God, and the gift by grace, which is *by one man,* Jesus Christ, hath abounded unto many. And not as it was *by one* that sinned, so is the gift: for the judgment was *by one* to condemnation, but the free gift is of many offenses unto justification. For if *by one man's offense* death reigned by one; much more they which receive abundance of grace and of the gift of righteousness shall reign in life *by one,* Jesus Christ.) Therefore as by *the offense of one* judgment came upon all men to condemnation; even so by *the righteousness of one* the free gift came upon all men unto justification of life. For as by *one man's disobedience* many were made sinners, so by *the obedience of one* shall many be made righteous. Moreover the law entered, that the offense might abound. But where sin abounded, grace did much more abound: That as sin hath

reigned unto death, even so might grace reign through righteousness unto eternal life by Jesus Christ our Lord (Rom. 5:12-21).

For since by man came death, by man came also the resurrection of the dead. For as in Adam all die, even so in Christ shall all be made alive. And so it is written, the first man Adam was made a living soul; the last Adam was made a quickening spirit. Howbeit that was not first which is spiritual, but that which is natural; and afterward that which is spiritual. The first man is of the earth, earthy, the second man is the Lord from heaven. As is the earthy, such are they also that are earthy: and as is that heavenly, such are they also that are heavenly. And as we have borne the image of the earthy, we shall also bear the image of the heavenly (I Cor. 15:21-22, 45-49).

What holds true in our relationship with Adam will basically hold true in our relationship to the second Adam, the Lord Jesus Christ.

Our relationship to Adam was first to all a *legal* relationship, i.e. a relationship created and sustained by divinely ordained law. Our relationship to Adam was not a product of evolution or chance. Neither was it product of social contract. The legal relationship which we have to Adam which bound us to his success or failure is an arrangement of God's absolute sovereignty. This answers the question, "Why did God place us in a legal relationship to Adam?" God did so simply to advance His glory. Beyond this, all we can say is that God did what He wanted to do.

Oh, how the hearts of rebellious sinners kick against this relationship to Adam. "It is not fair." I didn't ask Adam to represent me." "Who does God think He is?" "Why should I be punished for Adam's sin?" How well did the Apostle Paul answer such objections in Rom. 9:19-23,

Thou wilt say then unto me, Why doth he yet find fault? For who hath resisted His will? Nay but, O man, who art thou that repliest against God? Shall the thing formed say to Him that formed it, Why hast thou made me thus? Hath not the potter power over the clay, of the same lump to make one vessel unto honour, and another unto dishonour? What if God, willing to shew His wrath, and to make His power known, endured with much long-suffering the vessels of wrath fitted to destruction: And that He might make known the riches of His glory on the vessels of mercy, which He had afore prepared unto glory.

Our relationship to Adam is binding on all his descendents due to the divine law of God. To seek to go beyond God's will to discern other motives is to tread the sharp razor's edge between curiosity and blasphemy (Deut. 29:29).

In the same way, we are "in Christ" by a *legal* relationship. Union with Christ is by sovereign divine appointment. It is interesting to note that the very ones who deny the imputation of Adam's sin and guilt, will often comfort themselves with the hope of the imputation of Christ's righteousness. Do they not realize that if they are not "in Adam" then there is no need to be "in Christ"? How foolish is the unregenerate heart of man!

Our relationship to Adam is also an *organic* relationship. In him resided the sum total of humanity. All men are thus organically related to Adam by their constitution.

We are related to Christ organically because He was the first man of the new humanity. As all men are made in the image of Adam (Gen. 5:3), so the new humanity, God's elect from all ages, is being conformed to the image of Christ (Rom. 8:29). This conforming is at first moral and spiritual (Eph. 4:24) then at the resurrection it will be bodily (Phil. 3:20, 21).

> For our conversation is in heaven; from whence also we look for the Saviour, the Lord Jesus Christ: Who shall change our vile body, that *it may be fashioned like unto His glorious body,* according to the working whereby He is able even to subdue all things unto Himself.

Adam was by legal and organic relationship appointed by God to act for us as our *representative.* He represented us in the Garden of Eden. Thus when he fell into sin and guilt, we fell with him.

When Congress or Parliament declares war, these representative bodies speak for their citizens. As an individual citizen you may not declare war but once your representatives have done so, you are at war whether you like it or not.

Adam sinned and started a war between God and man. God's wrath, alienation, and man's total depravity are the direct result of Adam's fall into sin and guilt.

Christ Jesus is the representative of God's elect who took the punishment for us which we deserve to Adam's fall and our own sin (Lk. 22:19, 20; John 17:19). As the representative of God's people, He lived a perfect life of obedience to fulfill all righteousness for us. Thus His life and death are saving because they are viewed as being done by our divinely appointed representative.

Adam not only acted as a representative *for* us but also *as* us in terms of *substitution*. His sin was accounted by God as *our sin*. We sinned in Adam just as much as Adam sinned for us (Rom. 5:12). We are guilty because *we* sinned against God in Adam. This is the only possible understanding of Romans 5.

Likewise, Christ Jesus is explicitly said to be our *substitute* (Matt. 20:28; John 1:29; etc.). When He was crucified, *we* were crucified (Gal. 2:20). When He died, we died. When he was raised, *we* were raised (Rom. 6:3-14). We obeyed God for thirty-three and a half years. We were deserted by man and God at the crucifixion. We were there in Christ.

II. Subjective Union with Christ

We have seen what it means to be objectively "in Christ." But what does it mean subjectively for Christ to be "in us" and for us to be "in Christ"?

Our subjective union with Christ involves the application of redemption while objective union concerns the plan and accomplishment of redemption.

First, our union with Christ is *spiritual*. Spiritual in two different senses.

1. Spiritual in references to the work of the Holy Spirit. We are created in Christ Jesus or engrafted into Christ by the almighty power of the Holy Spirit (Jn. 3:3, 5).

2. Spiritual in opposition to any pantheistic union of natures or essences. We do not become Christ nor He us. Christ is said to indwell the believer without any confusion, mixing or blending of their respective natures.

Second, our union with Christ is *vital*. Vital in two senses.

1. Vital, because it is life giving. When we are brought into union with Christ we are raised from spiritual death (Eph. 2:1-10). It means eternal life is given us in Christ.

> And this is the record, that God hath given to us *eternal life*, and this *life* is in *His Son*. He that hath the Son hath *life*, and he that hath not the Son of God hath not *life*. These things have I written unto you that believe on the name of the Son of God; that ye may know that ye have *eternal life*, and that ye may believe on the name of the Son of God (I Jn. 5:11-13).

2. Vital, in the sense of being absolutely necessary for salvation.

Third, our union with Christ is *saving*. It delivers us from the wrath of God (Jn. 3:13, 36; Eph. 2:1-10; I Thess. 1:10). We are translated into the Kingdom of Christ out of the kingdom of darkness (Col. 1:13). We are made new creatures (II Cor. 5:17).

Fourth, our union with Christ is *sanctifying*. We are delivered not only from the guilt of our sin but also from its power (Rom. 6:17). And one day our union with Christ will result in the entire sanctification of body and soul (I Thess. 5:23, 24).

Fifth, our union with Christ means *intimate communion with God*. We can now have fellowship with God (I John 1:30). We now can go before God boldly without fear (Eph. 3:12). Communion is like a bridge broken at either end if we are not "in Christ" or Christ is not "in us."

Sixth, our union with Christ is *indissolvable*. No one can sever us from our union with Christ.

> What shall we then say to these things? If God be for us, who can be against us? He that spared not His own Son, but delivered Him up for us all, how shall He not with Him also freely give us all things? Who shall lay anything to the charge of God's elect? It is God that justifieth. Who is He that condemneth? It is Christ that died, yea rather, that is risen again, who is even at the right hand of God, who also make intercession for us. Who shall separate us from the love of Christ? Shall tribulation, or distress, or persecution, or famine, or nakedness, or peril, or sword? As it is written, For thy sake we are killed all the day long; we are accounted as sheep for the slaughter. Nay, in all these things we are more than conquerors through Him that loved us. For I am persuaded, that neither death, nor life, nor angels, nor principalities, nor powers, nor things present, nor things to come, nor height, nor depth, nor any other creature, shall be able to separate us from the love of God, which is in Christ Jesus our Lord (Rom. 8:31-39).

Though the ungodly may throw the child of God into prison, he cannot sever that Christian from Christ.

Seventh, our union with Christ is *corporate*. We are joined to the joys and sorrows of our spiritual brothers and sisters (I Cor. 12:26, 27). True spiritual unity is only possible where union with Christ is already a reality.

Eighth, our union with Christ is *effectual and infallible*. It cannot fail to bring about the eternal salvation of all in Christ. Christ came to do God's will and His will was that Christ would not lose one of the elect but infallibly raise them all up at the last day (John 6:37-40).

Ninth, our union with Christ is *perfect and complete*. Our union with Christ gives us all we need. There is nothing lacking. All has been done by Christ for us.

Tenth, our union with Christ is *personal*. Reader, you yourself must enter into union with Christ. You must receive Him as your Prophet, Priest, and King.

> *But as many as received Him, to them gave He power to become the sons of God*, even to them that believe on His name (John 1:12).

While union with Christ is corporate it is not genetic. Thus do not be deceived into thinking that you are "in Christ" merely because your parents are Christians or because you have been baptized. You personally must be saved for Paul said,

> Not as though the Word of God hath taken none effect. For they are not all Israel, which are of Israel: *Neither, because they are the seed of Abraham, are they all children*: but, in Isaac shall thy seed be called. That is, *They which are the children of the flesh, these are not the children of God: but the children of the promise are counted for the seed* (Rom. 9:6-8).

In conclusion to our study of the Biblical doctrine of union with Christ, we must answer several questions: Who is the author or originator of union with Christ: Is it man or God? Are we "in Christ" because we believe or do we believe we are "in Christ"?

In I Cor. 1:30 we find these clear words,

> But OF HIM are ye *in Christ*.

There is no room for any other interpretation but that God Himself is the author of our union with Christ. Our faith is a gift of God given to those objectively in Christ. Indeed, every aspect of salvation flows out of union with Christ, thus none of these things can serve as a human grounds for such a union.

No, we are thrust back upon the mysterious will of God. Why and how God chose only some to be "in Christ" from all eternity will remain a mystery until God reveals it in heaven, if He so pleases. It is enough to know that we are in Christ "of Him." Faith asks for no more.

> O mystery of love divine, That thought and thanks o'er pow'rs!
> Lord Jesus, was our portion thine, And is thy portion ours?
> Didst thou fulfill each righteous deed, God's perfect will express,
> That we th' unfaithful one might plead Thy perfect faithfulness?
> For thee the Father's endless grace, The song of victory?
> Our load of sin and misery Didst thou, the Sinless, bear?
> Thy spotless robe of purity Do we the sinners wear?
> Thou, who our very place didst tak, Dwell in our very heart:
> Thou, who thy portion ours dost make, Thyself, thyself impart.
>   Amen.

CHAPTER 10

Calling

Calling is one of the most frequently mentioned aspects of salvation. At the same time, it is difficult to ascertain exactly where calling should be placed in the order of salvation.

A case can be made to place calling between objective union and subjective union with Christ because we are told in I Cor. 1:9 that God *"called us into fellowship with His Son."* Thus calling has been viewed as being God's effectual means to bring all who are objectively in Christ into a subjective and saving union with Christ.

Others have placed calling before regeneration while some have placed it after regeneration. And even more, some have felt that calling and regeneration are the same thing viewed from different perspectives!

The confusion and disagreement over the placing of calling in the order of salvation is further evidence that a linear approach to this problem is hopeless. We have already offered in our chapter on the order of salvation another way of approaching this problem. This way is the use of a model in order to reveal the richness and manifold variety of ways in which the elements of salvation can be related to one another. In one way, calling can be viewed as being before regeneration and at the same time it can be viewed as being after it. We will deal with this issue later on in our study.

Our first task is to establish clearly the truth that *The New Testament concept of calling necessitates a distinction between two different kinds of calling.*

Those who simply state that "the call of God is one" do not do justice to the Biblical material. We must distinguish between the Gospel Call and the Effectual Call. They are not the same thing and should never be confused with each other.

The Gospel Call does not necessarily include the Effectual Call for the preaching of the Word can be "in word only," devoid of the power of the Holy Spirit (I Thess. 1:5). But the Effectual Call always comes in the context of the Gospel Call. Thus while the Effectual Call is always connected with the Gospel Call, the Gospel Call can be given without the Effectual Call being an attendant.

The following contrast between the Gospel Call and the Effectual Call should be helpful at this point.

THE Gospel Call	The Effectual Call
1. The Gospel Call is *universal* and *general* for it is given to all sinners irrespective of their race, rank, or religion: see Matt. 20:16; 28:19, 20; Mk. 16:15, 16.	1. The Effectual Call is *particular* and *special* for it is given only to the elect: see Matt. 22:14; Jn. 6:37-44, 65; Rom. 8:28-30; I Cor. 1:24-26; I Pet. 2:9; II Pet. 1:10; Rev. 17:14.
2. The Gospel Call comes *outwardly* and *objectively* to all sinners. It is the Gospel message put *in the ear* of man: see Matt. 28:19, 20; Mk. 16:15, 16; Acts 17:22-34.	2. The Effectual Call is *inward* and *subjective*. It takes place *in the heart* of elect sinners: see Jn. 6:44, 65; Acts 16:14; I Cor. 1:9.
3. The Gospel Call is God's gracious and sincere *command*, *summons* and *invitation* that all sinners everywhere should repent and turn to Him through Christ: see Matt. 22:2-14; Mk. 16:15, 16; Lk. 14:16-24; 29:47; Acts 17:22-34.	3. The Effectual Call is God's supernatural *act* in which He *ushers* the elect sinner into salvation. Christ was "called out of Egypt" (Matt. 2:15). This "calling" cannot be understood as mere invitation but it actually means that God *brought* or *ushered* Christ out of Egypt. In this same way, sinners are "called" out of sin in salvation: see Act 2:39; I Cor. 1:9; Gal. 1:15; I Thess. 2:12.

4. The Gospel Call can be _rejected_ and _resisted_ by those who hear it: see Acts 7:51; 13:46; 17:22-34; II Thess. 1:8; 2:12; Heb. 4:1, 2; Jud. 4.

4. The Effectual Call is irrestible, and _immutable._ It is always effectual in bringing the elect sinner to Christ: see Jn. 6:37-44, 65; Acts 16:14; Rom. 1:6-8; 8:28-30; Gal. 1:15; I Thess. 2:12.

5. The Gospel Call is given by _man_ through the preaching or teaching of the Word of God: see Matt. 28:19, 20; Mk. 16:15, 16.

5. The Effectual Call is given by God, mysteriously and sovereignly working salvation in the hearts of sinners: see Acts 16:14; Rom. 8:28-30; 11; 29; I Cor. 1:9, 30; Gal. 1:15; I Thess. 2:12.

6. By itself, the Gospel Call can produce the _temporary blessings of common grace_ and thus act as a restraint against sin: see II Thess. 2:7; I Tim. 1:8-11.

6. The Effectual Call produces _eternal blessings of special grace unto salvation:_ see Matt. 11:25-30; Jn. 6:36-44, 65; 10:10, 27-29; 17:2; Heb. 9:15.

7. The Gospel Call is based on _the Creator-creature relationship._ All sinners are told to repent and believe the Gospel because God created them and it is the duty of all men to worship their Creator: see Acts 17:22-34; Rom. 1:18-32.

7. The Effectual Call is based on _the redemptive work of God._ Those chosen by the Father, and purchased by the Son will be called into eternal salvation. Because Christ died for them, all the elect will be effectually called unto salvation: see Jn. 6:37-44, 65; 10:10, 27-29; Heb. 9:15; Jude 1; Rev. 17:14.

SPECIAL NOTE

Not once did Christ or the Apostles tell sinners to believe the Gospel because Christ died for them. Christ's work is the _means_ through which rebellious creatures can make peace with their Creator.

Having established the distinction and differences between the Gospel Call and Effectual Call, we can now give their respective definitions.

The Gospel Call is the sincere and gracious command, summons and invitation of God given to and for all mankind.

It consists in a setting forth of man's true identity as a responsible creature of God, created in God's image, and a rebellious sinner who must give an account of himself on the Day of Judgment.

It centers in a presentation of Christ's work as the only Divinely appointed way for sinners to be reconciled to God. The duty of faith and repentance are pressed upon the consciences of all sinners because it is their moral responsibility to worship their Creator.

Rejection of or ignorance of the Gospel Call cannot excuse man from his creaturely responsibilities to serve his Creator. The fact of judgment is based on man's sinful nature while the degree of judgment is based on how men respond to the light that they have.* The Gospel Call, once rejected, becomes a savor of death unto death and increases the guilt and condemnation of the sinner (II Cor. 3:15-16; Rom. 1-3).

The Effectual Call is the work of the Truine God for the Father is the author of the call (Rom. 8:30; I Cor. 1:9), the Son is the object (Rom. 1:6; I Cor. 1:9) and the Spirit is the agent (Jn. 15:26; I Thess. 1:5). *It is that act of God in which He not only summons the sinner to come to Christ but He effectually draws him to Christ* (Jn. 6:37-44, 65) *by making him willing to come to Him* (Ps. 110:3; Phil. 2:13 cf.; Acts 16:14).

The sinner is not forced against his will to come to Christ but God so powerfully works in the heart of sinners so as to make them freely of their own will receive Christ as offered in the Gospel Call. Thus the Effectual Call comes to Lydia. Acts 16:14: "And a certain woman named Lydia, a seller of purple, of the city of Thyatira, which worshipped God, heard us: *whose heart the Lord opened, that she attended unto the things which were spoken of Paul.*"

Several other points should be added to our definition of Effectual Calling at this point.

1.   The Gospel Call must be viewed as preceding regeneration and even the Effectual call itself. The application of salvation always takes place in the context of the preached or written Word of God (Acts 14:46; Rom. 10:14; James 1:18). In this sense calling *precedes* regeneration.

*See chapter 18 on the heathen.

2. The Effectual Call should not be confused with regeneration, in which sinners are viewed as being dead in sins; i.e., totally passive. This is an obvious contrast to Effectual Calling where sinners are viewed as freely and actively responding to the Gospel Call.

3. In this light, Effectual Calling must be viewed as being logically *after* or *simultaneous* with regeneration.

Perhaps the parallel of physical resurrection would clarify this point. In John 5:25 Christ said,

> Verily, verily, I say unto you, The hour is coming, and now is, when the dead shall hear the voice of the Son of God: and they that hear shall live.

It is obvious that the words "and now is" must refer to some present exercise of Christ's resurrection power. It is not surprising therefore to read that the raising of Lazarus was accomplished by the voice of the Son of God when He said in John 11:43, "Lazarus, Come Forth."

It is said that if Christ had not explicitly named Lazarus, all the dead would have been resurrected! But what is important for us to notice is that:

1. A verbal calling took place first just as the Gospel Call must take place first.

2. This verbal call was seen to be accomplished by an effectual call for Lazarus did come forth.

3. It was impossible for Lazarus to respond to the call of Christ to come to Him until he had been quickened or raised from the dead. *His response to Christ was the reflex reaction of his resurrection by Christ.*

In the Scriptures, regeneration is described as a spiritual resurrection (Eph. 2;1-10; etc.). In this light, no one can really deny that the words "and now is" of John 5:25 refer to Christ raising the spiritually dead as well as the physically dead. Thus there is a solid Biblical parallel between resurrection and regeneration.

This leads us to the following conclusion.

1. Chronologically, while the Gospel Call clearly precedes regeneration, effectual calling may be simultaneous with or after regeneration. The parallel with Lazarus' resurrection is too compelling to deny this proposition.

2. Casually, regeneration causes or enables the sinners to respond to God's call. We agree that effectual calling is God's act. But we must add that it is *God's act which effectually ushers the WILLING sinner into salvation.* Without regeneration, effectual calling is reduced to a general call because sinners cannot be ushered into salvation while they are still dead in sins.

3. Presuppositionally, we must presuppose regeneration in defining Effectual Calling.

4. Pedagogically, it is impossible to understand how and in what way God's call is effectual unless you understand regeneraion first.

5. Teleologically, regeneration take place with Effectual Calling as its goal. This seems to be self-evident. But that Effectual Calling would have regeneration as its goal seems to put the cart before the horse.

The objections to placing regeneration before Effectual Calling are not convincing.

Some have pointed to Rom. 8:28-30 where calling is mentioned first before the other elements of the application of redemption. But as all grant that when Paul referred to justification he included faith and repentance, so when he referred to calling, we feel that he assumed regeneration as well. We must also point out that Paul was not giving an exhaustive list but he had in view the distinctive work of God the Father and did not intend to give a complete order of all the elements of the application of redemption.

Another objection is urged from the New Testament's custom of placing calling and election together (Rom. 8:28-30; II Pet. 1:10). Since election is prior to regeneration, should we not also see calling as prior?

The only problem with this objection is that we would also place regeneration after faith for faith is linked to election in Acts 13:48; II Thess. 2:13; Titus 1:1, 2; etc. This would also hold for glorification or any element of salvation which is linked with election in the New Testament.

In conclusion, the New Testament concept of calling carries within itself a two-fold distinction between the Gospel Call and the Effectual Call. The Gospel Call is the context for the entire process of the application of redemption while Effectual Calling is a part of application. Effectual calling is preceded by the Gospel Call and simultaneous with regeneration. It is God's act wherein He ushers or brings elect sinners to Christ.

Reader, have you experienced God's Effectual Call? Has the Word of God ever come to you in power and in the Holy Spirit and with much conviction? Has the Gospel gripped you in its power? Have you been drawn to Christ by the power of the Father and influence of the Spirit?

If so, thank Him who spoke the words of the call and brought you out of spiritual deadness to life eternal. Thank God that He called you by His grace into salvation. The following hymn celebrates God's Gospel Call.

> Come, ye sinners, poor and wretched, Weak and wounded,
>   sick, and sore;
> Jesus ready stand to saves you, Full of pity joined with pow'r:
> He is able, He is able, He is able,
> He is willing, doubt no more.
>
> Come, ye needy, come and welcome, God's free bounty glorify;
> True belief and true repentance, Every grace that brings you
>   nigh,
> Without money, Without money, Without money,
> Come to Jesus Christ and buy.
>
> Come, ye weary, heavy laden, Bruised and broken by the fall;
> If you tarry till you're better, You will never come at all:
> Not the righteous, Not the righteous, Not the righteous —
> Sinners Jesus came to call.
>
> Let no conscience make you linger, Nor of fitness fondly dream;
> All the fitness he requireth Is to feel your need of him;
> This he gives you, This he gives you, This he gives you;
> 'Tis the Spirit's rising beam.
>
> Lo! the incarnate God, ascended, Pleads the merit of his blood;
> Venture on him, venture wholly, Let no other trust intrude:
> None but Jesus, None but Jesus, None but Jesus Can do help-
>   less sinners good. Amen.*

*Hymn: "Come, Ye Sinners, Poor and Wretched"

CHAPTER 11

Regeneration

The new birth or regeneration is the touchstone of the doctrine of salvation for it is in this doctrine that false teaching reveals itself in its clearest form.

While it would seem that all the various theories of the atonement give the glory to God and His grace, an examination of their respective views on regeneration will clearly reveal all the man-centered views of salvation which actually attribute salvation to man's work and not to God's sovereign grace.

All forms of sacramentalism (be it Romanism, Lutheranism or the Churches of Christ) will ultimately attribute regeneration to water baptism. If a sinner would come to a sacramentalist and ask the questions, "What must I do to be regenerated?", they would point him to the waters of baptism as well as personal faith in Christ. Instead of pointing the sinner to God and to Christ, the sacramentalist would be concerned to administer water baptism as soon as possible. Thus it is in its doctrine of regeneration that sacramentalism reveals its true nature. It is a "salvation-by-works" religion. It is a false gospel which falls under the condemnation of the Word of God (Gal. 1:6-9).

While some evangelical Christians would not attribute regeneration to anything so obviously a human work as baptism; nevertheless, they attribute the new birth to the inward work of man's will.

They would tell the seeking sinner, "You can regenerate yourself anytime you please by an act of your own will. Just choose or decide by your will to be born again, and you will be regenerated." Thus regeneration comes by the work of man and not by the sovereign work of the Spirit of God.

False views of salvation will always teach that regeneration can be obtained by something done by man outside or inside of himself. Some would point the sinner to the outward work of baptism while others would point him to the inward work of his own will.

Since regeneration serves as a touchstone or test, it is absolutely imperative for us to gain an accurate understanding of what the Scriptures teach about this subject.

When we turn in our New Testaments to find verses which mention regeneration, we only find two passages which contain the word "regeneration" itself (Matt. 19:28 and Titus 3:5). Yet, we are not confined to the mere appearance of the word "regeneration" for the concept of regeneration is spoken of in different terminology throughout the entire Bible.

Perhaps the best way to begin a study of the Biblical concept of regeneration is to use *the principle of full mention.*

This principle emphasizes the truth that some doctrines are dealt with in a full manner in a particular passage in Scripture.

In a passage of full mention, a given doctrine is in central focus and receives a detailed treatment by the author whereas elsewhere it is always referred to in connection with some other great truth.

Once you have discovered a passage of full mention on a particular doctrine, you should interpret all other scattered references to this doctrine in the light of this passage of full mention.

Perhaps several examples will clarify this principle of interpretation. Matt. 24-25 is the passage of full mention on the Second Coming of Christ. I Cor. 15 is the passage of full mention which deals with the relationship between Christ's bodily resurrection and our future resurrection. John 1 is the passage of full mention on the deity of Christ. Rom. 4-5 is the passage of full mention on divine sovereignty in salvation and reprobation. The book of Hebrews is the passage of full mention on the superiority of Christ's person and work to the Old Covenant administrations and religious leaders. I John is the passage of full mention on the doctrine of assurance of salvation. Gen. 1-2 is the passage of full mention on creation. Isa. 40 is the passage of full mention on God's transcendence, etc.

We are now warranted to ask, "Is there a passage of full mention in the Word of God which deals with the subject of regeneration?"

To this question we must answer, "Yes." Our Lord's discourse on the new birth to Nicodemus in John 3 is the passage of full mention which deals with regeneration. Indeed, it is beyond dispute that John 3 is the clearest and plainest passage in God's Word which deals with the subject of the new birth. Since John 3 is the passage of full mention on regeneration, we will examine this passage in detail in order to discover the mind of God on this subject.

In order to establish the Biblical context of our Lord's teaching on regeneration, it is necessary to quote the passage starting from John 2:13-3:16.

I.   The Context of the Discourse

Passover was at hand, and Jesus went up to Jerusalem, And found in the temple those that sold oxen and sheep and doves, and the changers of money sitting: And when He had made a scourge of small cords, He drove them all out of the temple, and the sheep, and the oxen; and poured out the changer's money, and overthrew the tables; And said unto them that sold doves, Take these things hence; make not my Father's house a house of merchandise. And his disciples remembered that it was written, The zeal of thine house hath eaten me up. Then answered the Jews and said unto him, What sign showest thou unto us, seeing that thou doest these things? Jesus answered and said unto them, Destroy this temple, and in three days I will raise it up. Then said the Jews, Forty and six years was this temple in building, and wilt thou rear it up in three days? But he spake of the temple of his body. When therefore He was risen from the dead, His disciples remembered that He had said this unto them; they believed the Scripture, and the word which Jesus had said.

Now when He was in Jerusalem at the passover, in the feast day, many believed in His name, when they saw the miracles which He did. But Jesus did not commit Himself unto them, because he knew all men, And needed not that any should testify of man; for He knew what was in man.

There was a man of the Parisees, named Nicodemus, a ruler of the Jews: The same came to Jesus by night, and said unto him, Rabbi, we know that thou art a teacher come from God: for no man can do these miracles that thou doest, except God be with him. Jesus answered and said unto him, Verily, verily, I say unto thee, Except a man be born again, he cannot

see the Kingdom of God. Nicodemus saith unto him, How can
a man be born when he is old? Can he enter the second time
into his mother's womb, and be born? Jesus answered, Verily,
verily, I say unto thee, Except a man be born of water and
of the Spirit, he cannot enter into the Kingdom of God. That
which is born of the flesh is flesh; and that which is born of
the Spirit is spirit. Marvel not that I said unto thee, Ye must
be born again. The wind bloweth where it listeth, and thou
hearest the sound thereof, but canst not tell whence it cometh, and whiter it goeth: so is every one that is born of the
Spirit. Nicodemus answered and said unto him, How can these
things be? Jesus answered and said unto him, Art thou a master of Israel, and knoweth not these things? Verily, verily, I
say unto thee, We speak that we do know, and testify that
we have seen; and ye receive not our witness. If I have told
you earthly things, and ye believe not, how shall ye believe,
if I tell you of heavenly things? And no man hath ascended
up to heaven, but He that came down from heaven, even the
Son of man which is in heaven. And as Moses lifted up the
serpent in the wilderness, even so must the Son of man be lifted
up: That whosoever believeth in him should not perish, but
have eternal life. For God so loved the world, that He gave
His only begotten Son, that whosoever believeth in Him should
not perish, but have everlasting life.

Upon His baptism, Christ entered into His public ministry. John
picks up the beginning of His ministry with His public appearance at
Jerusalem where Jesus brought dramatic attention to Himself by cleansing the temple and by performing many miracles.

Because of His miracles, "many believed in His name" (v. 23). But
their faith was founded on an awe of the miraculous and not on a true
and saving knowledge of the person and work of Christ. For this reason, "Jesus did not commit Himself of them" (v. 24). His non-
commitment was based on His omniscient knowledge of the hearts of
all men (vs. 24-25).

While still at Jerusalem, one of "many" who had a miracle-centered,
non-saving faith decide to visit Jesus in the night. This "nominal" believer was Nicodemus. The reason for his night visit has been attributed
to his timid character and fear of his fellow Jews. This is puzzling in
the light of his being a Pharisee and a ruler of the Jews (3:1).

Nicodemus began his visit with Christ by pouring forth what he thought were great compliments. He called Christ "Rabbi." Then he gave the general consensus of the "many who believed in His name" as to the person and work of Jesus. Thus he said, "*We* know that thou art. . . . "

Nicodemus stated that he understood Jesus to be a "man" who had been "sent by God" to be a "teacher." Jesus' "miracles" were proof of this position.

Evidently, Nicodemus also thought that he was already a member of God's kingdom and that he really understood spiritual matters.

It is important at this point to mention that Nicodemus is singled out by the Apostle John as an example of the popular misunderstanding of the person and work of Christ.

Nicodemus did not know that Jesus was the Christ, or that He was the divine Son of God. Neither did he understand that Jesus came to die for sinners. In blunt terms, Nicodemus did not have a clue as to the true identity of Jesus or the purpose of His coming. Nicodemus is much like the millions of nominal Christians who do not really understand who Christ is and what He has done for sinners.

It is understandable, therefore, to find in this passage a detailed exposition on the new birth (vs. 3-12) and on the person and work of Christ (vs. 13-16).

How mercifully and skillfully did Jesus correct Nicodemus' false concepts and replace them with Gospel truths. Nicodemus could not be saved until the truth was preached to him.

At this point there is an important truth which must be emphasized once again in these days of darkness in which we live: *The message of the new birth should be preached to all without exception regardless if they are church members, professing Christians or considered covenant children.*

There are some who feel that it is not proper to preach evangelistically on the new birth to church members. But was not Nicodemus a member of the visible church? Was not his church the revealed religion of the Jews? And was it not the *only* true church in all the earth? Yet Jesus said to him, "You must be born again."

There are some who feel that as long as people are professing Christians and attend church faithfully, they do not need the message of the new birth. But was not Nicodemus a faithful and strict adherent of the most orthodox and fundamental sect or denomination within Judaism? Was he not a teacher of religion widely known for his knowledge of the Scriptures? Yet, Jesus said to him, "You must be born again."

Some have said that baptism of covenant infants is based on the assumption that they are regenerated automatically from their mother's womb due to one or more parent being a Christian. Therefore, it is urged that covenant children should never be told that they need the new birth. But did not Nicodemus receive the covenant sign as an infant? Was he not viewed as a covenant child from birth? Was he not moral, upright and a believer in the Scriptual religion? Is it not the case that there was not any outward evidence to indicate that he was not regenerate? Yet, Jesus said to this covenant child, "You must be born again."

Christ here teaches us that the new birth needs to be preached to all without exception. To withhold the gospel of salvation from any group or segment of social or church life is to claim omniscient knowledge of men's hearts. We should assume someone to be regenerate only when there is clear and credible evidence of regeneration. To do otherwise may delude the souls of thousands and lead them to eternal perdition.

With our brief survey of the context completed, we will now begin to examine the teaching of our Lord on regeneration.

II.   The Absolute Necessity of Regeneration

In verses 3 and 5 our Lord clearly indicates that *the new birth is an absolute necessity binding on all sinners everywhere in all ages.*

First, did not our Lord use certain key words which reveal absolute necessity?

> *Except* a man be born again, he *cannot see* the kingdom of God.

> *Except* a man be born . . . he *cannot enter* the kingdom of God.

Second, did He not explicitly place the necessity of the new birth upon all men when he said, "Except *a man.* . . . " The original simply says *"Except one"*; i.e. anyone and everyone.

Because Nicodemus did not apply the general truth of the necessity of regeneration to himself, Christ pointedly applied this truth to his conscience in v. 7.

> Marvel not that I said unto *thee,* Ye must be born again.

Let the reader be here instructed not to be so foolish and dull of hearing as was Nicodemus. Have *you* ever applied the need of regeneration to yourself? Are you trusting in church membership, baptism or a moral life? Be here warned that none of these things can save you. *You* must be born again.

Third, would you notice that the necessity of the new birth is *inescapable* and *unchangeable* as well as *universal*.

When Christ said that no one shall ever see or enter God's kingdom without experiencing regeneration, no loop holes were left through which unregenerate sinners could slip into heaven.

We must also view the necessity of the new birth as a royal law which is unchangeable as long as King Jesus reigns.

The following illustration may be helpful.

Suppose you wanted to ride the train but you did not have a ticket. You approach the conductor and say that you do not have a ticket but you are sure that he will let you on the train anyway. But he says, "No one can ride this train unless he has a ticket. Since this rule applies to everyone, it applies to *you*. So kindly disembark."

Well, you are not easily discouraged, so you ask, "What if I come back tonight or tomorrow, will you let me ride without a ticket?" The conductor replies, "The rule is that no one *at anytime* shall ride a train without a ticket. As long as this rule is in effect, you will *never* ride this train without a ticket."

The conductor then ordered you off the train. You get off but you were determined to ride the train anyway you could. But you could not find any opened doors except the one where the conductor was standing. Since he was obviously more powerful than you, all you could do was to stand and watch the train pull away.

In the same way, unless we experience the new birth, we will never see or enter God's kingdom. This law is inescapable, universal and unchanging.

Having established that the new birth is necessary, we are warranted to ask, "Why is it necessary? Did Jesus explain the basis of this necessity?"

> That which is *born of the flesh is flesh*; and that which is born
> of the Spirit is spirit.

When the word "flesh" is found in the New Testament, in a context where it is used in opposition to the word "spirit," it always has reference to man's sinful or fallen nature.

Jesus is not referring to man's natural or physical birth when He speaks of "flesh." He is speaking of man's sinful depravity which is transmitted from generation to generation. We are born sinners: i.e., "flesh." We can give birth only to sinners: i.e., "flesh."

The contrast between flesh and spirit in the New Testament can be illustrated by the following passages.

> There is therefore now no condemnation to them which are in Christ Jesus, who walk not after the *flesh*, but after the *Spirit*.

> For what the law could not do, in that it was weak through the *flesh*, God sending His own Son in the likeness of sinful *flesh*, and for sin, condemned sin in the *flesh*.

> That the righteousness of the law might be fulfilled in us, who walk not after the *flesh*, but after the *Spirit*.

> For they that are after the *flesh* do mind the things of the *flesh*; but they that are the *Spirit*, the things of the *Spirit*.

> *So then they that are in the flesh* cannot please God.

> But ye are not in the *flesh*, but in the *Spirit*, if so be that the *Spirit* of God dwell in you. Now if any man have not the *Spirit* of Christ, he is none of his (Rom. 8:1, 3, 4, 5, 8, 9).

> This I say then, walk in the *Spirit*, and ye shall not fulfil the lust of the *flesh*.

> For the *flesh* lusteth against the *Spirit*, and the *Spirit* against the *flesh*: and these are contrary to the one to the other: so that ye cannot do the things that ye would.

> But if ye be led of the *Spirit*, ye are not under the law.

> Now the works of the *flesh* are manifest, which are these; adultery, fornication, uncleaness lasciviousness.

> Idolatry, witchcraft, hatred, variance, emulations, wrath, strife, seditions, heresies.

> Envyings, murderers, drunkenness, revelings, and such like: of the which I tell before, as I have also told you in time past, that they which do such things shall not inherit the kingdom of God.

> But the fruit of the *Spirit* is love, joy, peace, longsuffering, gentleness, goodness, faith.

> Meekness, temperance: against such there is no law (Gal. 5:16-23).

In John 3:6 Jesus is saying that *all men need the new birth because they are constituted sinners from birth and, as such, are alienated from the life of God and under the just condemnation of God.*

Is it not true that by our first birth, we are the "children of the devil" (Jn. 8:38-47)? Therefore, we need a second birth so we can be born into God's family; i.e., to become the sons and daughters of God.

It is not also true that by our first birth, we are born into Satan's kingdom and remain under his power (Col. 1:13)? Therefore, we need to enter God's kindgom in order to be delivered from Satan's dominion.

Is it not true that we are born under God's wrath (Eph. 2:3; Jn. 3:36)? Therefore, we need a second birth se we can escape the wrath to come (I Thess. 1:10).

In summary, the new birth is an inescapable, unchangeable and universal necessity which is based upon man's sinful nature. We must be regenerate because we are sinners. Unregerate sinners will never see or enter God's kindgom or heaven (Rev. 21:27).

III. The Origin of Regeneration

From where or whom does regeneration or the new birth come? Who is the author of it? What or who is the origin of the new birth?

The question of the origin of the new birth is very important. If man is the ultimate author of his own regeneration, then to him belongs the credit for his salvation. God must be viewed only as man's "helper" and cannot be given all the glory. Salvation would be auto-salvation and not *God's* salvation. Thus there are but three options:

1. God alone regenerates sinners.
2. Man with God's help regenerates himself.
3. Man alone regenerates himself.

When we examine the words of our Lord in John 3, there can be no doubt but that He taught that *God the Holy Spirit is the ultimate origin, source and author of regeneration.* To Him belongs the glory and power forevermore!

In regeneration, we must view God as being active while sinners must be viewed as totally passive. Thus regeneration is not a cooperative program between God and man. God *alone* regenerates. And He does so without the work, help or even consent of sinners. God's work of regeneration is sovereign and free and is based on His own sovereign purposes which were decreed in Christ before the world began (II Tim 1:9).

The proof of the Divine Sovereignty in regeneration rests upon the following observations.

> A.   *In John 3, our Lord speaks of regeneration in terms of human birth.*

Ye must be born again.

Stop and ask yourself, "What did I contribute toward my physical birth?" You cannot but answer, "Absolutely nothing! I did not choose to be conceived or to be born. I was passive from beginning to end."

As you were totally passive in your physical birth, so you were totally passive in your spiritual birth. This teaching is further strengthened by the two other Biblical illustrations of regeneration: creation and resurrection.

Regeneration is spoken of in terms of creation in the following passages:

Therefore if any man be in Christ, he is a *new creature*: old things are passed away; Behold, all things are become new (II Cor. 5:17).

For we are *his workmanship, created* in Christ Jesus unto good works, which God hath before ordained that we should walk in them (Eph. 2:10).

And that ye put on the new man, which after God is *created* in righteousness and true holiness.

You had nothing to do with your creation as you had nothing to do with your birth. God created the universe without man's help for we read in Gen. 1:1, "*God* created the heavens and the earth."

Resurrection is another Biblical illustration of regeneration.

Even when we were dead in sins, hath *quickened* us together with Christ, (by grace ye are saved;)

And hath *raised* us up together, and made us sit together in heavenly places in Christ Jesus (Eph. 2:5, 6).

Will you help God to resurrect your body? Or, will God do this all by Himself? Even so, regeneration is something that God does all by Himself.

In creation, birth, and resurrection, God alone is active while man is passive. Since these three Divine activities are used to illustrate regeneration, we cannot fail to grasp the truth that God alone is the author of regeneration.

> B.   Does not the Apostle John clearly indicate who is the author of regeneration in John 1:13?

> Which were born, not of blood, nor of the will of the flesh, nor of the will of man, but *of God*.

John first tells us that *regeneration is not given via the blood lines or genes*. Just because you parents are Christians does not make you regenerate for:

> They which are the children of the flesh, these are not the children of God (Rom. 9:8).

To say that your children are regenerate just because they are *your* children is to say that they are regenerate because of a blood tie to you. To say this is to contradict the direct statement of John 1:13.

Secondly, John states that *regeneration cannot be traced to any decision made by fallen human nature or "flesh."*

In our fallen state of sin and rebellion, we do not seek, understand or fear God (Rom. 3;10-18). "The will of the flesh" is never the will of God (Rom. 8:7). Therefore, God must "draw us" or "work in us" before regeneration takes place (Jn. 6:44; Phil. 2:13). We read in I Cor. 12:3,

> Wherefore I give you to understand, that no man speaking by the Spirit of God calleth Jesus accursed: and that *no man can say that Jesus is the Lord, but by the Holy Ghost*.

Having shown that the origin of regeneration is not family ties or man's fallen nature, John then states that *regeneration cannot be said to be the result of "the will of man" or "the will of a man."*

No man can say that he is regenerated as a result of the exercise of his will. *We are not born again because we believe but we believe because we have been born again.* Jesus plainly states this when He places "see the Kingdom of God" after the new birth. When we are born again, then and only then can we see or believe.

How then or from where does regeneration come to us? "Born of God" is John's answer.

God alone is active while man is passive. God's will and not man's will determines regeneration. Thus we read in James 1:18,

> Of *His own will* begat he us with the word of truth, that we
> should be a kind of firstfruits of his creatures.

Or again we read in Rom. 9:16,

> So then it is not of him that willeth, nor of him that runneth,
> but of God that showeth mercy.

> C.   *Notice the direction from which regeneration comes for Christ
>   says that we must be born "from above."*

The KJV says "born *again.*" Yet the word translated "again" is translated "from above" in every other place in John's Gospel (see 3:31; 19:11,
23). This same word is also translated "from above" in James 1:17; 3:15.
Thus we must conclude that "from above" is the proper translation.

When Jesus said, "you must be born *from above,*" He was emphasizing that regeneration comes from God. That this is true is seen from
places such as James 1:17 where "from above" has references only to
God.

> Every good gift and every perfect gift is *from above,* and com-
> eth down *from the Father* of lights, with whom is no variable-
> ness, neither shadow of turning.

The new birth comes from God above and not from man below.

> D.   *Did not our Lord explicitly state that the Holy Spirit is the au-
>   thor and origin of regeneration when He said, "born of the spirit"
>   in vs. 5, 6, 8?*

> Jesus answered, Verily, verily, I say unto thee, Except a man
> be born of water and of *the Spirit,* he cannot enter into the
> kingdom of God.

> That which is born of the flesh is flesh; and that which is born
> of the *Spirit* is spirit.

> The wind bloweth where it listeth, and thou hearest the sound
> thereof, but canst not tell whence it cometh, and whither it
> goeth; so is every one that is *born of the Spirit.*

Regeneration is the sovereign work of the third person of the Trinity.
*He regenerates helpless sinners who cannot and do not do anything toward
their own regeneration.*

But someone may object and say, "If regeneration is solely God's work and not man's, this will make men sit back and wait for God to regenerate them! There is no reason for us to urge sinners to believe in Christ if regeneration does not come by virtue of their faith."

To this we must reply that we do not feel that Christ's view of regeneration entails a denial of fervent and earnest evangelism. The sovereignty of God in regeneration does not negate the duties and responsibilities of man to seek salvation but, rather, it should make men even *more* zealous and fervent in seeking God's grace. After all has been said, we must all confess that to shut sinners up to God as their only hope is good. This is exactly the effect of a proper understanding of God's work of regeneration.

IV.   The Nature of Regeneration

Having examined the necessity and origin of regeneration, it is only natural that we ask, "What is the nature of regeneration? What does it do to the sinner? What happens to a sinner when he or she experiences the new birth?"

The answer to this question is crucial for our assurance of salvation because only when we understand the Biblical nature of regeneration, can we truly judge whether or not we have ever experienced it! The standard or test of our regeneration must be the Biblical standard or false assurance may result.

Our Lord Jesus sets forth at least three elements of regeneration in John 3.

A.   *Illumination of the mind of the Spirit*

When we experience the new birth, this regeneration causes us to "see the Kingdom of God."

The Biblical usage of the word "see" indicates that it means to perceive, understand, comprehend or grasp. Hence, the Apostle speaks of "the eyes of understanding" in Eph. 1:18.

By the nature we are born spiritually blind. The eyes of our soul are blinded by Satan for we read in II Cor. 4:3, 4,

> But if our gospel be hid, it is hid to them that are lost:

> In whom the god of this world hath blinded the minds of them which believe not, lest the light of the glorious gospel of Christ, who is the image of God, should shine unto them.

In regeneration, our eyes are opened. We are made to see for the first time in our spiritual history. As II Cor. 4:6 states,

> For God, who commanded the light to shine out of darkness,
> hath shined in our hearts, to give the light of the knowledge
> of the glory of God in the face of Jesus Christ.

Once our eyes are opened "by the illuminating and quickening work
of the Holy Spirit," we are said to "see the Kingdom of God." Therefore, we must ask, "What is this 'Kingdom of God' which we see when
regenerated?"

By a careful study of Scripture we are enabled to perceive spiritual
truths about the nature of the Kingdom of God. There are several things
about this Kingdom which are immediately clear from the Bible.

    1.   *"The Kingdom of God" exists now in the present age.*

The Old Testament prophesied that the Messiah would set up God's
Kingdom upon earth when He came to die for sinners. In Dan. 2:44
we read,

> And in the days of these kings shall the God of heaven set
> up a kingdom, which shall never be destroyed: and the king-
> dom shall not be left to other people, but it shall break in pieces
> and consume all these kingdoms, and it shall stand forever.

The present existence of God's Kingdom is also mentioned in Dan.
7:27; 9:24-27. The preaching of John the Baptist proclaimed,

> And saying, Repent ye: for the kingdom of heaven is at hand
> (Matt. 3:2).

Some scholars feel that the translation "at hand" is not accurate.
The text should read, "The Kingdom of God is *present.*" And this translation would conform to places in Scripture where "at hand" meant
"present."

Our Lord stated that the Kingdom of God had come in Matt. 12:28,

> But if I cast out devils by the Spirit of God, then the *kingdom
> of God is come* unto you.

Thus, we find Him preaching the Kingdom of God as a present reality into which Nicodemus could enter by the new birth.

According to Christ, the preaching of the Kingdom shall go on until
the end of the present age.

> And this gospel of the kingdom shall be preached in all the

world for a witness unto all nations; and then shall the end come (Matt. 24:14).

Even though some have thought that the preaching of the Kingdom has no place in the church age, the Apostle Paul viewed it as being synonymous with preaching the Gospel. The last glimpse we have of the aged Apostle is found in the last verses of the book of Acts, which is well into the church age, and in these verses we read,

> And Paul dwelt two whole years in his own hired house, and received all that came in unto him,
>
> *Preaching the kingdom of God*, and teaching those things which concern the Lord Jesus Christ, with all confidence, no man forbidding him (Acts 28:30-31).

In I Cor. 15:24, 25 the Apostle states that Christ is now reigning over God's Kingdom, and at the end of the present age He will turn over the Kingdom of the Father,

> Then cometh the end, when *he shall have delivered up the kingdom to God*, even the Father; when he shall have put down all rule, and all authority and power.
>
> For *he must reign*, till he hath put all enemies under his feet (I Cor. 15:24-25).

Christ is reigning because He is now sitting on David's throne according to Peter in Acts 2:29-33,

> Men and brethren, let me freely speak unto you of the patriarch David, that he is both dead and buried, and his sepulchre is with us unto this day.
>
> Therefore being a prophet, and knowing that God had sworn with an oath to him that of the fruit of his loins, according to the flesh, *he would raise up Christ to sit on his throne*;
>
> He, *seeing this before, spake of the resurrection of Christ*, that his soul was not left in hell, neither his flesh did see corruption.
>
> *This Jesus hath God raised up*, whereof we all are witnesses. Therefore, being by the right hand of God exalted, and having received of the Father the promise of the Holy Ghost, he hath shed forth this, which ye now see and hear (Acts 2:29-33).

Or again, Col. 1:13 states that we presently enter into Christ's kingdom when regenerated.

> Who hath delivered us from the power of darkness, and hath translated us into *the kingdom of his dear Son.*

When Jesus told Nicodemus that he could see and enter God's Kingdom if he experienced the new birth. He was speaking of a present reality.

> 2.   *"The Kingdom of God"* refers to the present spiritual realities of salvation.

The Apostle states in Rom. 14:17,

> For the *kingdom of God is* not meat and drink; but *righteousness,* and *peace,* and *joy in the Holy Ghost.*

Upon regeneration, Nicodemus would understand that he was a sinner under the just condemnation of God's law for the Holy Spirit was sent to convince and convict sinners of their sinfulness. Our Lord stated this in John 16:8-11.

> And when he is come, he will reprove the world of sin, and of righteousness, and of judgment:
>
> Of sin, because they believe not on me;
>
> Of righteousness, because I go to my Father, and ye see me no more;
>
> Of judgment, because the prince of this world is judged (John 16:8-11).

Upon regeneration, Nicodemus would understand that he could not save himself by Pharisaical obedience to the Law. He would see Christ as the sinner's substitute and faith in Him as the only way to receive everlasting life. This is exactly what Jesus pointed out to him in John 3:14-16.

> And as Moses lifted up the serpent in the wilderness, even so must the Son of man be lifted up:
>
> That whosoever *believeth in him* should not perish, but have eternal life.
>
> For God so loved the world, that he gave his only begotten

Son, that *whosoever believeth in him* should not perish, but have everlasting life.

Upon regeneration, Nicodemus would understand for the first time in his life who and what he really was in the sight of God, the nature of true salvation, the true identity of Christ and a true understanding of the work of Christ.

Dear Child of God, rejoice and praise God because He has shown you these spiritual truths. Regardless of culture, nationality, race or education, every true regenerate child of God will confess with John Newton,

Amazing grace, how sweet the sound
   That saved a wretch like me!
I once was lost, but now am found;
   Was blind, but now I see.

'Twas grace that taught my heart of fear,
   And grace my fears relieved;
How precious did that grace appear
   The hour I first believed.

Thro' many dangers, toils and snares,
   I have already come;
'Tis grace has brought me safe thus far,
   And grace will lead me home.

And when this flesh and hear shall fail,
   And mortal life shall cease,
I shall possess within the veil
   A life of joy and peace.

When we've been there ten thousand years,
   Bright shining as the sun,
We've no less days to sing God's praise
   Than when we've first begun. Amen.

B.   *Full possession of all the blessings and responsibilities of salvation.*

When one is regenerated, Christ said that they would not only "see the Kingdom of God" but also actually "enter" it. *Entering the Kingdom is to be understood as coming into full possession of all spiritual blessings of the Kingdom of God.*

Upon regeneration, you become a member and citizen of God's Kingdom.

Upon regeneration, you become a child of God, a member of the royal family, a brother of Christ, a joint-heir with Christ, a prophet, priest and king.

Upon regeneration, you receive all the blessings of the Kingdom: justification, adoption, forgiveness of sins, sanctification, etc.

Upon regeneration, you receive all the duties and responsibilities of a citizen in God's Kingdom. Your allegiance is now to King Jesus and His court. For Him you are to live and die if necessary. Your purpose in life is now to glorify God and enjoy Him forever.

Upon regeneration, you take up arms and declare a holy war against Satan and his kingdom. You will wage a life-long battle to mortify the remaining elements of depravity within your own heart as well as fight Satanic attacks and temptation which come from outside.

Upon regeneration, you are recreated in the image of God. You are born all over again and begin your spiritual life as an infant. You are resurrected from spiritual death and now walk in newness of life. In short, you are now alive forevermore.

C.   *The constitution of the spiritual nature of man.*

In verse 6 of John 3, Christ speaks of a third element in regeneration.

That which is born of the Spirit is spirit.

When a person experiences regeneration by the Spirit, he becomes spiritual in nature, i.e. he is "spirit."

Jesus did not say that we would become "*a* spirit" but "spirit." This verse cannot be twisted to mean that the new birth awaits a future resurrection of the spirit or that the spirit now sleeps in the grave as such cults as Armstrongism and Jehovah's Witnesses maintain.

The Twentieth Century Translation of the New Testament simply translates that he who is born of the Spirit "*is spiritual.*" This is the proper understanding of the words.

When you are regenerated, you become "spiritual" in that the Holy Spirit now dwells within you.

But ye are not in the flesh, but *in the Spirit,* if so be that *the Spirit of God dwell in you.* Now if any man have not the Spirit of Christ, he is none of his (Rom. 8:9).

You are constituted "spiritual" when the indwelling Spirit causes you to desire and to love "the things of the Spirit." Romans 8:4-8,

> That the righteousness of the law might be fulfilled in us, who walk not after the flesh, but *after the Spirit.*

> For they that are after the flesh do mind the things of the flesh; but they that are *after the Spirit, the things of the Spirit.*

> For to be carnally minded is death; but to be *spiritually minded* is life and peace.

> Because the carnal mind is enmity against God: for it is not subject to the law of God neither indeed can be.

> So then they that are in the flesh cannot please God.

You are constituted "spiritual" when you are led by the Spirit to mortify sin and seek holiness of life. Romans 8:12-14,

> Therefore, brethren, we are debtors, not to the flesh, to live after the flesh.

> For if ye live after the flesh, ye shall die: but if ye through the Spirit do mortify the deeds of the body, ye shall live.

> For as many as are *led by the Spirit of God*, they are the sons of God (Rom. 8:12-14).

You are constituted "spiritual" when the fruit of the Spirit is manifested in your life. Gal. 5:22-25,

> But *the fruit of the Spirit* is love, joy, peace, long-suffering, gentleness, goodness, faith,

> Meekness, temperance: against such there is no law.

> And they that are Christ's have crucified the flesh with the affections and lusts.

> If we live in the Spirit, let us also walk in the Spirit.

You are constituted "spiritual" because the indwelling Spirit applies the benefits of Christ's work to you. In Rom. 8:15, 16 and Gal. 4:6 we see the Spirit as the one who makes our adoption known to us.

> For ye have not received the spirit of bondage again to fear; but ye have received *the Spirit of adoption*, whereby we cry, Abba, Father.

The Spirit itself heareth witness with our spirit, that we are the children of God.

And Because ye are sons, God hath sent forth *the Spirit* of his Son into your hearts, crying, Abba, Father.

In summary, you are constituted "spiritual" when you partake of the indwelling presence and work of the Holy Spirit.

This is why the Apostle Paul speaks of only two types of people in I Cor. 2:14-15. One is either "natural" (i.e., devoid of the person and work of the Spirit) or "spiritual" (i.e., partaking of the person and work of the Spirit).

But *the natural man* receiveth not the things of the Spirit of God: for they are foolishness unto him: neither can he know them, because they are spiritually discerned.

But *he that is spiritual* judgeth all things, yet he himself is judged of no man.

At this point, it is important to notice that Christ did *not* say,

"He that is born of the Spirit has *a new nature as well as an Old nature.*"

It is a shame that the myth of the two natures in the Christian still persists unto this day. To speak of "old man vs. new man" or "Adam vs. Christ" or "nature vs. grace" as existing in the Christians at the same time is not only contradictory of Christian experience and psychology but also unbiblical.

1.   *Regeneration is nowhere described in Scripture as giving you a new nature or that only a part of you was affected by regeneration.* Where does Scripture ever say that you "have" a new nature as a "thing" which the Spirit has given you?
2.   *Regeneration is described as making you into something and not as just giving you something.*

In John 3:6, he that is born of the Spirit *becomes spiritual*. It does not say that he becomes a half-spirit and half-flesh creature.

I Cor. 2:14, 15 speaks of the whole Christian as being spiritual.

II Cor. 5:17 states,

Therefore if any man be in Christ, *he is a new creature*: old things are passed away; behold, all things are become new.

It if obvious that the whole person is a new creation. It does not say that he received a new nature but that he became a new creature. Regeneration constitutes us a spiritual people and not as spiritual split-personalities.

  3. *The two-nature theory is hopelessly confusing when certain questions are pressed upon it.*

a. The old nature is said to be completely evil. It will never change and will be destroyed at death. The old nature is called "the old man" or "the Adamic nature." It is further qualified as being the "ego" or "self." The old man or nature is "in" me. When I sin, it can be said that my "old nature" or "old man" did it. The "old nature" never repents and never seeks or receives forgiveness.

b. The "new man" or nature is completely good. It never sins. It is created perfect. It always does God's will. The "new nature" is "Christ in me." He is the man.

Question 1 — Isn't it true that the two nature theory actually puts forth *three* individual forces in the Christian?

There is: (1) the old man; (2) the new man; (3) and there is the believer himself who possesses these two natures.

The believer is said to be sovereign over his two natures. Both natures are like caged animals with the believer having the freedom and ability to let the old man or the new man out.

If the Christian chooses to sin, he lets the old man out of his cage. The old man does evil because it is his nature. But when the Christian want to do good, he lets the new man out of his cage. He can only do good by nature.

Question 2 — Is forgiveness of sins ever received?

The old man does the sinning. But he is incorrigibly evil and never confesses sin or seeks forgiveness. He will never receive forgiveness for he will be destroyed.

The new man never sins so he never seeks, asks for, or receives forgiveness. He is perfect and thus can never sin.

Who then is forgiven?

Question 3 — Is salvation ever accomplished?

The old man will never be saved while the new man doesn't need saving. Who then shall be saved?

Question 4 — Who will go to heaven?

The old man will not go to heaven. And if, indeed, the old man is you, or your ego or self-life as some have stated, then *you* do not go to heaven.

The new man goes to heaven. But the new man is not I but "Christ who liveth in me." Therefore, Christ goes to heaven but not me! I get destroyed along with the old man who is the real me.

Question 5 — Who is responsible for sin?

The new man is perfect so he never sins. And neither am I responsible for sin for *I* do not do the sinning, but the old man does it. Who then is responsible for sin?

Some may object at this point and say, "But are you teaching us a form of perfectionism?" No, not at all. We state our position as follows:

All Christians are spiritual but in varying degrees.

We must not forget that our Lord taught that there are "30-60-100 fold" degrees of fruit bearing (Matt. 13:8).

The Corinthian Christians were considered "spiritual" and yet, they manifested a low degree of sanctification and a high degree of carnality (I Cor. 1:2, 2:10; 3:3).

Someone else may object that our teaching does not do justice to Romans 7 where Paul said,

For we know that the law is spiritual. But I am carnal sold under sin.

For that which I do, I allow not. For what I would, that do I not; but what I hate, that do I.

If then I do that which I would not, I consent unto the law that it is good.

Now then it is no more I that do it, but sin that dwelleth in me.

For I know that in me (that is, in my flesh) dwelleth no good thing: for to will is present with me; but how to perform that which is good I find not.

For the good that I would, I do not: but the evil which I would not, that I do.

Now if I do that I would not, it is no more I that do it, but sin that dwelleth in me.

I find then a law, that, when I would do good, evil is present with me.

For I delight in the law of God after the inward man:

But I see another law in my members, warring against the law of my mind, and bringing me into captivity to the law of sin which is in my members.

O wretched man that I am! Who shall deliver me from the body of this death?

I thank God through Jesus Christ our Lord. So then with the mind I *myself* serve the law of God but with the flesh (I *myself* serve) the law of sin (Rom. 7:14-25).

There are several things in this passage which deserve particular notice.

1. Paul is speaking of the normal Christian life. This passage is not speaking of the unregenerate or of the backslidden saint. Does not Paul use the present tense through the passage in obvious distinction to the use of the past tense in vs. 9-13? Does not v. 22 reveal the heart of the believer? Will not all true believers confess their inability to live a perfect life which is bemoaned in vs. 15, 16-24? Does not the conclusion found v. 25 reveal that Paul is discussing the Christian life?

2. Nowhere in the text do we read that the believer is struggling with two *natures*. All we find is a believer struggling with *sin*. This sin is said to "indwell" him (v. 17). It is said to be present in whatever he does even when he does good (v. 21). But Paul does not lay the sin-problem in the Christian life on the presence of an "old man" but rather he views the Christian himself as the problem.

I am carnal, sold under sin. For that which I do I allow not; for what I would, that I do not; but what I hate, that I do (vs. 14, 15).

O wretched man *that I am* (not wretched old man in me), who shall deliver *me* from the body of this death (vs. 24)?

The end of v. 25 renders any higher life or deeper life interpretation of this passage impossible. It has been rightly said that Romans 7 keeps us from inferring too much from Romans 6.

We are not created perfect by regeneration. We are born as spiritual infants and grow into young men and women until we are old in the faith. This progress from infancy to maturity is clearly taught in such places as I Jn. 2:12-14.

> I write unto you, little *children*, because your sins are forgiven you for His name's sake.

> I write unto you, *fathers*, because you have known him that is from the beginning. I write unto you, *young men*, because ye have overcome the wicked one. I write unto you, little children, because ye have known the Father.

> I have written unto you, *fathers*, because ye have known him that is from the beginning. I have written unto you, *young men*, because ye are strong, and the word of God abideth in you, and ye have overcome the wicked one (I Jn. 2:12-14).

In conclusion, regeneration does not merely give us a new nature which will exist alongside of our old nature. But, rather, it recreates us, quickens us, and raises us from spiritual death. By it we are illumnated and come into full possession of the blessings and responsibilities of the Kingdom of God. By regeneration we are constituted spiritual; i.e., made to partake of the person and work of the Spirit.

V.   The Pattern or Manner of Regeneration

In verse 8 our Lord clearly draws a parallel between the ways or manner of the wind and the ways of manner of the Spirit in His work of regeneration. A paraphrase of this verse would be as follows:

> The wind blows where it wants to. And although you may hear the sound of it, you cannot tell where it comes from or even where it is going. So it is with the Spirit when He gives birth to someone.

There is an obvious parallel between the operations of the wind and the Spirit. Thus by examining several of the clear parallels between the wind and the Spirit, we can discern certain truths concerning the pattern or manner of the Spirit's operation in regeneration.

First, the wind and Spirit are both sovereignly free in their actions.

The wind comes and goes without the consent or control of man. It blows wherever and whenever it wishes.

The Spirit is sovereign and free in His work of regeneration. No individual or organization can control the work of regeneration because they cannot control the Spirit.

Secondly, the ways of the wind and Spirit are unpredictable because they are ultimately mysterious.

We may see two men and suppose that one is too hard to be saved while the other looks like a good candidate for conversion. Then the mysterious work of the Spirit surprises and confounds us because He passes over the one we had chosen and brings the harder sinner to his knees in repentance and faith.

Third, the wind and the Spirit are both irresistable in their work.

No building can withstand the tornado. Even so no sinner can resist the Spirit's work of regeneration. After all, could the world resist its creation by God? Or, a child resist its birth? Or, the dead resist their resurrection? No, the Spirit is irresistable in His work.

In John 3, our Lord establishes the principle that the Gospel message is the context of regeneration. The Gospel must be present in order to make the new birth possible. Why? The Spirit always works in conjunction with the Word and never apart from it.

This is one of the reasons why we believe that John 3:16 came from the lips of Jesus. The major purpose of Christ's lesson was to instruct Nicodemus concerning a true and proper understanding of His person and work, as well as the necessity and nature of the new birth.

VI. Old Testament Background on Regeneration

In verse 10, our Lord reminds Nicodemus that the subject of the new birth or regeneration is not something just invented or discovered but, rather, Nicodemus should have known about this truth from the Old Testament Scriptures. Christ is actually giving a mild rebuke for the ignorance and amazement of Nicodemus when he says,

> Jesus answered and said unto him, Art thou a master of Israel, and knowest not these things?

Some people teach that salvation in the Old Testament was radically different from salvation today. But this notion is not correct especially when it comes to regeneration; for our Lord Himself points Nicodemus back to the Old Testament to see the truth of the new birth.

Nicodemus should have remembered the following Old Testament passages.

1. The true child of God was said to have a spiritually circumcised heart.

    Circumcise therefore the foreskin of *your heart*, and be no more stiffnecked (Deut. 10:16).

    And the Lord thy God will *circumcise* thine *heart*, and the *heart* of thy seed, to love the Lord thy God with all thine *heart*, and with all thy *soul*, that thou mayest live (Deut. 30:6).

2. The unbelieving Jew or Gentile was said to have an uncircumcised heart.

    And that I also have walked contrary unto them, and have brought them into the land of their enemies; if then their *uncircumcised hearts* be humbled, and they then accept of the punishment of their iniquity (Lev. 26:41).

    To whom shall I speak, and give warning, that they may hear? Behold, their ear is *uncircumcised*, and they cannot harken: behold, the word of the Lord is unto them a reproach; they have no delight in it (Jer. 6:10).

    Egypt, and Judah, and Edom, and the children of Ammon, and Moab, and all that are in the utmost corners, that dwell in the wilderness: for all these nations are uncircumcised, and all the house of Israel are *uncircumcised* in the heart (Jer. 9:26).

3. The New Testament picks up the Old Testament concept of the circumcised heart and equates it with regeneration.

    For he is not a Jew, which is one inwardly; neither is that circumcision, which is outward in the flesh:

    But he is a Jew, which is one inwardly; and *circumcision is that of the heart, in the spirit*, and not in the letter; whose praise is not of men, but of God (Rom. 2:28-29).

    For we are *the circumcision*, which worship God in the spirit, and rejoice in Christ Jesus, and have no confidence in the flesh (Phil 3:3).

    In whom also ye are circumcised with the *circumcision made without hands*, in putting off the body of the sins of the flesh by the circumcision of Christ (Col. 2:11).

4.   The true child of God was said to have a new heart given them by God Himself.

Behold, the days come, saith the Lord, that I will make a new covenant with the house of Israel, and with the house of Judah:

Not according to the covenant that I made with their fathers, in the day that I took them by the hand to bring them out of the land of Egypt; which my covenant they brake, although I was a husband unto them, saith the Lord:

But this shall be the covenant that I will make with the house of Israel, After those days, saith the Lord, I will put my law in their inward parts, and write it in their hearts; and will be their God, and they shall be my people.

And they shall teach no more every man his neighbor, and every man his brother, saying, Know the Lord: for they shall all know me, from the least of them unto the greatest of them, saith the Lord: for I will forgive their iniquity, and I will remember their sin no more (Jer. 31:31-34).

And *I will give them one heart*, and I will put *a new spirit* within you; and I will take the stony heart out of their flesh, and will give them *a heart of flesh*:

That they may walk in my statutes, and keep mine ordinances, and do them: and they shall be my people, and I will be their God (Ezk. 11:19-20).

Then I will sprinkle clean water upon you, and ye shall be clean: from all your filthiness, and from all you idols, will I cleanse you.

A new heart also will I give you, and *a new spirit* will I put within you: and *I will take away the stony heart out of your flesh, and I will give you a heart of flesh.*

And I will put *my Spirit* within you, and cause you to walk in my statutes, and ye shall keep my judgments, and do them (Ezk. 36:25-27).

5.   The disobedient and the unbelieving are said to lack a new heart.

> O that there were such a *heart* in them, that they would fear me, and keep all my commandments always, that it might be well with them, and with their children for ever (Deut. 5:29)!

> Yet the Lord hath *not* given you a *heart* to perceive, and eyes to see, and ears to hear, unto this day (Deut. 29:4).

The Old Testament saints experienced regeneration. They knew that they were born with original sin and therefore needed a regenerate nature (Psa. 51:5, 10).

Christ's rebuke was valid. Nicodemus should have known the doctrine of regeneration from the Old Testament Scriptures.

And what excuse can you give, dear reader? You have read much concerning regeneration but are you still unregenerate? Or, have you seen and entered the Kingdom of God? If so, you cannot help but sing with Issac Watts,

> As when the Hebrew prophet raised
>   The brazen serpent high,
> The wounded looked, and straight were cured,
>   The people ceased to die:

> So from the Saviour on the cross
>   A healing virtue flows;
> Who looks to Him with lively faith
>   Is saved from endless woes.
> For God gave up His Son to death,
>   So gen'rous was His love,
> That all the faithful might enjoy
>   Eternal life above.

> Not to condemn the sons of men
>   The Son of God appeared;
> No weapons in His hand are seen,
>   Nor voice of terror heard.

> He came to raise our fallen state,
>   And our lost hopes restore;
> Faith leads us to the mercy seat,
>   And bids us fear no more.

>   Amen.

In order to seal the truth to our hearts that God regenerates us according to His sovereign will, perhaps the following story will be of some help.

There is a certain park in England which has become famous because of all the public speakers who come to air their different viewpoints while standing on wooden boxes. On one Sunday afternoon, two speakers drew a large crowd because of their diametrically opposite positions. One speaker was a communist and the other a Christian.

As the communist tried desperately to out-do the Christian, he saw a derelict dressed in obviously dirty, shabby clothing, standing in the crowd. With triumph, he pointed to the derelict and said, "Communism will put a suit on that man." The Christian immediately responded by saying "Christianity will put a new man in that suit."

CHAPTER **12**

Conversion

In I Thessalonians 1:2 the Apostle begins this epistle with his customary giving of thanks to God.

> We give thanks to God always for you all, making mention
> of you in our prayers.

After giving thanks to God, he then states the basis of his thankfulness in verses 3 and 4.

In verse 3, he gives thanks to God for the dynamic Christian life displayed by the Thessalonians.

> Remembering without ceasing your *work of faith*, and *labor of love*, and *patience of hope* in our Lord Jesus Christ, in the sight of God and our Father.

In verse 4, Paul bases his thankfulness on his certain knowledge of their election by grace.

> *Knowing*, brethren beloved, *your election of God.*

Having stated their election in verse 4, the Apostle points to three evidences in their lives upon which he based his assumption of their election. In verse 5, he points to his Spirit-empowered ministry among them.

> For our gospel came not unto you in word only, but also in power, and in the Holy Ghost, and in much assurance; as ye know what manner of men we were among you for your sake.

In verse 6, Paul refers to their joyous reception of the Gospel in spite of opposition and affliction.

> And ye became followers of us, and of the Lord, having received the word in much affliction, with joy of the Holy Ghost.

In verse 7, Paul points out the third evidence of election. They were shining examples of true believers.

> So that ye were examples to all that believe in Macedonia and Achaia.

In what particular aspect were they examples to all believers? Paul points to their aggressive personal evangelism in verses 8 and 9.

> For from you sounded out the word of the Lord not only in Macedonia and Achaia, but also in every place your faith to God-ward is spread abroad; so that we need not to speak any thing.

> For they themselves show of us what manner of entering in we had unto you, and how ye turned to God from idols to serve the living and true God.

The Thessalonian evangelism was bold for from them "sounded out" or "trumpeted forth" the gospel.

They engaged in "saturation evangelism" for their faith was "spread abroad" and "in every place."

Their evangelism was not shallow but as deep as it was extensive for the apostles "need not to speak any thing."

Having mentioned their exemplary evangelism, Paul points to one aspect of their witness which made a great impression on the non-Christians (verses 9-10).

> For they themselves show of us what manner of entering in we had unto you, and how ye turned to God from idols to serve the living and true God; And to wait for his Son from heaven, whom he raised from the dead, even Jesus, which delivered us from wrath to come.

The non-Christians were impressed by the conversion stories of the Thessalonian Christians.

Why were the ungodly so impressed by the testimonies of personal conversion which they heard from the Thessalonians?

Unbelievers are impressed with someone's conversion because it is something that can be seen with their own eyes. A changed life cannot be ignored. This is in distinction from the other aspects of salvation such as election, regeneration, justification, etc., which deal with unseen realities.

We are reminded of a well-known minister who was asked to debate the validity of historic Christianity with a notorious atheist. The minister agreed on one condition. The atheist must bring with him at least one person who had been delivered from a life of crime, prostitution or drunkenness by embracing atheistical beliefs. The minister would appear with one hundred such men and women who had been raised from the depths of depravity to become good upstanding citizens of society by the power of the Gospel of Jesus Christ. The atheist never showed up. So the debate was turned into a meeting of testimony and evangelism.

But we must not simply view conversion as a powerful element in personal evangelism. We must also understand that it is *necessary for salvation*. Did not our Lord stress this truth in Matthew 18:37.

> And said, Verily I say unto you, *Except ye be converted*, and become as little children, *ye shall not enter into the kingdom of heaven*.

Did not Peter speak of conversion as necessary for forgiveness of sins in Acts 3:19?

> Repent ye therefore, and *be converted, that your sins may be blotted out*, when the times of refreshing shall come from the presence of the Lord.

Does not James speak of conversion in terms of personal salvation in James 5:20?

> Let him know, that he which converteth the sinner from error of his way shall save a soul from death, and shall hide a multitude of sins.

Seeing that personal conversion is necessary for salvation, we must ask, "What brings it about?" To discover the cause of conversion, we need but look to the conversion story of the Thessalonians in I Thessalonians 1:9-10, where we are told what conversion meant to them. In this passage, it is abundantly clear that conversion flows from FAITH for we read that they "turned to God" (verse 9). And conversion flows out of REPENTANCE for they "turned from idols" (verse 9). Then faith and repentance caused the Thessalonians "to serve the living and true God; and to wait for his Son from heaven" (verse 10).

Conversion takes place when a sinner consciously turns away from sin to God in response to the Gospel. This is why repentance is joined to conversion in Acts 3:19.

> *Repent* ye therefore, and *be converted*, that your sins may be blotted out, when the times of refreshing shall come from the presence of the Lord.

Thus a sinner who will not believe in Jesus Christ is described as refusing conversion in Acts 28:27.

> For the heart of this people is waxed gross, and their ears are dull of hearing, and their eyes have they closed; *lest they* should see with their eyes, and hear with their ears, and understand with their heart, and *should be converted*, and I should heal them.

Faith and repentance are therefore both *necessary to* and the *efficient cause* of true spiritual conversion.

Some have confused conversion with regeneration. Therefore it is necessary to distinguish clearly between these two different operations of the Spirit. The following diagram may help to distinguish conversion from regeneration.

Regeneration	Conversion
1. God is *active* while man is *passive*.	1. *Both* God and man are active.
2. God regenerates man in his inner being on his *unconscious* level.	2. Conversion takes place on man's *conscious* level.
3. Regeneration is *hidden* and *private*, taking place *unseen* within man.	3. Conversion is *open* and *public* as well as inward.
4. No response from man included in regeneration.	4. The response of faith and repentance included in conversion.
5. No man is ever said to regenerate a sinner. Only God can "recreate," "give birth to," or "raise from spiritual death" sinners.	5. A believer can be said to "convert" sinners in the limited sense of the validity of the secondary cause or agent (Psa. 51:13; Jas. 5:19-20).

Because it is true that God works in us the desire and the accomplishing of His sovereign will (Phil. 2:13), in conversion we consciously turn to God by the gifts of faith and repentance. Taking this view of conversion, we strengthen the necessity of God's sovereign grace in the securing of salvation.

The Holy Spirit was sent to *convince* sinners of their sin and need of salvation and to *convict* sinners of their guilt before the Law of God and to *convert* sinners to Christ (John 16:7-14).

The importance of the Spirit's work in conversion means that conversion should never be viewed merely as an automatic effect of regeneration. Conversion is organically connected to regeneration, not by any inherent power in regeneration but by the direct operation of the Spirit. Conversion always follows regeneration simply because this is the way the Spirit works.

Having examined in general the necessity and origin of conversion, we now turn to a closer examination of faith and repentance.

1. FAITH

The Apostle speaks of saving faith when he says that the Thessalonians "turned to God" (I Thess. 1:9). That Paul urged his hearers to believe the Gospel is clear from Acts 20:21, where he summarized his message as follows.

> Testifying both to the Jews, and also the Greeks, repentance toward God, and *faith* toward our Lord Jesus Christ.

Since conversion is necessary for salvation, it is not surprising to find that faith is said to be necessary in Hebrews 11:6.

> But *without faith it is impossible to please him*: for he that cometh to God *must believe* that he is, and that he is a rewarder of them that diligently seek him.

Indeed the necessity of faith for salvation is so clear in Scripture that no one can deny it. All the popular Gospel texts emphasize the necessity of faith in salvation.

> For God so loved the world, that he gave his only begotten Son, that whosoever *believeth* in him should not perish, but have everlasting life" (John 3:16). "And brought them out, and said, sirs, what must I do to be saved? And they said, *Believe* on the Lord Jesus Christ, and thou shalt be saved, and thy house" (Acts 16:30-31).

The necessity of faith implies the necessity of hearing the Gospel. The logic of the Apostle Paul in romans 10:13-15 is devastating.
1. Salvation comes from faith.
2. *Faith comes in the context of the Word of Christ.*

No word of Christ means no hearing.

No hearing means no faith.

No faith means no salvation.

Since faith is necessary for salvation, it is important to set forth the Biblical concept of *the nature of true saving faith*. The following points are a summary of the nature of faith.

1. *Faith is the gift of God.*

Can a sinner believe in Christ or come to Christ by virtue of some kind of inherent natural power of his own soul or, is faith a gift of God? Does God save us because we believe by an act of our own free will? Or, does God give us the faith which saves?

The Scriptures are clear that *no one can confess Christ* (I Cor. 12:3, or *come to Christ* (John 6:44, 65) by their own power. God is the one who works "in us the willing and doing" of His will (Phil. 2:13). God was the one who opened Lydia's heart (Acts 16:14). It is unbiblical to picture Christ as patiently waiting for sinners to open the door of their heart. Revelation 3:20 refers to Christ's dealings with His church.

Thus while some picture Christ as standing before the door of the heart with the latch on the inside so that Christ cannot come in until the sinner decides for Christ, the Scriptures consistently picture God as causing sinners to willingly receive Christ by the power of His sovereign grace. We believe through grace and not in order to receive grace (Acts 18:27). God makes His people willing by His sovereign power.

Man's spiritual inability because of his depraved nature is clearly and abundantly taught in Scripture. Notice in the following Scriptures what man *cannot* do.

> Verily, verily, I say unto thee, Except a man be born again, he *cannot see the kingdom of God*. Verily, verily, I say unto thee, Except a man be born of water and of the Spirit, he *cannot enter into the kingdom of God* (John 3:3, 5).

> *No man can come to me, except the Father which hath sent me draw him*: and I will raise him up at the last day. Therefore said I unto you, that *no man can come unto me, except it were given unto him of my* Father (John 6:44, 65).

> For to be carnally minded is death; but to be spiritually minded is life and peace. Because the carnal mind is enmity against God: for it is not subject to the law of God, *neither indeed can it be*. So then they that are in the flesh cannot please God (Rom. 8:6-8).

But the natural man *receiveth not the things of the Spirit of God:* for they are foolishness unto him: *neither can he know them,* because they are spiritually discerned (I Cor. 2:14).

Wherefore I give you to understand, that no man speaking by the Spirit of God calleth Jesus accursed: and that *no man can say that Jesus is the Lord,* but by the Holy Ghost (I Cor. 12:3).

As it is written, There is none righteous, no, not one: There is *none that understandeth,* there is *none that seeketh after God* (Rom. 3:10-11).

In Acts 18:27, Luke tells us of the brethren at Achaia who "believed *through grace." Their faith was given to them as the unmerited gift of God.* Since faith is "through grace," it cannot be a work of man as Romans 11:6 states:

And *if by grace,* then *is it no more of works:* otherwise grace is no more grace: otherwise work is no more work.

The Apostle Paul mentions that faith is *"the gift of God"* in Ephesians 2:8-9 in order to make salvation the work of God.

In Philippians 1:29 we read:

For unto you it is given . . . *to believe in him.*

In describing the fruit of the Spirit, Paul includes faith in Galatians 5:22-23:

But the fruit of the Spirit is love, joy, peace, long-suffering, gentleness, goodness, *faith,* meekness, temperance."

Romans 12:3 states quite clearly that:

God hath *dealt* to every man the measure of *faith.*

Thus the disciples knew that if their faith was to increase, God was the one who had to do it, for faith is His gift.

And the apostles said unto the Lord, *Increase our faith* (Luke 17:5).

The Psalmist praised God in Psalm 65:4, saying,

Blessed is the man whom thou choosest, and *causest to approach unto thee.*

II Thessalonians 3:2 states that "all men have not faith." Therefore we are warranted to ask, "Who has faith?"

When we search the Scripture, it is clear that faith belongs to the elect of God. The following passages obviously relate saving faith to divine election.

    a. *"as many as were ordained to eternal life* believed" (Acts 13:45).
    b. "the faith of God's elect" (Tit. 1:1).

Faith is viewed as being one of the blessings which God gives to the elect. Thus faith is said to be ours *"in Christ"* because it comes *from* Christ as a gift of free grace. I Timothy 1:14 states,

> And *the grace of our Lord was exceeding abundant with faith and love which is in Christ Jesus.*

The true child of God upon his knees in prayer or on his feet in praise knows in his heart that faith is a gift of God. How often does he cry out to God to give him more faith!

Certain hymns beautifully express the truth that faith is the gift of God.

> *I know not why God's wondrous grace*
> *To me He hath made known,*
> *Nor why unworthy — Christ in love*
> *Redeemed me for His own.*

> *I know not how this saving faith*
> *To me He did impart,*
> *Nor how believing in His Word*
> *Wrought peace within my heart.*

> *I know not how the Spirit moves,*
> *Convincing men of sin,*
> *Revealing Jesus thro' the Word,*
> *Creating faith in Him.*

> *Come, ye sinners, poor and wretched,*
> *Weak and wounded, sick and sore;*
> *Jesus ready stands to save you,*
> *Full of pity joined with pow'r:*
> *He is able, He is able, He is able,*
> *He is willing; doubt no more.*

> *Come, ye needy, come and welcome,*
> *God's free bounty glorify;*
> *True belief and true repentance,*
> *Every grace that brings you nigh,*
> *Without money, Without money, Without money,*
> *Come to Jesus Christ and buy.*

> *Let not conscience make you linger,*
> *Not fitness fondly dream;*
> *All the fitness he requireth*
> *Is to feel your need of Him;*
> *This He gives you, This He gives you,*
> *This He gives you: Tis the Spirit's rising beam.**

Despite the clear teaching of Scripture that faith is the gift of God, some have rejected this truth because they are convinced that unless faith is viewed as an act of man's free will which all men everywhere can do at anytime they so choose, personal evangelism becomes a useless activity. If sinners cannot believe unless God gives them the faith, then why urge men to believe in Christ?

Once again we must defend God at all costs even if this means that all men are liars.

The doctrine of man's total spiritual inability to believe or to repent does not in any way detract from or diminish the urgency and necessity of calling sinners to Christ. Rather, the doctrine of man's inability will increase the urgency and desperation of sinners. It will compel them to seek God diligently. Perhaps the following illustrations will make this point clear.

Imagine that you found yourself in a room which had only one exit. This one exit was a locked door and there were no windows in the room by which you could escape.

Now, if you had the key to this door in your pocket and could unlock the door and leave at any time you so chose, there would be no urgency, panic, or desperation about leaving this room. Even if a fire would begin in a corner of the room, since you have the key in your pocket, there is no reason to feel frightened or concerned.

But, on the other hand, if you did *not* have the key to this locked door and a fire started in the corner of the room, you would be seized and gripped by a true sense of urgency and desperation. You would pound at the door and desperately shout for someone on the outside to come and save you.

In the same way, the doctrine that all men have a free will and that they can believe at any time they so choose, actually promotes and fosters an attitude of procrastination in spiritual things. How often do we hear sinners making the excuse that they will believe one day in the future when they are old or after they have had a chance to sin. They con-

---

*Hymn: "I Know Not Why God's Wondrous Grace"

tinue in a course of rebellion confident that they can believe and repent any time they wish. They experience no urgency or desperation.

But when the doctrines of God's sovereign grace are preached in the power of the Spirit, the doctrine of man's total inability will make sinners desperate enough to plead urgently with God that He would give them salvation. They will be desperate for God to save them for they know they cannot escape from the fires of hell unless God Himself unlocks the door and delivers them.

If we would only return to preaching the full Biblical Gospel, perhaps we would see a mighty revival such as Whitefield witnessed in his own day as he fearlessly preached man's total inability.

2. **Faith is the responsibility of all men.**

We must accept human responsibility along with God's sovereignty because both are taught in God's Word. Faith is a gift of the sovereign God while at the same time all men will be held responsible for the duty of believing although they are spiritually incapable of saving faith.

Man's responsibility to believe God and His word is rooted in the Creator-creature relationship. Adam and Eve originally had the spiritual ability of faith. This ability was lost in the Fall of man into sin and guilt.

The Gospel Call goes forth to all men in general (Acts 17:30) and is urged upon every individual sinner (Mark 16:15 or Acts 16:31).

Faith is therefore the duty of all men because it is, by its very nature, something that man "ought" to do as God's image-bearer. This "oughtness" of faith is the creation basis for the warrant of faith.

The redemptive basis of the warrant of faith is based upon the universal Gospel Call, the perfection of Christ's work, and the truth that Christ is a ready, willing and able Saviour.

3. **Faith adds nothing to Christ's work.**

Why is faith chosen among all the virtues as being the means of salvation? The answer is found in the observation that faith is an "empty" virtue.

Faith is not our giving to Christ but a reception of what Christ gives to us. Faith contributes nothing. It is an open hand held out to receive the free gift of salvation. It is the helpless cry of help. Faith is self-emptying and self-denying.

Faith has Christ as its object. It has in focus *His* work of salvation. Faith turns you away from yourself to Christ. In this sense, faith must never be viewed as the basis of salvation.

Faith is not obedience. Obedience is a virtue which carries merit in its hand. It should never be confused with faith. While faith leads to obedience, they are not the same thing.

Some have mistakenly thought that we are saved or justified "because of" or "by virtue of" faith. This is not true.

The Scriptures always speak of faith as the *means* by which we receive the salvation which is *based* on Christ's life and death. We are saved *by* grace which comes to us "by virtue of" or "because of" Christ's work and this salvation is received *through* faith.

> For *by grace* are ye saved *through faith*; and that not of yourselves: it is the gift of God (Eph. 2:8):

Faith is always pictured as being an activity in which the whole man participates for what is said of love can surely apply to faith. Thus faith must be "with *all* thy heart . . . soul . . . mind" (Matt. 22:37).

Faith is active in its dealings with Christ. Thus it is illustrated by *"looking"* to Christs (John 3:14-15), *"eating"* and *"drinking"* of Christ (John 6:50-58), *"coming"* to Christ (John 7:37), and *"receiving"* Christ (John 1:12).

Since saving faith is active, it is alive and fruitful. If it is a dead or unfruitful faith, it cannot be true saving faith as James 2:14-26 says,

> What doth it profit, my brethren, though a man say he hath faith, and have not works? Can faith save him?

> If a brother or sister be naked, and destitute of daily food,

> And one of you say unto them, Depart in peace, be ye warmed and filled; notwithstanding ye give them not those things which are needful to the body; what doth it profit?

> Even so faith, if it hath not works, is dead, being alone.

> Yea, a man may say, Thou hast faith, and I have works: show me thy faith without thy works, and I will show thee my faith by my works.

> Thou believest that there is one God; thou doest well: the devils also believe, and tremble.

> But wilt thou know, O vain man, that faith without works is dead?

Was not Abraham our father justified by works, when he had offered Isaac his son upon the altar?

Seest thou how faith wrought with his works, and by works was faith made perfect?

And, the Scripture was fulfilled which saith, Abraham believed God, and it was imputed unto him for righteousness: and he was called the Friend of God.

Ye see then how that by works a man is justified, and not by faith only.

Likewise also was not Rahab the harlot justified by works, when she had received the messengers, and had sent them out another way?

For as the body without the spirit is dead, so faith without works is dead also.

One great man of God said, "Works will never save you — but you will never be saved without works." Saving faith will be a working faith, i.e., alive and active.

4. **Non-saving faith is possible.**

The Scriptures plainly point out that some people have a kind of faith which will not save them.

Non-saving faith is referred to in the following Scriptures:

   a.   A multitude in Jerusalem including Nicodemus (John 2:33; 3:2).
   b.   The disciples who turned away from Christ in John 6:60-66.
   c.   Certain unconverted disciples in John 8:30-31, 40-41.
   d.   Simon in Acts 8:13 or 19-23.
   e.   The stony-ground hearer and the thorny-ground hearer in Matthew 13:20-22.

Non-saving faith can be of several kinds. It has been called historical faith, temporary faith, dead faith and miraculous faith.

   1.   Historical faith is the non-saving faith which is characteristic of the vast majority of professing Christians in our day. It is an acknowledgement of the existence of one called Jesus Christ who lived in Palestine nearly 2,000 years ago, who was the Son of God. Thus while the faith is orthodox in that it affirms the historical existence of Jesus Christ, it is non-saving because He

Himself is never personally trusted or received. In this sense, Jesus becomes only one historical figure among many. Historical faith would also affirm the past existence of such people as Alexander the Great, Abraham Lincoln, or Queen Elizabeth I.

2. Temporary faith is the non-saving faith characteristic of so many "converts" from modern evangelistic techniques. We often meet people who tell us, "Oh, I used to believe in Jesus but I don't need religion any more," or "I went forward when I was nine years old and received Christ. But I don't believe in that kid's stuff any more." The Scriptures teach that only those who endure in faith and holiness until the end shall be saved (Matt. 24:13).

3. Dead faith is a non-saving faith which never produces a changed life. It does not bear the fruit of good works. It is still-born. It is empty and nothing but mere professions. James describes this kind of non-saving faith in chapter 2 of his epistle.

4. A miraculous faith is produced in those who witness or experience what they consider to be a "miracle." During the last great war, "fox-hole religion" was experienced by many who felt they escaped death by divine intervention. Yet, their faith was non-saving because it was only temporary and quite dead. After the war very few of those who experienced divine deliverance fulfilled their promise to live for God. The important thing to remember is that any faith which fails to bring together the sinner and Christ is non-saving for,

He that *hath* the Son *hath* life; and he that hath *not* the Son of God hath *not* life (I John 5:12).

5. Faith's essential ingredients.

True saving faith is composed of knowledge, assent and trust.

a. "Ignorance is bliss" can never be said in the realm of salvation. To be ignorant of God is to come under the judgment of God at the last day, for Christ shall come.

In flaming fire taking vengeance or *them that know not God*, and that obey not the gospel of our Lord Jesus Christ: Who shall be punished with everlasting destruction from the presence of the Lord, and from the glory of his power; When he shall come to be glorified in his saints, and to be admired

in all them that believe (because our testimony among you was
believed) in that day (II Thess. 1:8-10).

It is often asked, "Exactly what must be known to make salvation
possible? What is the irreducible minimum of knowledge a sinner can
have and yet be saved?"

While the Scriptures do not give us a complete list of doctrines which
must be believed before salvation is possible, there are passages which
do point out some of the essential truths of the Gospel which must be
believed for salvation.

In Hebrews 11:6, the author of Hebrews points out that *true saving
faith must embrace general Biblical theism.*

> But without faith it is impossible to please Him. For he that
> cometh to God *must believe that He is,* and that He is a re-
> warder of them that diligently seek Him.

This text tells us that we must believe in the existence of the infinite personal God of the Bible and that we must also believe that God
is the Judge of the universe for He is the one who gives out rewards.
This means there must be a basic understanding of God's moral character as well as His existence.

True saving faith must also understand that God must be diligently
sought for God will not allow Himself to be found by hypocritical or
insincere seekers.

> And ye shall seek me, and find me, when ye shall search for
> me with all your heart (Jer. 29:13).

In Romans 10 we find several places where the Apostle Paul points
out different truths which must be believed for salvation.

The deity and bodily resurrection of Christ are necessary beliefs according to verse 9:

> That if you confess with your mouth that *Jesus is Lord (i.e.,
> Jehovah)* and believe in your heart that *God raised him from
> the dead* you shall be saved.

In Romans 10:13, Paul quotes Joel 2:32 where we read, "whosoever
calls upon the name of Jehovah, shall be saved." It is undeniable that
the "Lord" or "Jehovah" of verse 13 is the same "Lord" of verse 9. Therefore, Paul is affirming the deity of Christ in verse 9.

A basic knowledge of the person and work of Christ is therefore
necessary for salvation just as is a knowledge of general theism.

If we do not know of or believe in the Biblical Christ, it only stands to reason that we will not call upon His name. If we do not call upon Him, salvation is not possible.

> For whosoever shall call upon the name of the Lord shall be saved (Rom. 10:13).

Paul then sets forth the position that saving faith is only possible in the context of the Word of God.

> How then shall they call on him in whom they have not believed? And how shall they believe in him of whom they have not heard? And how shall they hear without a preacher? And how shall they preach, except they be sent? as it is written. How beautiful are the feet of them that preach the gospel of peace, and bring glad tidings of good things! But they have not all obeyed the gospel. For Esaias saith, Lord, who hath believed our report? So then faith cometh by hearing, and hearing by the Word of God (Rom. 10:14-17).

But how much of the person and work of Christ must be understood and received?

From our previous study of John 3, we saw that a sinner must understand that Christ is the Saviour of sinners and that salvation is received from Him through faith. This much is clear.

At this point we must make the distinction between conscious rejection and ignorance.

A sinner may be sincere and yet be very untaught. He may not know of the virgin birth, the orthodox view of inspiration, the full meaning of Christ's life or death, the second coming of Christ, etc. All he may know is that he is a terrible sinner and that Jesus is a wonderful Saviour. He would gladly accept all Biblical truths if explained to him for he is sincerely open to all of God's Word. He does not believe in certain doctrines because he is untaught.

On the other hand, someone may know about the virgin birth, the inspiration of the Bible, the vicarious death of Christ, etc., and consciously reject these truths. This person is rejecting the light he has. Therefore he cannot be placed in the same category with the untaught sinner who humbly believes what little light he has. The conscious rejectors should not be viewed as being saved for Jesus said in John 10:26-27:

> But ye believe not, because ye are not of my sheep, as I said unto you. My sheep hear my voice, and I know them, and they follow me.

While we say that a basic acquaintance with general theism and the person and work of Christ is necessary for salvation, it is impossible to discover the precise irreducible minimum.

If we sit in a theological "ivory tower" and are out of contact with the real world of sinners and saints, it would be very easy to put forth what we think is the irreducible minimum. It would be very easy to pass judgment on the spiritual nature of professing Christians and to develop a critical attitude toward anyone or any group who differs theologically from us.

But we have had to develop a more charitable attitude toward our untaught brothers and sisters in the Lord. We have met many saints who know very little theology. But, Oh, how they know Him personally! Therefore, we have come to accept this truth: God does not so much measure the knowledge in the head as He does the love in the heart.

If we want to win the ear of the millions of untaught Christians throughout the world today, we must not have a hypercritical attitude toward them. We must love them and obey Romans 14:1 and 15:1.

> Him that is weak in the faith receive ye, but not to doubtful disputations. We then who are strong ought to bear the infirmities of the weak, and not to please ourselves.

b. It is not enough to merely understand the basic doctrines of Christianity, we must also give our intellectual *assent* that they are true. There must come the moment when we accept the Gospel as the infallible Word of God.

The Apostle's ministry to the Thessalonians was not "in word only but also in power and in the Holy Spirit and with full conviction" (I Thess. 1:5). The response of the Thessalonians to Paul's ministry involve their intellectual assent as well as their understanding.

> For this cause also thank we God without ceasing, because, when ye received the word of God which ye heard of us, *ye received it not as the word of men, but as it is in truth, the word of God*, which effectually worketh also in you that believe (I Thess. 2:13).

Intellectual assent may come immediately upon hearing the Gospel or it can be a gradual process.

When Paul preached to the Athenians, some believed at once (Acts 17:34). But the Bereans gave their intellectual assent only after searching the Scriptures for we read in Acts 17:11-12:

These were more noble than those in Thessalonica, in that *they received the word with all readiness of mind, and searched the Scriptures daily,* whether those things were so." "*Therefore many of them believed;* also of honorable women which were Greeks, and of men, not a few.

Intellectual assent can be partial or full as well as being immediate or progressive. Some true converts begin by assenting to very little. But true saving faith will grow and will finally accept the Gospel.

That intellectual assent may come in progressive degrees and be partial at first is particularly clear in John 9 where we read of a blind man whom Jesus healed:

And as Jesus passed by, he saw a man which was blind from his birth. And his disciples asked him, saying, Master, who did sin, this man, or his parents, that he was born blind? Jesus answered, Neither hath this man sinned, nor his parents: but that the works of God should be made manifest in him. I must work the works of him that sent me, while it is day. The night cometh, when no man can work. As long as I am in the world, I am the light of the world. When he had thus spoken, he spat on the ground, and made clay of the spittle, and he anointed the eyes of the blind with the clay. And said unto him, go wash in the pool of Siloam (which is by interpretation, Sent). He went his way therefore, and washed, and came away seeing. The neighbors therefore, and they which before had seen him that he was blind, said, Is not this he that sat and begged? Some said, This is he: others said, He is like him: but he said, I am he. Therefore said they unto him, how were thine eyes opened? He answered and said, *A man that is called Jesus* made clay, and anointed mine eyes, and said unto me, Go to the pool of Siloam, and wash: And I went and washed, and I received sight. Then said they unto him, Where is he? He said, I know not. They brought to the Pharisees him that aforetime was blind. And it was the sabbath day when Jesus made the clay, and opened his eyes. Then again the Pharisees also asked him how he had received his sight. He said unto them, He put clay upon mine eyes, and I washed, and do see. Therefore said some of the Pharisees, This man is not of God, because he keepeth not the sabbath day. Others said, How can a man that is a sinner do much miracles? And there was a division among them.

They say unto the blind man again, what sayest thou of him, that he hath opened thine eyes? He said, *He is a prophet.* But the Jews did not believe concerning him, that he had been blind, and received his sight, until they called the parents of him that had received his sight. And they asked them, saying, Is this your son, who ye say was born blind? How then doth he now see? His parents answered them and said, We know that this is our son, and that he was born blind: But by what means he now seeth, we know not; or who hath opened his eyes, we know not: he is of age; ask him: he shall speak for himself. These words spake his parents, because they feared the Jews: for the Jews had agreed already, that *if any man did confess that he was Christ, he should be put out of the synagogue.* Therefore said his parents, He is of age, ask him. Then again called they the man that was blind, and said unto him, Give God the praise: we know that this man is a sinner. He answered and said, *Whether he be a sinner or no, I know not:* one thing I know, that, whereas I was blind, now I see. Then said they to him again, What did he do to thee? How opened he thine eyes? He answered them, I have told you already, and ye did not hear: wherefore would ye hear it again? will ye also be his disciples? Then they reviled him, and said, Thou art his disciple; but we are Moses' disciples. We know that God spake unto Moses: as for this fellow, we know not from whence he is. The man answered and said unto them, Why herein is a marvelous thing, that ye know not from whence he is, and yet he hath opened mine eyes. Now we know that God heareth not sinners: but if any man be a worshipper of God, and doeth his will, him he heareth. Since the world began was it not heard that any man opened the eyes of one that was blind. *If this man were not of God, he could do nothing.* They answered and said unto him, Thou was altogether born in sins, and dost thou teach us? And they cast him out. Jesus heard that they had cast him out; and when he had found him, he said unto him, *Dost thou believe on the Son of God?* He answered and said, *Who is he, Lord, that I might believe on him?* And Jesus said unto him, Thou hast both seen him, and *it is he that talketh with thee.* And he said, *Lord, I believe.* And he worshipped him. And Jesus said, For judgment I am come into this world, that they which see not might see; and that they which see might be

made blind. And some of the Pharisees which were with him
heard these words, and said unto him, Are we blind also? Jesus
said unto them, if ye were blind, ye should have no sin: but
now ye say, We see; therefore your sin remaineth.

After Christ healed the blind man (verse 7), the Pharisees questioned
the man as to what he believed about Jesus. The man replied that Jesus
was a prophet (verse 17). This is all the man initially believed about Jesus.

Upon a second questioning by the Pharisees, the man now confessed
that Jesus could not have been a sinner (verses 24-25).

When questioned again, we see that he had grown in his understanding and assent for he boldly rebukes the Pharisees and confesses
that Jesus came from God (verse 33).

In response to the man's confession, the Pharisees cast him out of
the synagogue (verse 34) as they had planned to do if he confessed that
Jesus was the Christ (verse 22).

When Jesus heard of the man's confession and excommunication,
He came to him and asked him, "Do you believe in him?" (verse 30).
Christ responded by revealing Himself to the man.

And Jesus said unto him, Thou hast both seen Him, and it
is He that talketh with thee.

This man's faith was partial at first but it progressively grew by degrees and now it comes to a full understanding and assent to the truth
of who Jesus really was.

And he said, Lord, I believe. And he worshipped Him.

The man not only understood who Jesus was but he gave his full
assent and worshipped him.

Now it must be pointed out that understanding and assent primarily concern truths *about* the person and work of Christ. *Thus true
faith involves understanding and giving assent to propositional revelation.*

When we speak of propositional revelation *we are not saying that God
gave us the Scriptures only in propositional form.* The Word of God comes
to us in *many* different literary forms. But we do mean that there are
propositions in the Bible which we must understand and to which we
must give our intellectual assent in order to be saved.

By the word "proposition," we simply mean that God has given to
us in Scripture declarative sentences in which He gives us statements
of fact to which understanding and assent are demanded. A proposition demands that we believe that such and such is a fact.

We find in Scripture many places where we are commanded to understand and give assent to various propositions. In the following examples the propositional aspect of the verse is italicized.

I believe that *Jesus Christ is the Son of God* (Acts 8:37).

If you confess with your mouth that *Jesus is LORD* and that *God raised him from the dead*, you shall be saved (Rom. 10:9).

I delivered to you as of first importance what I also received, that *Christ died for our sins* according to the Scriptures, and that *he was buried*, and that *he was raised on the third day* according to the Scriptures (I Cor. 15:3-4).

Who is the liar but the one who denies that *Jesus is the Christ* (I John 2:22).

By this you know the Spirit of God: every spirit that confesses that *Jesus Christ has come in the flesh* is from God (I John 4:2).

Whoever believes that *Jesus is the Christ* is born of God (I John 5:1).

In the above passages, saving faith is not said to be *in* Christ Himself but, rather, faith is seen as confessing or believing certain propositional statements *about* Christ. A proposition can be *believed* (Acts 8:37), *confessed* (Rom. 10:9), or *even denied* (I John 2:22).

But someone may ask, "Does this mean that you believe in propositional truth? Do not all of the modern existential theologians reject the idea of truth in propositional form?"

Again we must clarify that we do not mean to say that *all* the truth in the Bible comes to us in the form of propositions. *It is false to assume that truth must be either entirely propositional or not propositional at all.*

There are some modern theologians who state dogmatically that the Bible never uses the word "truth" in a propositional sense but, instead, truth always means an existential relationship of faithfulness or honesty. According to Liberal thought, truth should never be viewed as being in propositional form. It is even said that the concept of "truth in propositional form" comes from Greek philosophy and not from the Scriptures!

What shall we say to the above present Liberal popular view? We must say that those who embrace the above position are a sad example of the apostate existential age in which we live. They simply echo whatever the wisdom of this world comes up with because they have been squeezed into the world's mold (Rom. 12:1-2). They have never learned that "the world though its wisdom did not come to know God" (I Cor. 2:21) or that "God has made foolish the wisdom of this world" (I Cor. 2:20). We would urge them in Paul's words found in Colossians 2:8 and I Timothy 6:20-21:

> Beware lest any man spoil you through philosophy and vain deceit, after the tradition of men, after the rudiments of the world, and not after Christ (Col. 2:8).

> O Timothy, keep that which is committed to thy trust, avoiding profane and vain babblings, and oppositions of science falsely so called.

> Which some professing have erred concerning the faith (I Tim. 6:20-21).

As to the claim that the Bible never uses the word "truth" in a propositional sense, we simply reply that this is *not* true.

In order to develop a Biblical concept of truth, we have examined the Biblical usage of the words truth, true, truly, truths, verily (and the opposite words such as liar, lie, lied, liars, lies, lying and leasing).

We found that the words for truth are used as follows:

1. The word "truth" and its derivations are sometimes used as an adverb to describe the way an activity is carried out. We must walk, speak, and live truly, i.e., faithfully and honestly before God and man (see I John 1:6; 3:8; II John 4, etc.)

2. The word "truth" and its derivations are sometimes used as an adjective to describe a thing or a person.

Thus we read of the "true God" (John 17:3). Christ as being "the Truth" (John 14:6), Christ as "true light" (John 1:9) or "true vine" (John 15:1), etc. It is obvious that when Jesus said, "I am the true vine," He did not mean, "I am a propositional vine" or "I am an existentially faithful vine." He meant that He was the *real* and *saving* vine as opposed to the *counterfeit* and *damning*.

3. We have seen so far that "truth" and its derivations can be used to describe a person and his activities. In these cases, truth cannot be reduced to propositions. But the Scriptures also use the word "truth" and its derivations in propositional sentences.

A true person who speaks truly will speak the truth, i.e., the propositional sentences which the person speaks will be found to be factual. The word "truth" and its derivations are thus sometimes used to describe the validity and factuality of statements. A sentence is true if it is in accord with the facts.

Notice how the words for truth are used in this sense in the following passages.

> Thou shalt not sacrifice unto the LORD thy God any bullock, or sheep, wherein is blemish, or any evil-favoredness: for that is an abomination unto the LORD thy God.

> If there be found among you, within any of thy gates which the LORD thy God giveth thee, man or woman, that hath wrought wickedness in the sight of the LORD thy God, in transgressing his covenant,

> And hath gone and served other gods, and worshipped them, either the sun, or moon, or any of the host of heaven, which I have not commanded,

> and it be *told* thee, and thou hast *heard of it*, and *inquired diligently*, and, behold, *it be true*, and *the thing certain*, that such abomination is wrought in Israel:

> Then shalt thou bring forth that man or that woman, which have committed that wicked thing, unto thy gates, even that man or that woman, and shalt stone them with stones, till they die (Deut. 17:1-5).

> If any man take a wife, and go in unto her, and hate her,

> And give *occasions of speech* against her, and bring up an evil name upon her, and *say*, I took this woman, and when I came to her, I found her not a maid:

> But if this thing be *true*, and *the tokens* of virginity *be not found* for the damsel:

> Then they shall bring out the damsel to the door of her father's house, and the men of her city shall stone her with stones that she die. Because she hath wrought folly in Israel, to play the whore in her father's house: so shalt thou put evil away from among you (Deut. 22:13-14, 20-21).

> And when the queen of Sheba *heard* of the *fame* of Solomon concerning the name of the LORD, she came to *prove* him with *hard questions*.

And she came to Jerusalem with a very great train, with camels
that bare spices, and very much gold, and precious stones: and
when she was come to Solomon, she communed with him of
all that was in her heart.

And she said to the king. It was a *true report* that I *heard* in
mine own land of thy wisdom.

Howbeit I believed not *the words*, until I came and mine eyes
had seen it; and, behold, the half was not told me: thy wisdom and prosperity exceedeth *the fame which I heard* (I Kings
10:1-2, 6-7).

So he came to the king. And the king said unto him, Micaiah,
shall we go against Ramoth-gilead to battle, or shall we for-
bear? and he *answered* him, Go, and prosper: for *the LORD
shall deliver it into the hand of the king.*

And the king said unto him, How many times shall I adjure
thee that thou *tell* me nothing but *that which is true* in the name
of the LORD? (I Kings 22:15-16).

Wherefore at that time certain Chaldeans came near, and *ac-
cused* the Jews.

There are certain Jews whom thou hast set over the affairs of
the province of Babylon, Shadrach, Meshach, and Abednego;
these men, O king, have not regarded thee; they serve not thy
gods, nor worship the golden image which thou hast set up.

Then Nebuchadnezzar in his rage, and fury commanded to
bring Shadrach, Meshach, and Abednego. Then they brought
these men before the king.

Nebuchadnezzar spake and said unto them, *Is it true*, O Shadrach, Meshach, and Abednego? Do not ye serve my gods,
nor worship the golden image which I have set up? (Dan. 3:8,
12-14).

Then spake Jesus again unto them, saying, I am the light of
the world: he that followeth me shall not walk in darkness,
but shall have the light of life.

The Pharisees therefore said unto him, Thou bearest *record* of
thyself; thy *record is not true.*

Jesus answered and said unto them, Though I bear *record* of myself, yet *my record is true*: for I know whence I came, and whither I go; but ye cannot tell whence I come, and whither I go.

It is also written in your law, that *the testimony* of two men is *true* (John 8:12-14, 17).

And he that saw it bare record, and his *record* is *true*. And he knoweth that he *saith true* (John 19:35).

This is the disciple which *testifieth* of these things, and *wrote* these things: and we know that *his testimony is true* (John 21:24).

But *speaking the truth in love*, may grow up into him in all things, which is the head, even Christ:

Wherefore putting away *lying, speak* every man *truth* with his neighbor: for we are members one of another (Eph. 4:15, 25).

Whereunto I am ordained a preacher, and an apostle (I *speak the truth* in Christ, and *lie not*,) a teacher of the Gentiles in faith and verity (I Tim. 2:7).

Truth as proposition can be either denied (II Thess. 2:12) or believed (II Thess. 2:13). Truth as proposition is opposed to sentences of lies and falsehoods in many passages in Scriptures (ex. Eph. 4:24; I Tim. 2:7).

In conclusion, a Biblical concept of truth will see truth as proposition as well as being used to describe the character and activity of someone. We must speak and believe the truth as well as be true and live truly.

c. While knowledge and assent have in focus propositional revelation, personal trust is directed to Christ Himself. We trust or believe *in* Christ having understood and assented to the Gospel propositions *about* Christ.

Trust is the heart or central core of saving faith because it is the key element in salvation. We may know of and assent to the truths of Scripture about Christ but if we do not then personally *trust* in Him, we shall not be saved. Knowledge and intellectual assent are not enough. We must come into union with Christ Himself.

Whenever the Scriptures emphasize personal faith in Christ, it is referring to trusting in Him.

For God so loved the world, that he gave his only begotten Son, that whosoever *believeth in him* should not perish, but have everlasting life (John 3:16).

And they said, *Believe on the Lord Jesus Christ,* and thou shalt be saved, and thy house (Acts 16:31).

For the Scripture saith, Whosoever *believeth on Him* shall not be ashamed (Rom. 10:11).

Saving faith is active because it moves one out of self-trust to trust upon Christ and to receive from Him eternal life. There are two acrostics made from the word "FAITH" which emphasizes the necessity of personally closing with Christ.

These acrostics are based upon John 1:12.

Forsaking	Forsaking
All	All
I	I
Trust	Take
Him	Him

Reader, have you taken the step of personal trust in Christ? Please do not be satisfied with mere knowledge and assent. Turn to Him. Have direct dealings with Him. Trust and take Him as your personal Lord and Saviour.

II. **Repentance**

The Thessalonians not only "turned to God" (faith) but they turned "From idols" (repentance). Thus repentance must also be viewed as causing conversion.

There are several things about repentance which must be emphasized in our age because repentance is a much ignored truth of God's Word.

1. *Repentance is necessary for salvation and should be preached today.*

Did not our Lord plainly state that repentance is necessary in Luke 13:3, 5?

I tell you, Nay: but except ye *repent,* ye shall all likewise *perish.*

Is it not true that both Peter and Paul preached repentance as well as faith?

Repent ye therefore, and be converted, that your sins may be blotted out, when the times of refreshing shall come from the presence of the Lord (Acts 3:19).

Testifying both to the Jews, and also to the Greeks, *repentance toward God*, and faith toward our Lord Jesus Christ (Acts 20:21).

The preaching recorded in the book of Acts was in response to the Great Commission given by our Lord Himself. In this commission, Christ included the preaching of repentance.

And that *repentance* and remission of sins *should be preached in his name among all nations*, beginning at Jerusalem (Luke 24:47).

Thus we find that repentance is viewed as being one of the basic principles of Christianity in Hebrews 6:1.

Therefore leaving the principles of the doctrine of Christ, let us go on unto perfection; not laying again *the foundation of repentance from dead works*, and of faith toward God.

2. *Repentance is the gift of God.*
The apostles stated in Acts 5:31 concerning Christ that,

Him hath God exalted with his right hand to be a Prince and a Saviour, for *to give repentance* to Israel, and forgiveness of sins.

Paul in II Timothy 2:24-25 encourages Timothy to persevere in witnessing to the lost, not because they have free wills and there is a chance that they may repent by their own power. But, rather, he states,

And the servant of the Lord must not strive; but be gentle unto all men, apt to teach, patient; In meekness instructing those that oppose themselves; if *God* peradventure *will give them repentance* to the acknowledging of the truth.

The New Testament's emphasis on repentance being the gift of God echoes the Old Testament teaching that repentance is the work of God. Thus we find Old Testament saints pleading God to work true repentance in their hearts.

Turn us, O God of our salvation, and cause thine anger toward us to cease (Psa. 85:4).

I have surely heard Ephraim bemoaning himself thus, Thou has chastised me, and I was chastised, as a bullock unaccustomed to the yoke: turn thou me, and I shall be turned; for thou art the LORD my God. Surely after that I was turned, I repented; and after that I was instructed, I smote upon my thigh: I was ashamed, yea, even confounded, because I did bear the reproach of my youth (Jer. 31:18-19).

3. Repentance is the duty and responsibility of all mankind because they are God's creatures and image-bearers.

Once again we must simply accept Scripture for what it says. God is sovereign and repentance is His gift. Yet, all men are held responsible to repent. Notice how in Acts 17:24-31, the Apostle bases the duty of all to repent on the Creator-creature relationship.

> *God that made the world and all things therein,* seeing that *he is Lord of heaven and earth,* dwelleth not in temples made with hands; Neither is worshipped with men's hands, as though he needed any thing, seeing *he giveth to all life, and breath, and all things;* And *hath made of one blood all nations of men for to dwell on all the face of the earth,* and hath determined the times before appointed, and the bounds of their habitation; That they should seek the Lord, if haply they might feel after him, and find him, though he be not far from every one of us: For *in him we live, and move, and have our being;* as certain also of your own poets have said, For we are also his offspring. Forasmuch then as we are the offspring of God, we ought not to think that the Godhead is like unto gold, or silver, or stone, graven by art and man's device. And *the times of this ignorance God winked at, but now commandeth all men everywhere to repent:* Because he hath appointed a day, in the which he will judge the world in righteousness by that man whom he hath ordained; whereof *he hath given assurance unto all men, in that he hath raised him from the dead.*

In trying to solve the seeming contradiction between God's sovereignty and man's responsibility, a wise man once said, "Faith must swim when reason can no longer wade." True faith is simply taking God at His word and going your way (see Matt. 8:5-13).

4. Repentance is a change of mind.

A word study of the Biblical usage of repentance will clearly show that repentance takes place in the mind or heart and it consists of a change of mind or attitude about God, Christ, sin and one's self.

When repentance comes, you begin to see God as the Holy Judge of all the earth. His judgment upon sinners is seen as right and just.

When repentance comes, you see that Christ is the only way of salvation. You no longer try to save yourself.

When repentance comes, sin is no longer viewed as something innocent or the occasion of fun. Sin becomes odious for it is seen as damning. Thus the sin-problem becomes very serious.

When repentance comes, you view yourself as a lost, hell-deserving sinner who is not worthy to be saved. You cannot but pray the publican's prayer.

God be merciful to me a sinner (Luke 18:13).

The change in the sinner's attitude toward God, Christ, sin and himself, produces sorrow and grief. This sorrow is pointed out as being good by the Apostle Paul in II Corinthians 7:8-11.

> For though I made you *sorry* with a letter, I do not repent, though I did repent: for I perceive that the same epistle hath made you *sorry*, though it were but for a season. Now I rejoice, not that ye were made *sorry*, but that *ye sorrowed to repentance: for ye were made sorry after a godly manner, that ye might receive damage by us in nothing. For godly sorrow worketh repentance to salvation not to be repented of:* but the sorrow of the world worketh death. For behold this selfsame thing, that *ye sorrowed after a godly sort*, what carefulness it wrought in you, yea, what clearing of yourselves, yea, what indignation, yea, what fear, yea, what vehement desire, yea, what zeal, yea, what revenge! In all things ye have approved yourselves to be clear in this matter.

While there are different degrees of sorrow and grief over sin due to different personalities, a turning away from sin to Christ must be present in some degree.

5. *Repentance requires the preaching of the Law.*

If repentance involves an understanding of and a turning away from sin, the Law of God must be preached. Why?

The Apostle tells us in Romans 3:20 that "by the law is the knowledge of sin." We would not know of our sinfulness if the Law of God had not come. If we do not *know* that we are sinners, we will not see our *need* of Christ or His salvation.

Paul's own conversion story is particularly powerful in illustrating the use of the law in bringing sinners to a conviction of their condemnation and need of salvation.

What shall we say then? Is the law sin? God forbid. Nay, *I had not known sin, but by the law: for I had not known lust, except the law had said, Thou shalt not covet.*

But sin, taking occasion by the commandment, wrought in me all manner of concupiscence. For without the law sin was dead.

For I was alive without the law once: but *when the commandment came,* sin revived, and I died.

And the commandment, which was ordained to life, I found to be unto death.

For sin, taking occasion by the commandment, deceived me, and by it slew me.

Wherefore the law is holy, and the commandment holy, and just, and good.

Was then that which is good made death unto me? God forbid. *But sin, that it might appear sin, working death in me by that which is good; that sin by the commandment might become exceeding sinful* (Rom. 7:7-13).

Thus the law of God needs to be preached in order for men and women to know their sinful condition before God and their need of Christ and His salvation.

We know a pastor who had the convicting work of the Law brought home to him through the conversion of a lady who came to him to be saved so she could sleep at night.

It seems that this lady's neighbor and herself had a problem of not being able to sleep at night. Then the neighbor was saved and could sleep soundly.

The lady went to her doctor and explained how her neighbor could sleep at night because she was now "saved." In response, the doctor told her that if being "saved" would help her sleep at night, by all means try it!

So she made an appointment with her neighbor's pastor thinking she could be saved at once and sleep soundly that night.

The pastor was amazed to discover that the woman did not have any basic knowledge of God, Christ, sin or herself. Despite lengthy explanations of her sin and need of Christ, the woman did not understand her true spiritual condition. So the pastor said to her, "I am sorry but you can't be saved today. You must attend my church for at least six weeks and then we will meet again." The woman agreed to do this.

After the six weeks were up, the woman met with the pastor once again. Upon sitting down she at once burst into tears and pleaded with him that she must be saved for she saw herself as a lost sinner who needed Christ. With great pleasure the pastor pointed her to Christ who freely receives all who come to Him. She was soon baptized and became a faithful member of the church — as well as sleeping at night.

What happened during those six weeks? The woman was instructed from the Law of God as to her sinfulness and need of salvation. The Law did its work and brought her to faith in Christ.

In summary, conversion is the necessary work of God and responsibility of man. It flows out of repentance toward God and faith in our Lord Jesus Christ.

Stop and meditate on the following hymn.

> With broken heart and contrite sigh,
> A trembling sinner, Lord, I cry;
> Thy pard'ning grace is rich and free:
> O God, be merciful to me.
>
> I smite upon my troubled breast,
> With deep and conscious guilt oppressed,
> Christ and his cross my only plea:
> O God, be merciful to me.
>
> Far off I stand with tearful eyes,
> Nor dare uplift them to the skies;
> But thou dost all my anguish see:
> O God, be merciful to me.
>
> Nor alms, nor deeds that I have done,
> Can for a single sin atone;
> To Calvary alone I flee:
> O God, be merciful to me.
>
> And when, redeemed from sin and hell,
> With all the ransomed throng I dwell,
> My raptured song shall ever be,
> "God has been merciful to me." Amen.*

*Hymn: "With Broken Heart and Contrite Sigh"

CHAPTER **13**

Justification

In his epistle to the Romans, the Apostle Paul at the outset establishes the basic truths of man's sinfulness and God's judicial wrath upon man for his sin. Thus he begins his epistle by saying in 1:18,

> For *the wrath of God* is revealed from heaven against all *ungodliness* and *unrighteousness* of men, who hold down the truth in unrighteousness.

Paul argues from 1:18 to 3:23 that all men are sinners and are therefore rightfully condemned before the Law of God. He demonstrates from Scripture that both Gentile and Jew are without excuse before the bar of God's justice.

> That every mouth may be stopped, and all the world become guilty before God (Rom. 3:19).

In Chapter 3, Paul points out the two major results of man's sin. First, man is rendered unrighteous in his *person* or *condition* (vs. 10-18). Second, man is rendered guilty in his *position* or *standing* before God and His Law (v. 19). These two problems constitute the basis of man's need for salvation. Indeed, the rest of Romans is simply God's answer to the problems of man's sinful condition and guilty position.

In Chapters 4-5, the Apostle explains how a sinner's guilty position before God and His Law can be removed by God's plan of salvation. Then in Chapters 6-8, the apostle explains how God deals with the sinful condition of man.

It is in the context of dealing with the problem of man's guilty standing before God that Paul introduces justifications as God's answer to this problem.

It is necessary to emphasize in our day that *man has a problem with real judicial* guilt *before God and His Law.*

Paul is not referring to mere guilt feelings or pangs of conscience. But he refers to real guilt before the Judge of all the earth.

Various pyschological techniques can be used to remove guilt feelings but they can never remove a sinner's real guilt before God. *Our real problem is not our guilt feelings but our guilty standing or position before God.*

Perhaps one of the main reasons for a general lack of joy and peace among 20th century Christians is their woeful ignorance of the Biblical doctrine of justification. The Reformation was created by men and women who understood, embraced, and proclaimed the doctrine of justification by grace alone-through faith alone-in Christ alone. They were Christians who turned their world upside down (or rather rightside up!)

If we are going to witness a true reformation or revival in our day, we must preach the Biblical doctrine of justification. The great themes of salvation must be thundered once again from pulpits across the land. We have no time to major on minors. We must preach the doctrines of grace if we desire to see a true reformation of religion in our generation.

With these thoughts in mind, let us now examine what the Scriptures teach us concerning justification.

I.   The Origin of Justification

Man's guilt is of such a nature that only God Himself could ever remove it. Thus the Apostle Paul states in Gal. 2:21,

> I do not frustrate the grace of God: for if righteousness comes by the law, then Christ is dead in vain.

Or, again, Paul argues in Gal. 2:16,

> Knowing that a man is not justified by the works of the law, but by the faith of Jesus Christ, even we have believed in Jesus Christ, that we might be justified by the faith of Christ, and not by the works of the law: for by the works of the law shall no flesh be justified.

The Scriptures are particularly clear that it is God the Father who is the author and origin of justification.

> Seeing it is one God, *which shall justify* the circumcision by faith, and uncircumcision through faith (Rom. 3:30).

> But to him that worketh not, but believeth on *him that justified the ungodly,* his faith is counted for righteousness (Rom. 4:5).

> Moreover, whom he did predestinate, them he also called: and whom he called, them *he also justified:* and whom he justified, them he also glorified (Rom. 8:30).

> Who shall lay anything to charge of God's elect? It is *God that justifieth* (Rom. 8:33).

Since it is the Father who justifies us, we can see how sinful it is to neglect the Father in our prayers and praise.

We hear very much today of praying to Jesus, praising Jesus, praying to and for the Holy Spirit. Yet, we hear very little about God the Father.

The Holy Spirit was sent to point us to Christ, *not* to Himself. Jesus said in John 16:13, 14.

> Howbeit when he, the Spirit of truth, is come, he will guide you into all truth: for *he shall not speak of himself;* but whatsoever he shall hear, that shall he speak: and he will show you things to come. *He shall glorify me:* for he shall receive of mine and shall show it unto you.

When we turn to Christ under the Spirit's guidance, we find Him pointing us to the Father. Christ is the way to the Father and not a dead end street (Jn. 14:6). Christ is the mediator between God and man (I Tim. 2:5). Thus Paul places all members of the Godhead in their proper order in Eph. 2:18,

> For through him we both have access by one Spirit unto the Father.

It is on this basis that we must judge as spurious any religious revival which does not lead to the glorification of the Father. True revivals in the past always quickened and renewed the believer's love and devotion to his Father.

Dear Christian reader, do you praise the Father for justification? Do you wish a quickened devotion to your Father? Then study those aspects of salvation which are His particular work.

II.   The Nature of Justification

Justification is a judicial, legal and forensic declaration or verdict of God. As such, justification takes place in heaven and not on earth. It deals with our guilty position or standing before God and His law. Thus justification concerns what God *says* about us in His capacity as the Judge of all the earth.

The Scriptures speak of God justifying us in the sense of judicially declaring us righteous before the Law of God. This declaration of righteousness involves two things: (1) God declares before the Law that we have never sinned. Thus it is a declaration of our *perfect sinlessness*. (2) God declares before the Law that we have lived in total obedience to the Law and have, therefore, merited the blessings of eternal life. Thus it is a declaration of our *perfect obedience*.

Justification is more than mere pardon for pardon means "declared guilty but delivered from punishment" while justification is God's declaration that we are *not* guilty and therefore *not* worthy of punishment. But, instead, God positively declares that we are *righteous* before Him and, therefore *worthy* to receive all the blessings and privileges of the righteous.

It is for this reason that forgiveness should not be confused with justification. In justification, God declares us perfect in righteousness. Thus there is nothing to forgive for no sin is judicially recognized by God.

That justification means *to declare righteous* in a legal, judicial or forensic sense is almost universally accepted. Since the arguments for this position have been presented in great detail by such scholars as James Buchanan, we will only present a brief summary of the chief arguments which demonstrate the forensic or judicial character of justification.

1. The word justification is not confined to the pages of Holy Scripture but it was a well-known and commonly used word in the Greek language. When we investigate the meaning of justification as used in everyday speech, we discover that justification as used in everyday speech, we discover that justification meant "to declare righteous" 100% the time. Furthermore, it was used in Roman law as the judicial term to declare someone "not guilty," i.e., righteous.

2. When we turn to study how the word justification is used in Scripture, we again find that it *always* means to declare someone righteous.

First, its usage in non-theological or everyday speech contexts always means to declare righteous. Examine the following passages and substitute the phrase "declare righteous" wherever the word justification is found.

> Keep thee far from a false matter; and the innocent and righteous slay thou not: for I will not *justify* the wicked (Ex. 23:7).

> If there be a controversy between men, and they come unto judgment, that the judges may judge them. Then they shall *justify* the righteous, and *condemn* the wicked (Deut. 25:1).

> He that *justifieth* the wicked, and he that *condemneth* the just, even they both are abomination to the Lord (Prov. 17:15).

> Which *justify* the wicked for regard, and take away the righteousness of the righteous from him (Isa. 5:23)!

> And the Lord said unto me, The backsliding Israel hath *justified* herself more than treacherous Judah (Jer. 3:11).

> Neither hath Samaria committed half of thy sins; but thou hast multiplied thine abominations more than they, and hast *justified* thy sisters in all thine abominations which thou hast done (Ezk. 16:51).

> The Son of man came eating and drinking, and they say, Behold a man gluttonous, and a winebibber, a friend of publicans and sinners. But wisdom is *justified* of her children (Matt. 11:19).

> But he, willing to *justify* himself, said unto Jesus, and who is my neighbor (Lk. 10:29).

> And he said unto them, Ye are they which *justify* yourselves before men; but God knoweth your hearts: for that which is highly esteemed among men is abomination in the sight of God (Lk. 16:15).

Second, man is said to "justify" God. It is obvious that while we cannot *make* God righteous we can *declare* Him to be righteous. No other meaning is possible.

> Against thee, thee only, have I sinned, and done this evil in thy sight: that *thou mightest be justified* when thou speakest, and be clear when thou judgest (Psa. 51:4).

And all the people that heard him, and the publicans *justified God,* being baptized with the baptism of John (Lk. 7:29).

Third, judicial condemnation is the opposite of justification. A judge cannot make a person guilty or righteous. He can only declare him condemned or justified.

If there be a controversy between men, and they come unto judgment, that the judges may judge them; then they shall justify the righteous, and *condemn* the wicked (Deut. 25:1).

If I justify myself, mine own mouth shall *condemn* me: if I say, I am perfect, it shall also prove me perverse (Job 9:20).

Shall even he that hateth right govern? And wilt thou *condemn* him that is most just (Job 34:17)?

He that justifieth the wicked, and he that *condemneth* the just, even they both are abomination to the Lord (Prov. 17:15).

Which justify the wicked for reward, and *take away the righteousness* of the righteous from him (Isa. 5:23)!

Behold, the Lord GOD will help me; who is he that shall *condemn* me? lo, they all shall wax old as a garment; the moth shall eat them up (Isa. 50:9).

Who shall lay any thing to the charge of God's elect? It is God that justifieth (Rom. 8:33).

Who is he that *condemneth?* It is Christ that died, yea rather, that is risen again, who is even at the right hand of God, who also maketh intercession for us (Rom. 8:34).

Fourth, the different words and phrases which are sometimes substituted for justification mean to declare righteous.

Blessed is the man unto whom the LORD *imputeth not iniquity,* and in whose spirit there is no guile (Psa. 32:2).

What shall we say then that Abraham our father, as pertaining to the flesh, hath found? For if Abraham were justified by works, he hath whereof to glory, but not before God. For what saith the Scripture? Abraham believed God, and it was *counted* unto him *righteousness.* Now to him that worketh is the reward not reckoned of grace, but of debt. But to him that worketh not, but believeth on him that justifieth the ungodly, his faith is *counted for righteousness*. Even as David also describeth the blessedness of the man, unto whom God *imputeth righteousness* without works. Saying, Blessed are they whose sins are covered. Blessed is the man to whom *the Lord will not impute sin* (Rom. 4:1-8).

3. In the book of Romans, Paul introduces justification as God's answer to man's problem of his sinful record or standing before God and His Law. Justification is always dealt with in the context of the Law and its demands. Thus justification and the Law are the two main topics discussed in Galatians as well as in Romans 4 and 5. Therefore, the context of justification reveals its judicial character.

III.   The Foundation of Justification

Having established that God declares us righteous in justification, we are warranted to ask, "On what grounds or foundation does God make such a declaration? How can He declare us righteous while we are yet unrighteous? How can God justify the ungodly (Rom. 4:5)? How can God be just and, at the same time be the justifier of sinners (Rom. 3:26)?"

The righteousness which is imputed to our account in God's act of justification must be understood as *an evangelical righteousness which is revealed to us in the Gospel*. Thus the Apostle Paul begins his epistle to the Romans by stating that there is a righteousness revealed in the Gospel which must be received by faith.

For therein is the righteousness of God revealed from faith to faith: as it is written. The just shall live by faith (Rom. 1:17).

The righteousness revealed by the Gospel is declared to be *God's* righteousness. This is not to be understood as referring to God's general attribute of righteousness, but, rather, as a righteousness which comes from God and not from man. Thus justifying righteousness is not the product of our obedience to the Law but it is the gift of God. Paul stated this beautifully in Phil. 3:9,

And be found in him, not having mine own righteousness, which is of the law, but that which is through the faith of Christ, the righteousness which is of God by faith.

Even though we have seen that the righteousness of justification comes from God and is revealed in the Gospel, we still must answer the question, "Upon what grounds does God declare us righteous?"

The Gospel reveals the righteousness of Jesus Christ as the foundation of our justification. By His life, death, and resurrection Christ Jesus accomplished all that was necessary for our complete justification.

The work of Jesus Christ is the key to justification. We are justified on the basis of His work for us while upon earth nearly 2,000 years ago. Justification is based upon three great transactions rooted in the historical redemptive work of Christ.

1. Christ's perfect life of sinlessness and total obedience to the Law of God is imputed to our account. God accepts us as righteous by the virture of the substitutionary obedience of Christ in His life. Thus Paul declares in Rom. 5:18,

> Therefore, as by the offense of one judgment came upon all men to condemnation; even so by the righteousness of one the free gift came upon all men unto justification of life.

2. Our life of sin and guilt was imputed to Christ's account and He bore the curse of the Law in our place.

> For he hath made him to be sin for us, who knew no sin; that we might be made the righteousness of God in him (II Cor. 5:21).

> Christ hath redeemed us from the curse of the law, being made a curse for us: for it is written, cursed is every one that hangeth on a tree (Gal. 3:13).

3. By resurrecting Christ from the grave, God demonstrated that He accepted the obedience of Christ in life and death. Thus Christ's resurrection is viewed by the apostle as being foundation to our justification in Rom. 4:25,

> Who was delivered for our offenses, and was raised again for our justification.

In summary, God declares us righteous because we *are* legally righteous by virtue of the imputation of Christ's perfect righteousness to our account.

The reality and preciousness of justification through Christ's righteousness can perhaps be emphasized by the following illustration.

Imagine that you found yourself in the courtroom of heaven. Your name was called and you were given a book entitled, *This Was Your Life*, in which was recorded every single thought, word, deed and desire of your entire life.

As you looked into your book, you found it divided into two sections. The first section was headed by this question, _"Did you always perfectly keep God's Law and do that which was pleasing in God's sight?"_ The second section began by asking, _"Did you ever transgress God's Law by failing to obey its commands or by doing what it forbids?"_

When you examine the first section you find that all the pages are blank because you never did any good in God's eyes. But when you turn to the second section, you find a detailed account of all of your many sins of omission and commission.

The full impact of your sinfulness before God suddenly rushes upon you. You realize that justice cannot do otherwise than demand and receive your eternal condemnation.

Your fear is increased as you hear a man before you receive this verdict, "Depart from me, ye cursed, into the eternal fire." You shake as your case is now called up. But then there arose One who willingly took upon Himself the task of representing and defending you before the Judge of all the earth.

He held a book in His hand. And now He asked you for your book. After He had both books, He switched the covers so that your cover received the contents of His book while the contents of your book were put into the covers of His book.

As you examine your book, you see that according to the record written therein, you always perfectly kept God's Law and did that which was pleasing before God. You turn to the second section and see blank pages because you never sinned.

The full realization of what just happened had come to you when you hear the Judge pronounce your representative guilty and hand Him over for Justice to crucify. Then you are declared "not guilty," even as your representative cries out, "My God! My God! Why have you forsaken me?"

His righteous life was put to your account while your sins were put to His account. O, the matchless grace of God!

IV.   The Attributes of Justification

Perhaps the best way to give the attributes of justification is to state them in comparison with regeneration and sanctification. In this way, we can establish wherein these redemptive works of God are alike and different. The following chart illustrates the similarities and differences between regeneration, justification and sanctification.

Regeneration	Justification	Sanctification
1. Work of the Holy Spirit.	1. Work of the Father.	1. Work of Holy Spirit.
2. Takes place in the sinner.	2. Takes place in heaven.	2. Takes place in the sinner.
3. Deals with the pollution and power of sin.	3. Deals with the guilt of sin.	3. Deals with the pollution and power of sin.
4. Impartation of new nature.	4. Impartation of Christ's righteousness.	4. Impartation of Christ's righteousness.
5. We are created righteous.	5. We are reckoned righteous.	5. We are made righteous.
6. The focus is on our person or condition.	6. The focus is on our standing.	6. The focus is on our person or condition.
7. Finished.	7. Finished.	7. Progressive.
8. Complete.	8. Complete.	8. Incomplete.
9. Instantaneous.	9. Instantaneous.	9. Gradual.
10. Perfect.	10. Perfect.	10. Imperfect.
11. Not repeatable.	11. Not repeatable.	11. Growth.
12. Act of God.	12. Act of God.	12. Work of God.

V. The Application of Justification

That justification is received by faith as the free gift of God's unmerited grace is apparent even to the most superficial reader of Scripture. The Apostle again and again emphasizes that the grace of justification comes to those who believe in Christ and not as a result of the works of the Law.

But now the righteousness of God without the law is manifested, being witnessed by the law and the prophets;

Even the righteousness of God which is *by faith* of Jesus Christ unto all and upon all them that *believe: for there is no difference:*

For all have sinned, and come short of the glory of God;

Being justified freely by his grace through the redemption that is in Christ Jesus:

Whom God hath set forth to be a propitiation through faith in his blood, to declare his righteousness for the remission of sins that are past, through the forbearance of God;

To declare, I say, at this time his righteousness: that he might be just, and the justifier of him which believeth in Jesus.

Where is boasting then? It is excluded. By what law? of works? Nay: but by the law of *faith.*

Therefore we conclude that a man is justified by faith without the deeds of the law (Rom. 3:21-28).

What shall we say then that Abraham our father, as pertaining to the flesh, hath found?

For if Abraham were justified by works, he hath whereof to glory; but not before God.

For what saith the Scripture? Abraham believed God, and it was counted unto him for righteousness.

Now to him that worketh is the reward not reckoned of grace, but of debt.

But to him that worketh not, but *believeth* on him that justifieth the ungodly, his *faith* is counted for righteousness (Rom. 4:1-5).

Therefore being justified *by faith*, we have peace with God through our Lord Jesus Christ (Rom. 5:1).

Knowing that a man is not justified by the works of the law, but *by the faith* of Jesus Christ, even we have believed in Jesus Christ, that we might be justified *by the faith* of Christ, and not by the works of the law: for by the works of the law shall no flesh be justified (Gal. 2:16).

I do not frustrate the grace of God: for if righteousness come by the law, then Christ is dead in vain (Gal. 2:21).

But that no man is justified by the law in the sight of God, it is evident: for, The just shall live *by faith* (Gal. 3:11).

Wherefore the law was our schoolmaster to bring us unto Christ, that we might be justified *by faith* (Gal. 3:24).

Faith is the means or channel through which justification comes to the believing sinner. Faith is the open hand extended to receive the free gift of justification.

It is important to point out that the Scripture *never* say that we are *justified because we believe*. Faith is never viewed as the grounds or foundation of justification. Thus the Biblical authors were very careful to use only those prepositions which in the Greek refer to faith as the *means* and *not* as the *grounds*. We are *not* justified *because* we believe, but *through* faith or *by means* of faith we receive justification.

VI.   The Time of Justification

Some confusion has centered around the exact point in time when justification takes place. This confusion has resulted from two basic errors of thought.

1. There is a failure to distinguish between the plan, the accomplishment and the application of salvation.

God planned or decreed from eternity past to justify all elect sinners. Then in the fulness of time, God sent forth Christ to accomplish the basis of justification by His obedience in life and death. At some point in the personal history of each elect sinner, they believe and are justified.

Justification cannot be reduced to God's *plan* to justify or to Christ's *accomplishing* the basis of justification. The Scriptures never place justification first and faith second as if we believe because we are justified. The order is always faith, then justification.

Also, if the elect were justified from all eternity or from the historical life of Christ, this would deny the transition from wrath to grace which is true of all elect sinners. If they were justified, i.e. declared righteous before they were born, no elect sinner was ever under the wrath of God. Yet, Scripture is clear that we are all born sinners under God's wrath and do not come into God's grace until conversion. Is this not the plan teaching of Eph. 2:1-3, where the apostle speaks of the transition from wrath to grace evident in the Ephesian believers?

And you hath he quickened, *who were dead* in trespasses and
sins; Wherein in time past ye walked according to the course of
this world, according to the prince of the power of the air, the
spirit that now worketh in *the children of disobedience*: Among
whom also we all had our conversation in times past in the lusts
of our flesh, fulfilling the desires of the flesh and of the mind;
and were by nature *the children of wrath*, even as others.

2. Confusion concerning the time of justification in relationship to
the other aspects of the application of redemption has arisen because
of the failure to avoid linear reasoning.

Justification and the other elements of salvation are related to each
other in *many* different ways. Thus while a chronological order will see
faith and justification as simultaneous, the casual order would place
faith before justification. Or again, while justification and adoption are
chronologically simultaneous, justification is placed first as the basis
of adoption in the legal order. Justification is interrelated to all the other
aspects of the application of redemption.

VII.   The Fruit or Results of Justification

The blessedness of justification is found not only in the act of justification wherein God declares us righteous in Christ, but, also, in the results of justification. Let us briefly consider three of the direct results of
justification.

1. Justification Secures Peace with God

Therefore being justified by faith, *we have peace with God* through
our Lord Jesus Christ.

The first and foremost result of justification is the obtaining of peace
with God. That peace with God could be obtained at all by any means
is astounding when one considers that we are viewed by God as "without
strength," "ungodly," "sinners," and "enemies" (Rom. 5:6, 8, 10).

By nature, we are at war with God and God is at war with us. The
futile revolt of sinful mankind and its utter defeat is graphically described
in Psalm 2.

Peace with God is something which every sinner should earnestly seek.
But this seeking must take into account the terrible price of peace. The
Son of God had to suffer and die under the wrath of God in order to
obtain peace for His people.

Christ must die for justice demands that either the rebel sinner or his
substitute must die for the crimes committed against God and His king-

dom. Thus Paul says in Col. 1:20 that Christ accomplished peace "through the blood of his cross."

> Blessed are the sons of God, they are bought with Christ's own blood; they are ransomed from the grave, life eternal they shall have: with them numbered may we be, here and in eternity.

> They are justified by grace, they enjoy the Saviour's peace; all their sins are washed away, they shall stand in God's great day:

> With them numbered may we be, here and in eternity; they are lights upon the earth, children of a heav'nly birth; one with God, with Jesus one, glory is in them begun: with them numbered may we be, here and in eternity. Amen.

2. Justification Secures the Righteousness of Christ

We, like Joshua, stand before God in filthy garments (Zech. 3:3) for all our righteousness are as filthy rags before Him (Isa. 64:6). Like Joshua, we need to be clothed with the pure white linen of the righteousness of Christ (Zech. 3:4 of. Rev. 19:8).

Is not Christ our only righteousness (I Cor. 1:30)? Was it not by Christ's righteousness that justification came to sinners (Rom. 5:18)? Does not Peter ascribe the obtaining of "like precious faith" to "the righteousness of our God and Saviour Jesus Christ" (II Pet. 1:1)?

We are acceptable before God because we are robed in the righteousness of Christ. Well did the hymn writer pen these beautiful words.

> Jesus, thy blood and righteousness my beauty are, my glorious dress; "Midst flaming worlds, in these arrayed, With joy shall I lift up my head."

> Bold shall I stand in the great day; For who aught to my charge shall lay? Fully absolved through these I am from sin and fear, from guilt and shame.

> When from the dust of death I rise to claim my mansion in the skies, Ev'n then this shall be all my plea, Jesus, Jesus hath lived, hath died for me.

> Jesus, be endless praise to thee, whose boundless mercy hath for me, for me a full atonement made, an everlasting ransom paid.

> O let the dead now hear thy voice; Now bid thy banished ones rejoice; Their beauty this, their glorious dress, Jesus, thy blood and righteousness. Amen.*

*Hymn: "Jesus, Thy Blood and Righteousness"

3. Justification Secures Judicial Forgiveness

While justification does not consist of forgiveness, it does result in forgiveness and pardon. Thus the Apostle quotes Psa. 32:1 where David ascribes forgiveness of sin to justification.

Saying, Blessed are they whose iniquities are forgiven and whose sins are covered (Rom. 4:7).

The focus of justification is on the righteous life of Christ while the focus of forgiveness is on the death of Christ. Thus while justification and forgiveness should not be viewed as being the same thing, neither should they be viewed as being totally apart from each other. They are like the head and tail of a coin. Even though they are different, they always attend each other.

The forgiveness which comes to us in justification is called *judicial* forgiveness to distinguish it from *parental* forgiveness. Perhaps the best way to clarify the difference between judicial and parental forgiveness is by the following comparison.

Judicial Forgiveness	Parental Forgiveness
1. Has in view our relationship as *sinners* before God the Judge of all the earth.	1. Has in view our relationship as *children* before God our heavenly *father*.
2. The lack of it means eternal torment in *hell*.	2. The lack of it means *loss of fellowship* with God and *chastening* on earth.
3. It is once for all and not repeatable.	3. It is needed continuously every day and is repeatable.
4. It covers all sins past, present and future.	4. It covers only the past and present sins of omission and commission which we confess and forsake.
5. Once received, we never again need to ask for it. It is immutable and eternal.	5. We need to ask for it daily for it is mutable and needs constant revival.

Judicial forgiveness guarantees that at the moment of death the child of God goes to heaven regardless if he had just committed a sin. Thus judicial forgiveness is one of the foundations of the assurance of salvation.

Judicial forgiveness is the ground upon which we ask for parental forgiveness. We can pray,

> "O, my Father, forgive me this day of my sins which are before Thee and withhold thy hand of chastening because these sins have been judicially forgiven through Christ's blood."

VIII. The Evidence of Justification

One of the basic principles of the Christian life is that *position determines experiences*. If we are truly justified, there will be the evidence of good works in our lives for justification is organically and immutably connected to sanctification. Thus after completing his section on justification, the Apostle immediately deals with sanctification as an evidence of justification in Rom. 6-7.

If justification is by faith alone, and apart from works, will this not give sinners the license to sin? No! Paul responds to this question in Rom. 6:1, 2.

> What shall we say then? Shall we continue in sin, that grace may abound? God forbid, How shall we, that are dead to sin, live any longer therein?

Paul is not afraid of the subject of works for he has placed works in its proper order. Saving faith justifies and then the justified sinner produces works in his life. Faith-then-works is the proper order. That Paul believed that position determines experience particularly it terms of justification and works is clear from the following passages.

> For by grace are ye saved through faith; and that not of yourselves: it is the gift of God: Not of works, lest any man should boast. For we are his workmanship, *created in Christ Jesus unto good works, which God hath before ordained that* we should walk in them (Eph. 2:8-10).

> In all things showing thyself *a pattern of good works:* in doctrine showing uncorruptness, gravity, sincerity (Tit. 2:7).

> Who gave himself for us, that he might redeem us from all iniquity, and purify unto himself a peculiar people, *zealous of good works* (Tit. 2:14).

> This is a faithful saying, and these things I will that thou affirm constantly, that they which have believed in God might be

careful to _maintain good works_. These things are good and profitable unto men (Tit. 3:8).

And let ours also learn to _maintain good works_ for necessary uses, that they be not unfruitful (Tit. 3:14).

It is in this light that we must approach the book of James. Although they approach it from different angles, James and Paul are both teaching the same doctrine. They both say that a _justified sinner will evidence his salvation by living a life of good works._

It is obvious that James was dealing with people who professed to be justified but there was evidence in their lives to make it a questionable profession (see 2:14).

They were hearers and not doers of the Word (1:22). They did not bridle their tongue (1:26). They favored the rich and ignored the poor (2:1-6). They did not have compassion on their brethren (2:16). They all wanted to be leaders (3:1). They cursed men (3:9). Their hearts were full of envying and strife (3:14). They were given over to lustful fighting (4:1-3). They attempted to be friends of this world (4:4). They spoke evil of one another (4:11). They were not patient and held grudges one against the other (5:8, 9).

In the light of the lives of these professing Christians, is it any wonder that James casts doubt on their conversion and demands evidence to make their profession credible? Did not Paul do the same with the Corinthians in II Cor. 13:5? Did not Jesus teach this in John 8:31? Is this not the same teaching as found in I Cor. 6:9-11 and Gal. 5:17-24?

When we compare the teaching of the Apostle Paul on the relationship between justification and sanctification with what James says, we find them teaching the same thing:

> The faith that works is the faith that saves. A dead faith will not save for it is not true faith.

A seeming contradiction arises between Paul and James when we mistakenly confuse Paul's teaching on faith with James' teaching on works as an evidence of true faith. There is a difference between Paul and James because they are handling different subjects. The following diagram may help to show that James and Paul do not contradict each other because they are dealing with two different issues.

Paul	James
1. Deals with justification "before God" (Rom. 4:1, 2).	1. Deals with justification before men. (See 2:14 "though a *man* say"; 2:18 "*a man* may say"; 2:18 "show *me*," "I will show *you*"; 2:24 "ye see.")
2. He speaks of faith because God alone can see faith in the heart.	2. He speaks of a living faith which produces works in the outward life of a man which can be seen and examined by other men (James 2:14, 17-20).
3. He draws his illustration from Gen. 15:6, wherein the conversion of Abraham is recorded. Paul refers to Abraham's justification by faith alone. Thus he is dealing with Abraham's *salvation*.	3. He draws his illustration from Gen. 22:1-19, where, after being a believer for many years, Abraham is asked to give evidence to everyone of his love to and faith in God. James refers to Abraham *after* he was justified. Thus he dealt with Abraham's *sanctification*.
4. Paul's key phrase is "before God."	4. James' key phrase is "show *me*" (1:18). James could not see faith if it was not manifested by works.

From the above it is clear that Paul in Rom. 3-5 is dealing with a different topic than that which James dealt with in his book.

Dear Reader, meditate on these questions and apply them to your conscience.

Is there evidence in my life that I am justified? Would James agree that I was justified?
Is my faith living or dead?
Do I have compassion and an open hand to brothers and sisters in Christ?

In summary, justification is God's way of dealing with our guilty standing before Him and His Law. In this amazing provision of God's free grace, the righteousness of Christ is imputed to our account or record while our sins were imputed to Christ's record. God declares us not guilty before the moral universe and pronounces us righteous in His sight.

CHAPTER 14

Adoption

W hen Adam and Eve were created by God, they were created in a filial relationship to God in which they looked to Him as their Father and in which He viewed and treated them as His children. Thus in Luke 3:38, we are told that Adam was "the son of God."

The filial relationship between God and man at creation must be viewed as one of the aspects of the image of God which distinguished man from the rest of creation. Adam and Eve were not merely *creatures* of God but they were the *son* and *daughter* of God who bore the family image and likeness in a unique manner which was not shared by any other creature.

When we read the early chapters of Genesis, we find man's filial relationship to God characterized by a mutual communion and communication. The Father's love for His children is evident on every hand. Did He not place His children as head over and heir of the world (Gen. 1:28; Psa. 8:3-8)? Did not the Father provide a wife for His son when He saw that Adam needed a help mate (Gen 2:18)? It would seem that God walked with His children "in the cool of the day" instead of in the heat of the day because He was mindful of their physical comfort (Gen. 3:8). Out of love, God warned His children of the terrible consequences of disobedience and rebellion (Gen. 2:17).

In spite of all the fatherly care and love which God lavished upon His dear children, they followed Satan and rebelled against God. Thus man's filial relationship to God magnifies the awfulness of the original sin to such a degree that no one can possibly comprehend the wickedness and mystery of this most terrible and tragic event in human history.

189

How could Adam and Eve deliberately sin against their loving Father who always tenderly cared for them? How could they willfully disobey their Father's explicit command? O, the depths of the wickedness, foolishness and insantiy of man's first fall into sin and guilt! Only God knows the depths of human depravity (Jer. 17:9, 10).

Dear child of God, seeing you claim to love and know the Father, how is it that you sin against Him? Has He not chosen, called and justified you? Is He not the origin of every good and perfect gift? Has He ever failed you? Does He not tenderly care for you? Then why is it that you willfully and deliberately disobey His holy law? Sin is doubly tragic and heinous in the Christian for he is God's child by redemption as well as by creation.

As a direct consequence of man's rebellion, God disowned them, i.e. God no longer viewed or treated them as His children. The symbol of this act of divine judgment is found in God's casting man out of the Garden and in His taking away the blessings and privileges of sonship from them (Gen. 3:19, 23, 24).

Man was no longer the head over or heir of the world. His absolute dominion over the creatures was broken. No longer would animals or insects willingly obey men as their head. But now man would have to survive by hard work and cunning intelligence. Instead of dealing with a world which was cooperative and subservient to man's desires and needs, man now faced a hostile world.

The ground would only grudgingly bear food for man and would give him thorns and weeds whenever and wherever it could. The insects would now pester, attack and destroy man. The animals would flee from man and devour him for food.

Now to be sure, man was still physically a creature of God and is even spoken of as being God's offspring in Acts 17:28, 29. Man still retains his distinction from the rest of creation by virtue of being in the image of God (James 3:9). Even though these things are true, we must yet say that man is no longer viewed or treated by God as His sons and daughters.

In John 8:41-47, the Jews claimed in the presence of Jesus that God was their Father. If Christ taught the liberal doctrine that God was the Father of all mankind, this was the perfect situation in which Christ could affirm what these men were saying. But Christ did not affirm their claim. As a matter of fact, He absolutely rejected it by disclosing the real spiritual father of lost mankind, Satan.

Ye do the deeds of your father. Then said they to him, We

be not born of fornication; *we have one Father, even God.* Jesus said unto them, *If God were your Father, ye would love me:* for I proceeded forth and came from God; neither came I of myself, but he sent me. Why do ye not understand my speech? Even because ye cannot hear my word. *Ye are of your father the devil, and the lusts of your father ye will do.* He was a murdered from the beginning, and abode not in the truth, because there is no truth in him. When he speaketh a lie, he speaketh of his own: for he is a liar, and the father of it. And because I tell you the truth, ye believe me not. Which of you convicteth me of sin? And if I say the truth, why do ye not believe me? He that is of God heareth God's words: ye therefore hear them not, because ye are not of God (Jn. 8:41-47).

It is evident that the first adoption to take place in history was Satan's adopting of fallen mankind to bear his image and likeness. Since he is a liar and murderer, he wants his children to be liars and murderers as well. Thus Satan seeks to build in his children a sinful character which has attributes directly opposite and opposed to God's moral attributes.

Satan's father hood of unregenerate mankind is also found in those places in Scripture where he is said to rule the world (Matt. 4:8, 9), to be the god of this world who blinds men to the gospel (II Cor. 4:3-6) and the spirit who dictates the life style of lost humanity (Eph. 2:1-3).

Even though man rebelled against God and has been adopted into Satan's family as his children, God in His rich mercy and grace took the initiative to seek lost man and to rescue him from the penalty, power and presence of sin.

God could have justly abandoned man to Divine wrath but in mercy He devised a plan in which sinners could once again be restored to full sonship with all of its blessings and privileges. Thus the goal of the Father's decree of predestination is adoption according to Eph. 1:5, 6.

> Having *predestinated us unto adoption of children* by Jesus Christ to Himself, according to the good pleasure of his will, to the praise of the glory of his grace, wherein he hath made us accepted in the beloved.

According to God's plan, the Eternal Word who is the second person of the Trinity would become flesh, i.e. man of very man (Jn. 1:12, 14). He would accomplish all that is necessary for our adoption back into God's family. Thus God ordained that Jesus Christ would be the One who gives us adoption. As John 1:12 says,

> But as many received him, to them *gave he power to become
> the sons of God*, even to them that believe on his name.

We become the children of God by receiving Jesus Christ as our personal Lord and Savior. Thus Gal. 3:26 states,

> For we are all children of God by faith in Christ Jesus.

But how did Christ make our adoption possible? The Scriptures point us to the messianic sonship of Christ as the means whereby adoption was made possible.

At this point it would be wise to clearly distinguish between the Eternal Sonship of Christ as the second person of the Holy Trinity and the messianic sonship of Christ.

According to God's word, Jesus Christ is God the Son, the second person of the Trinity. As such, He maintains a unique relationship to God the Father in which no creature either participates or partakes. Christ's Eternal Sonship must not be viewed as being substitutionary or vicarious.

The above truth is directly stated in John 5:18 where Christ said that God was *His* Father in a unique relationship not shared by anyone else. Thus the Jews sought to kill Him.

Also, is it not true that Jesus never joined the disciples in communal prayers in which they all said together "Our Father"? Christ taught them to pray "Our Father" but He was careful to maintain His unique relationship to the Father as God the Son. Thus He said to Mary in John 20:17,

> Jesus saith unto her. Touch me not; for I am not yet ascended
> to my Father: but go to my brethren, and say unto them, I
> ascend unto *my* Father, and *your Father; and to my* God, and
> *your* God.

While Christ's Eternal Sonship is perfect in every respect and admits of no degrees of growth, the Scriptures do speak of Jesus *becoming* a son of God, i.e. of taking upon Himself at birth messianic sonship.

This messianic office of being the son of God:

(1) began when Christ was born and was, therefore, not eternal.
(2) is an office of the Messiah.
(3) is substitutionary, i.e. in our behalf.
(4) admits of degrees of growth.
(5) reaches its climax on the cross.
(6) was crowned by God with glory and honor.

Throughout the Old Testament we read of the promised coming of the Messiah who would redeem us from our sins. It is well known that He would take upon Himself the offices of a prophet, priest and King. Yet, no one teaches that Christ fulfilled these offices from all eternity as God the Son, but, rather, that Jesus as the Christ took these offices upon Himself at birth and faithfully fulfilled them in His life.

In the same way, the Messiah is said to become "the seed of the woman" in Gen. 3:15. Was He the "seed" or child of the virgin Mary from all eternity? NO. Was He the son of David from all eternity (Matt. 1:1)? NO.

We are further taught in Scripture that the Messiah would take up the *office* of son of God which Adam lost through his fall. The Messiah would thus be made heir of and head over all the earth and would be viewed as the 2nd Adam. He would do what Adam failed to do. Thus the Messiah is the "Son of God" whom God begat on a certain day (Psa. 2:7). He is God's son whom He brought out of Egypt (Hos. 11:1 of Matt. 2:15). The Messiah is given to us as a "child" and "son" (Isa. 9:6). He is placed over the creation like Adam (Psa. 8 of Heb. 2:5, 9). Therefore we find that God has placed the son of God as King over all the Earth (Psa. 2).

Since the Old Testament had clearly taught the deity of the messianic son of God, the Jews in Christ's day understood that His claim to be the messianic son of God meant that He was saying that He was God (Jn. 10:30-36).

Even the phrase "son of man" referred to the messianic sonship of the Son God (Jn. 22:67-71). Thus the concept of the messianic sonship of Christ gives us further proof of the deity of the Messiah.

In Heb. 3:6; 5:8, 9; 7:28, we see that Christ developed and fulfilled His messianic office of the son of God and son of man. How did He do this?

Christ fulfilled His sonship by living in a filial relationship to the Father. As a Son, He lived in total dependence upon His Father. He spoke and did only what His Father commanded (Jn. 5:19; 12:49, 50).

The prayers of Christ must be viewed as the manifestation of His sonship in that they are addressed to God as His Father and reveal a spirit of total submission to His will (Lk. 22:42).

As a Son, Christ was obedient to His Father even unto death (Phil 2:8; Matt. 26:42). Whereas Adam disobeyed God and was defeated by the tempter, Christ met and defeated the tempter at the beginning of His public ministry (Matt. 4:1-11). As the messianic son of Adam. He won the Father's approval in Matt. 3:17.

> And lo a voice from heaven, saying, "This is my beloved Son, in whom I am well pleased."

Because Christ fulfilled His messianic sonship. He was crowned with glory and honor (Phil 2:9-11; Heb. 2:5-8). As the exalted son of God, the Messiah, He now sits as King (Psa. 2) for He is the recipient of all the covenantal blessings which Adam would have received if he would have remained faithful to God.

In God's covenantal framework Adam and Christ did not act as private persons. As all mankind fell into sin and guilt when Adam fell, so all the elect were in Christ when He fulfilled His sonship as the 2nd Adam. Thus He fulfilled our sonship in our place for us. Therefore it is by virtue of our living union with Christ that we partake of sonship, and become the brothers of Christ, joint heirs with Christ and in the family of God with Christ. In and through Him we become head over and heir of the world to come (Heb. 2;12, 17; Rom. 8:17).

Adoption can be defined as follows:

God's gracious act in which He establishes a filial relationship with justified sinners wherein He views and treats them as His own children by virtue of the fulfillment of Christ's messianic sonship.

In this filial relationship God grants unto His children all the privileges, blessings, and responsibilities of sonship. This adoption takes place in three stages.

1. The establishments of a spiritual filial relationship with justified sinners at conversion. This means access to God through Christ by the Spirit and the reception of all the elements of the application of redemption which are given to the saints in this life (Jn. 1:12; Rom. 8:14, 15; Gal. 1:5, 6; 3:26; 4:5, 6).

2. The reconstruction of the sinful bodies of the saints unto Christ's glorious body at His second return to this earth (Rom. 8:23; Phil 3:20, 21). As we once bore the image of the 1st Adam, so we shall bear a body like the 2nd Adam (I Cor. 15:49). Then we shall be what we should be and will have bodies more consistent with our sonship (I Jn. 3:12).

3. The manifestation of our sonship to the world, our vindication before the wicked and our installation as the heads over and heirs of the new heavens and the new earth await

the last judgment (Rom. 8:19-21; I Jn. 3:1, 2).

In anticipation of our manifestation as the sons of God, one hymn writer wrote,

> Behold the amazing gift of love the Father hath bestowed on us, the sinful sons of men, to call us sons of God!

> Concealed as yet this honor lies, by dark would unknown, a world that knew not when he came, Even God's eternal Son.

> High is the rank we now possess; but higher we shall rise; though what we shall hereafter be is hid from mortal eyes:

> Our souls, we know, when God appears, Shall bear his image bright; for then his glory, as he is, shall open to our sight.*

Now it must be pointed out that adoption should not be confused with regeneration or justification. It is a separate act of God which can be clearly distinguished from the other elements of the application of redemption.

By regeneration, we become new creatures and enter God's kingdom (II Cor. 5:17; Jn. 3:3, 5). But in adoption we become the children of God and enter God's family. Regeneration deals with our sinful condition and imparts to us a new heart while adoption deals with our standing or position before God and grants to us a filial relationship to God.

Justification declares us righteous and guiltless before God our Judge while in adoption we are ushered into sonship and are embraced by God as our Father. As a Judge God justified us and as a Father He views us as His own children.

While different from regeneration and justification, adoption is inseparably connected to them for as God only justified those whom He has regenerated, so He adopts only those whom He has justified. Adoption follows justification and regeneration.

Let it further be stated that adoption involves the entire triune Godhead of Father, Son, and Holy Spirit.

Did not the Father plan our adoption in eternity past (Eph. 1:5)? Does not John state that it is the Father who bestows upon us the privileges of sonship in I John 3:1? Did not Christ direct us to pray to God as our Father in Matt. 6:9? It is not, therefore, surprising that Paul constantly addresses the first person of the Trinity as "our Father" (Rom.

*Hymn: "Behold th' Amazing Gift of Love"

1:7; I Cor. 1:3; II Cor. 1:2; Gal. 1:2; Eph. 1:2; Phil. 1:2; Col. 1:2; I Thess. 1:3; II Thess. 1:1; etc.)

While the central thrust of our adoption centers in our becoming the children of God the Father, the Scriptures also teach that adoption brings us into a filial relationship to Jesus Christ.

Does not John 1:12 state that it is Christ who gives us the right or power to become the sons of God? Do we not become brothers of Christ, joint-heirs and rulers with Christ (Rom. 8:17, 29; Heb. 2:11-12, 17)? Is it not the case that Christ is called "the everlasting Father" in Isa. 9:6 and like unto a "mother" in Matt. 23:37? Does not Heb. 2:13, 14 and Isa. 53:10 describe believers as "the children" or "seed" of Christ? We must not assume that adoption concerns only the Father when the Scriptures teach otherwise.

The Holy Spirit is so involved in our adoption that He is even called, "the Spirit of adoption" in Rom. 8:15. It is His distinct work to make us aware of our adoption (Rom. 8:16) and to cause us to exercise our filial relationship to our Father in personal prayer wherein we cry "Abba, Father" (Gal. 4:4).

We are dependent upon the ministry of the Holy Spirit to make our adoption real to us and to fully receive all the blessings and benefits of our adoption. Access to God by prayer, fellowship with God, parental forgiveness and chastisement all come to us by the work of the Spirit. Oh, how much we are dependent on Him!

Having examined the doctrine of adoption, we must ask, "Have you ever become a child of the Father by faith in Christ Jesus? Are you a brother of and a joint-heir with Christ Jesus? Has the Spirit born witness to your spirit that you are a child of the King?" If so, then let the Apostle John apply the doctrine of adoption to your conscience for in I John 3:1-3, he maintains that a true grasp of adoption will result in a Christ-centered hope which purifies the life.

> Behold, what manner of love the Father hath bestowed upon us, that we should be called the sons of God: therefore the world knoweth us not, because it knew him not. Beloved, now are we the sons of God, and it doth not yet appear what we shall be: but we know that, when he shall appear, we shall be like him; for we shall see him as he is. *And every man that hath this hope in him purifieth himself, even as He is pure* (I Jn. 3:13).

The great test of adoption is whether or not one bears the family likeness. The Scriptures use the phrases "child of God" and "child of the Devil" in a *qualitative* sense in which people either bear the attributes and characteristics of God or Satan.

A child of God will be godly, i.e. like God. A child of the Devil will be devilish, i.e. like Satan. Thus the Apostle John states in I Jn. 3:7-10,

> Little children, let no one deceive you; the one who practices righteousness is righteous, just as He is righteous; the one who practices sin is the devil; for the devil has sinned from the beginning. The Son of God appeared for this purpose, that He might destroy the works of the Devil. No one who is born of God practices sin, because His seed abides in him; and he cannot sin, because he is born of God. By this the children of God and the children of the devil are obvious: any one who does not practice righteousness is not of God, nor the one who does not love his brother.

Are you a child of the King? Do you attempt day by day to be conformed to moral character of Jesus Christ, God's only begotten Son? These questions touch on the subject of assurance which is discussed in the next chapter.

CHAPTER **15**

Assurance

One of the greatest aspects of true Biblical religion is that it puts forth the position that a believer can have a true and full assurance of his personal eternal salvation. We can know without a shadow of doubt that we have been chosen by the Father, purchased by the Son and sealed with the Spirit. Blessed God three in One!

That this is the Biblical position on assurance can be seen from the example, command, and precept of Holy Scripture.

We find many examples in Scripture of believers who possessed an absolute assurance of their eternal salvation. They knew that they were strangers and pilgrims on earth who were on their way to the celestial city of heaven. Did not Mary express her assurance that God was her Saviour in Luke 1:46-59? Simeon could face death for he knew that he had seen the Saviour-Messiah of Israel (Lk. 2:25-32). Does not Philip's statement, "We have found him" reveal his assurance (Jn. 1:45)? Can anyone question John the Baptist's statement of assurance in John 1:29? Did not Stephen face death with the absolute confidence that his spirit would ascend to heaven at death to be with Christ (Acts 7:56-59)? Is it not true that the Apostle Paul gives us in his epistles many expressions of his assurance (see Rom. 8:38, 39; Phil. 1:21-23; II Tim. 1:12; 4:7, 8)?

We not only find the above examples of assurance in Scripture, but we are also commanded and exhorted by the Apostles to seek personal assurance.

> Wherefore the rather, brethren, *give diligence to make your calling and election sure*: for if ye do these things, ye shall never

199

fall (II Pet. 1:10).

> And we desire that every one of you do show the same diligence to *the full assurance of hope* unto the end (Heb. 6:11).

> Let us draw near with a true heart in *full assurance of faith*, having our hearts sprinkled from an evil conscience, and our bodies washed with pure water (Heb. 10:22).

God in His mercy has also given us a passage of full mention on the doctrine of assurance so that we might learn this doctrine by way of precept as well as by way of example and command. Of course, I am referring to the epsitle of I John.

The Apostle John tells us his reason in writing his letter in 5:13.

> These things have I written unto you that believe on the name of the Son of God; *that ye may know that ye have eternal life.*

Some have thought mistakenly that John's statement in I John 5:13 only referred to the two verses immediately preceding it.

> *And this is the record, that God hath given to us eternal life, and this life is in His Son.*

> *He that hath the Son hath life; and he that hath not the Son of God hath not life.*

But a close analysis of verse 13 reveals that this is John's statement of purpose in writing the entire epistle. Thus the entire book was written in order to instruct Christians how to obtain a true and full assurance of their eternal salvation.

This understanding of I John 5:13 is further strengthened by the observation that throughout his epistle John is concerned to tell us by what standards we can judge ourselves and others to be true Christians. Thus we find him writing, "Hereby we do know that we know him, if . . . " (I John 2:3, etc.).

John's concern that believers would be assured on their salvation arose out of his desire that they could experience the fullness of joy and fellowship with God. Thus he states in I John 1:3, 4,

> That which we have seen and heard declare we unto you, that ye also may have fellowship with us: and truly our fellowship is with the Father, and with His Son Jesus Christ.

And these things write we unto you, that your joy may be full.

Assurance is not just a theoretical issue in Christian doctrine but it is one of the most important issues of the Christian life. It is the main stream from which flows the spiritual dynamic of the Christian life. Until a believer possesses true assurance, can he really worship God as his Father with all his heart while doubting his salvation at the same time? Can he apply all the commands and duties to himself if he doubts his sonship? Can he give himself to service in the world if he does not know if he is yet saved? Can he excel in any aspect of Christian living if he does not know if he is a Christian? Will not his witness to the non-Christian be robbed of its power and effectiveness because of his own inner insecurity of salvation?

When God the Holy Spirit gives the precious gift of assurance to a believer, the change in that believer's life is so powerful and dynamic that it is often confused with conversion, a deeper-life experience or a second work of grace. Why? Assurance causes holy joy to whelm up in the believer's heart and to put boldness and power in his walk and witness.

Because of all the benefits to be desired from true assurance, the Westminister Confession states,

> It is the duty of everyone to give all diligence to make his call-
> ing and election sure; that thereby his heart may be enlarged
> in peace and joy in the Holy Ghost, in love and thankfulness
> to God, in strength and cheerfulness in the duties of obedi-
> ence, the proper fruits of this assurance (XVIII, III).

Let the reader ask himself, "Am I sure of heaven? Do I know that my sins are forgiven? Have I been born of God? Upon what grounds do I base my assurance of my own personal salvation? Am I really saved or deceived?"

Despite the multitudes of professing Christians in our day who would quickly respond that they have assurance of salvation, a true Biblical understanding of assurance is actually a rare jewel! It is a pearl of great price which is not owned by many in our day. Indeed, in the light of the present times, we are warranted in saying that the 20th century church has, by in large, suffered itself to be decked with the cheap im- itation jewelry of false teaching on assurance instead of adorning her- self with the beautiful jewels of Biblical truth.

Our study will begin with a call of self-examination for God's Word tells us in II Cor. 13:5,

Examine yourselves, whether ye be in the faith; prove your own selves. Know ye not your own selves, how that Jesus Christ is in you, except ye be reprobates?

The Apostle also teaches us in I Cor. 11:20, "But let a man examine himself." This examination includes judging ourselves for we read in I Cor. 11:31, 32.

For if we would judge ourselves, we should not be judged. But when we are judged, we are chastened of the Lord, that we should not be condemned with the world.

Self-examination is very neglected in these days and much denied and resisted. This has happened because self-examination is humbling to the fleshly nature of man. When we examine ourselves, we look into the mirror of God's Law and see ourselves as we really are. This is a painful experience and many would rather go their way and forget their condition before God. James 1:22-25 states that only the true believer can abide in the spiritual duty of self-examination.

But be ye doers of the word, and not hears only, deceiving your own selves.

For is any be a hearer of the word, and not a doer, he is like unto a man beholding his natural face in a glass:

For he beholdeth himself, and goeth his way, and straightway forgetteth what manner of man he was.

But whose looketh into the perfect law of liberty, and continueth therein, he being not a forgetful hearer, but a doer of the word, this man shall be blessed in his deed.

With an attitude of self-examination, let us turn to a study of I John in order to discover true Biblical assurance.

I. The Tests of Assurance

Throughout his letter, we constantly find the Apostle John giving us ways to test the reality and validity of a profession of faith. The tests at first center on one's personal profession of salvation and whether or not you can consider yourself a true believer. At other times John gives us tests by which we can examine the professions of others to see if they are truly saved.

We will arrange these tests under two basic headings. Each of these headings are representative of two areas in which we are to examine ourselves to see if we are in Christ.

First, John calls us to examine our FAITH. And John stresses that there are two distinct areas of faith which we must examine to determine if we are the children of God or the children of the devil.

First of all, John tells us to examine the CONTENT of our faith. Faith in this sense is used in its noun form as the object of faith, i.e. the doctrines which constitute our beliefs.

John tells us that we must believe in the essential Biblical doctrines concerning the person and work of Jesus Christ. Thus if you are believing what you should be believing, then you have passed the first test. John emphasizes this in the following passages.

> Hereby know ye the Spirit of God: Every spirit *that confesseth that Jesus Christ* is come in the flesh is of God (I John 4:2).

> And we have seen and do testify *that the Father sent the Son to be the Saviour of the world* (I John 4:14).

> Whosoever shall confess that *Jesus if the Son of God*, God dwelleth in him, and he in God (I John 4:15).

> Whosoever believeth that *Jesus is the Christ* is born of God: and every one that loveth him that begat loveth him also that is begotten of him (I John 5:1).

If a person denies the fundamental doctrines of the person and work of Christ, John says that their profession and assurance of salvation is to be rejected. Thus if you are denying what you should be believing, you have failed this test.

Who is a liar but *he that denieth that Jesus is the Christ?* He is antichrist, that denieth the Father and the Son (I John 2:22).

Whosoever *denieth the Son* the same hath not the Father: (but) he that acknowledgeth the Son hath the Father also (I John 2:23).

Beloved, believe not every spirit, but try the spirits whether they are of God: because many false prophets are gone out into the world (I John 4:1).

And every spirit *that confesseth not that Jesus Christ is come in the flesh* is not of God: and this is that spirit of antichrist, whereof ye have heard that it should come; and even now already is it in the world (I John 4:3).

Evidently, John would never have anything to do with universalism. For John's doctrine does divide. It divides the children of God from the children of Satan. This division is good and must be urged all the more in a world which chooses to ignore doctrine and to seek unity in either service or experience.

Second, John tells us to examine the COMMITMENT of our faith. This is faith used in its verb form, i.e. as the activity of believing. It is not enough to understand and give assent to orthodox doctrine but you must also put your personal trust and faith in Christ Jesus Himself as well as in the Biblical truths concerning His person and work.

It is also important to point out that the Apostle John always emphasizes the present tense character of true saving faith, i.e. faith is never viewed as a decision made in the past and now over with or completed.

Faith is an ever-present exercise of the soul in receiving all that Christ gives to spiritually hungry sinners and saints. Thus John says in 5:1,

> Whoever *is believing* (i.e. right now in the present exercise of his soul in faith) that Jesus is the Christ is born of God.

Throughout the Gospel of John, John emphasizes this present tense character of faith in such places as John 3:16.

> For God so loved the world, that he gave his only Son, that whoever *is believing* (i.e. right now in the present tense) in Him should not perish but have everlasting life.

The proper question is not, "Did you believe and receive Jesus Christ one time in the past?" John does not *once* refer to past decisions as having anything to do with true assurance.

The proper question is, "Are you believing in Christ right now? Are you trusting Him for salvation right now?"

In order to drive home the present-tense character of true saving faith to someone, it is sometimes helpful to ask, "Do you want assurance in your heart that you are *right now* a true Christian? If so, then you assurance must be based on the *present* content and commitment of your faith."

In the light of this aspect of saving faith, John certainly would have condemned the popular doctrines of decisionism and easy believism. There are multitudes today who base their assurance of salvation on a past date or decision although they do not manifest any sign of a present living faith. We should not ask, "When did you receive Christ?" as much as we should ask, "What evidence is there in your life today

— i.e. right now — that leads you to believe that you to believe that you are truly saved?"

Let the reader ask himself the above question. In these times of false assurance, you must examine your profession of faith to see if it is genuine.

The second general area to which John would direct our self-examination is the area of our *LIFE*.

John first calls upon us to examine the *OUTWARD WALK* of our life, i.e. to examine our lives to see if we are conforming ourselves to God's Law.

John tells us to stand before the mirror of the Law and to ask ourselves,

> "Do I purposefully attempt to keep God's Law? Do I delight in God's Law? Or, do I purposely disobey the Law and look upon it as grievous?"

Not only must we be believing what we should be believing but we must also be doing what we should be doing. Namely, seeking to conform our lives to the standard of the Law of Christ.

John is not demanding perfect obedience before assurance is attainable for none can say that they are without sin (I John 1:8-10). He is talking about *purposeful* obedience, i.e. the intent of the heart, the general bent of the will and affections is toward God and His Law. In this sense he states that obedience to God's Law is necessary for true assurance.

> And hereby we do know that we know him, if we keep his commandments (I John 2:3).

> But who so keepeth his word, in him verily is the love of God perfected: hereby know we that we are in him (I John 2:5).

> He that saith he abideth in him ought himself also so to walk, even as he walked (I John 2:6).

> If ye know that he is righteous, ye know that every one that doeth righteousness is born of him (I John 2:29).

> Little children, let no man deceive you: he that doeth righteousness is righteous, even as he is righteous (I John 3:7).

> Whosoever is born of God doth not commit sin; for his seed remaineth in him: and he cannot sin, because he is born of God (I John 3:9).

> In this the children of God are manifest, and the children of the devil: whosoever doeth not righteousness is not of God, neither he that loved not his brother (I John 3:10).

> My little children, let us not love in word, neither in tongue; but in deed and in truth (I John 3:18).

> And hereby we know that we are of the truth, and shall assure our hearts before him (I John 3:19).

> For this is the love of God, that we keep his commandments: and his commandments are not grievous (I John 5:3).

On the other hand, if a person is not purposefully seeking to conform his life to God's Law and he lives a life of abandonment to sin in which he views the Law as restricting his happiness, John declares that this person has no right to be a professing Christian. Yea, he even goes further and calls such a person a liar.

> He that saith, I know him, and keepeth not his commandments, is a liar, and the truth is not in him (I John 2:4).

> Whosoever abideth in Him sinneth not: whosoever sinneth hath not seen him, neither know him (I John 3:6).

> He that committeth sin is of the devil; for the devil sinneth from the beginning. For this purpose the Son of God was manifested, that he might destroy the works of the devil (I John 3:8).

How many present day "converts" live a life of willful disobedience and rebellion against God's Law? They want to live "under grace" and "not law" in order to feed their lusts. The Apostle John's appreciation and presentation of the use of God's Law in discovering the children of multitudes of professing Christians who abound on every hand. Oh, that God would raise up men who boldly proclaim the precious truths of I John.

John also tells us to examine the *EMOTIONAL FOCUS* of our life, i.e. to discover the objects of our desires and feelings.

As a wise theologian, the Apostle John does not deal with every emotion of the human heart but he deals with the two major emotions from which all the other emotions flow: Love and Hate.

Love and hate are like the engine of a train. Where love goes, we see *all* the other virtues following. If we love we will find all the elements of I Cor. 13 present on the train. In the same way, if we hate, all the evil emotions follow where hate goes. If we hate, then we find the works of the flesh (Gal. 5:19-21). Thus John deals with the focus of one's love and hate to determine if one is truly a child of God. If we love what God loves and hate what He hates, then we have passed this test. Thus John says that true Christians love fellow believers and hate the world of sin.

He that loveth his brother abideth in the light, and there is none occasion of stumbling in him (I John 2:10).

Love not the world, neither the things that are in the world. If any man love the world, the love of the Father is not in him (I John 2:15).

For this is the message that ye heard from the beginning, that we should love one another (I John 3:11).

We know that we have passed from death unto life, because we love the brethren. He that loveth not his brother abideth in death (I John 3:14).

Beloved, let us love one another: for love is of God; and every one that loveth is born of God, and knoweth God (I John 4:7).

Beloved, if God so loved us, we ought also to love one another (I John 4:11).

No man hath seen God at any time. If we love one another, God dwelleth in us, and his love is perfected in us (I John 4:12).

And we have known and believed the love that God hath to us. God is love; and he that dwelleth in love dwelleth in God, and God in him (I John 4:16).

And this commandment have we from him, That he who loveth God love his brother also (I John 4:21).

Whosoever believeth that Jesus is the Christ is born of God: and every one that loveth him that begat loveth him also that is begotten of him (I John 5:1).

But if we hate Christians and love the world, we reveal that we are not born of God.

He that saith he is in the light, and hateth his brother, is in darkness even until now (I John 2:9).

But he that hateth his brother is in darkness, and walketh in darkness, and knoweth not whither he goeth, because that darkness hath blinded his eyes (I John 2:11).

Love not the world, neither the things that are in the world. If any man love the world, the love of the Father is not in him (I John 2:15).

Whosoever hateth his brother is a murderer: and ye know that no murderer hath eternal life abiding in him (I John 3:15).

He that loveth not, knoweth not God; for God is love (I John 4:8).

If a man say, I love God, and hateth his brother, he is a liar: for he that loveth not his brother whom he hath seen, how can he love God Whom he hath not seen (I John 4:20)?

What is the emotional focus of your life? Do you love God's Law and delight to do His will (Psa. 119:97; 40:8)? Or do you love the things of this world? These are the questions which John presses home on the conscience of his readers.

II.   The Spiritual Application of Assurance

Self-examination even along the lines of the Biblical tests of assurance, will not automatically give anyone assurance for assurance is the personal and sovereign work of the Holy Spirit. John points this out in his epistle,

And hereby we know that he abideth in us, *by the Spirit* which he hath given us (I John 3:24).

Hereby know we that we dwell in him, and he in us, *because he hath given us of his Spirit* (I John 4:13).

But, we must hasten to point out that the Holy Spirit does not give assurance to those who fail to manifest the Biblical evidences of salvation. Instead, John combines the evidences of saving faith with the work of the Holy Spirit in I John 3:24.

And he that keepeth his commandments dwelleth in him and he in him. And hereby we know that he abideth in us, by the Spirit which he hath given us.

The Spirit may give us assurance by making us realize that our life and faith meet the Biblical tests for it is "the Spirit who bears witness with our spirit that we are the children of God" (Rom. 8:16). Thus no amount of personal introspection or mental syllogism will automatically produce true assurance. The Sovereign Spirit is the Lord of Assurance and He gives it to whomever He wishes.

III.   The Grounds of Assurance

While evidences are important as tests of Salvation, they should never be viewed as the grounds or foundation of assurance. Our hope of eternal life is based on the person and work of Christ *alone*. His blood, His righteousness and His covenant form the sounds of assurance.

Some have confused their works with Christ's and have ended looking to their own performance as the basis of their hope or heaven. We know we are on our way to heaven because Jesus paid it all.

IV.   Remaining Questions

Having examined the tests for assurance and the ministry of the Spirit in assurance, there are still some questions which must be answered.

1. Is assurance a part of saving faith? Can a person be a Christian and still lack assurance?

Answer: I John was written to believers. Yet John wrote to them concerning their need of assurance (I John 5:13). Peter in his exhortation to seek assurance in II Peter 1:10 was addressing believers (II Pet. 1:1). If all believers automatically had assurance as part of saving faith, there would have never arisen the need to exhort them to seek assurance. Therefore, one can be saved but still lack assurance. And God has His reasons for this.

God in mercy knows that some believers need their doubts to keep them striving in the way of holiness. Others need assurance to keep them striving. Thus some will never have assurance while on earth as part of God's plan to conform them to the image of Jesus Christ. They will make it to heaven. But they will tremble all the way.

It is also interesting to note that God usually gives strong assurance to those whom He will use mightily for the cause of God and Truth. They must have an overwhelming assurance in order to stand the attacks of the Evil One and to face death as did Stephen.

2. Can we possess assurance and then lose it? And may we regain it?

Answer: Assurance is not a "thing" which is given to the believer and then he has it for good. Assurance is that personal ministry of the Holy Spirit to the heart or soul of a believer in which He effectually reveals to them God's love for them (Rom. 5:5) and causes them to be conscious of and to exercise their filial relationship to God as their Father (Rom. 8:16; Gal. 4:6).

When we grieve or quench the Spirit by unconfessed sin in our life, the personal ministry of the Holy Spirit in assurance may be taken away from us along with the other fruit of the Spirit (Eph. 4:30; I Thess. 5:19). This, undoubtedly, explains some of David's Psalms wherein he expressed a lack of assurance due to his sin (Psa. 51, etc.).

This also reveals that many cling to a merely intellectual assurance for their "assurance" is not affected by their sin. Their assurance goes on completely oblivious to whether or not they have quenched or grieved the Spirit of God. Thus their "assurance" is not true spiritual assurance but only carnal presumption.

Since assurance is due to the ministry of the Spirit, when He leaves us because of our sin, He takes His assurance with Him. Is it any wonder that every true Christian must confess that he knows from the heart the prayer and experience of David in Psa. 51:10-12?

> "Create in me a clean heart, O God; and renew a right spirit within me.
>
> Cast me not away from thy presence; and take not thy Holy Spirit from me.
>
> Restore unto me the joy of thy salvation; and uphold me with thy Spirit."

3. How can I obtain assurance of my salvation? Or, how can I regain it?

Answer: First, recognize that it is not in your power to produce assurance. Neither can any pastor or counselor give you real assurance. Assurance is the work of the Holy Spirit and thus it is in His hands and He gives it where, when, and to whom He wishes.

Second, realize that He may not want to give it to you because it would cause pride, self-confidence and complacency. Submit yourself to God's will.

Third, be much in prayer, the Scriptures, Christian fellowship, church attendance, the ordinances and seek to strengthen your faith.

Fourth, search your life to discover if you have committed some particular sin which has grieved and quenched the Holy Spirit. Repent of this sin following James 4:6-10, and Psa. 51.

Fifth, be much in those Psalms where David has doubts and then found the way out of them (See Psa. 8, 7, 10, 13, 25, 28, 32, 38, 39,

40, 42, 51, etc.)

Sixth, seek counsel from godly ministers who are wise in dealing with the spiritual needs of saints.

Seventh, we would recommend the chapter on assurance in J.C. Ryle's book entitled *Holiness,* as one of the most practical and helpful writings on this subject. Secure the book and carefully study the chapter asking God to grant you spiritual insight on the subject.

In summary, it would be helpful to clench the Biblical doctrine of assurance by studying some of the great hymns on assurance. Either read or sing the following hymns.

> I know now why God's wondrous grace
> To me He hath made known,
> Nor why unworthy — Christ in love
> Redeemed me for His own.
>
> I know not how this saving faith
> To me He did impart,
> Nor how believing in His Word
> Wrought peace within my heart.
>
> I know not how the Spirit moves,
> Convincing men of sin,
> Revealing Jesus thro' the Word,
> Creating faith in Him.
>
> I know not what of good or ill
> May be reserved for me,
> Of weary ways or golden days,
> Before His face I see.
>
> I know not when my Lord may come,
> At night or noon-day fair,
> Nor if I'll walk the vale with Him,
> Or "meet Him in the air."
>
> But "I know whom I have believed,
> And am persuaded that He is able
> To keep that which I've committed
> Unto Him against that day."*

*Hymn: "I Know Whom I Have Believed"

Blessed Assurance

Blessed assurance, Jesus is mine!
Oh, what a foretaste of glory divine!
Heir of salvation, purchase of God,
Born of His Spirit, washed in His blood.

Perfect submission, perfect delight,
Visions of rapture now burst on my sight;
Angels descending, bring from above
Echoes of mercy, whispers of love.

Perfect submission, all is at rest,
I in my Saviour am happy and blest;
Watching and waiting, looking above,
Filled with His goodness, lost in His love.

This is my story, this is my song,
Praising my Saviour all the day long;
This my story, this is my song,
Praising my Saviour all the day long.

CHAPTER 16

Sanctification

What is the goal of God's plan of salvation? No answer to this question can be complete if it does not include the entire sanctification of elect sinners. God has purposed not only to declare sinners righteous through the imputation of Christ's righteousneses to their record in heaven but He has also willed to make these justified sinners righteous through the impartation of Christ's righteousness to their body and soul.

Does not Ephesians 1:4 state that God the Father chose us "that we should be holy and blameless before him"? Are not we told that God's foreknowledge and predestination have in view our sanctification in Romans 8:29, where we read,

> For whom he did foreknow, He also did predestined to be conformed to the image of His Son.

Does not the Apostle Paul state in I Thessalonians 5:23 that God will bring about the entire sanctification of His people at the Second Coming of Christ? Thus God's will is our sanctification (I Thess. 4:3).

The discerning reader of Scripture soon discovers that the sanctifying of God's people formed the central burden of Christ's death for we read in Titus 2:14,

> Who gave himself for us, that he might redeem us from all iniquity, and purify unto himself a peculiar people, zealous of good works.

Not only was sanctification the burden of Christ in His death but it is also central to His present ministry of intercession for the saints. Thus we find our High Priest praying for us in John 17:15-19,

> I pray not that thou shouldest take them out of the world, but that thou shouldest keep them from the evil.
>
> They are not of the world, even as I am not of the world.
>
> Sanctify them through thy truth: thy word is truth.
>
> As thou hast sent me into the world, even so have I also sent them into the world.
>
> And for their sakes I sanctify myself, that they also might be sanctified through the truth.

Having seen the centrality of sanctification in the past and present work of Christ, it is surprising that modern Christians know so little of this Biblical truth. There is so much false teaching on sanctification today that it would take an entire volume just to record the various theories. And let not the reader think that false views of sanctification are harmless.

One great problem in modern missions is the staggering number of missionaries who quit after or before their first term is completed on the mission field. A good number of those returning must seek psychiatric help. Why is there such a large turnover of missionaries? Why do many zealous, sincere missionaries develop tremendous psychological problems?

At one particular missionary conference, the high dropout rate among missionaries was discussed with the purpose to define the major cause and then to seek its cure.

After some discussion it was evident that the vast majority of missionaries who must return home for psychiatric care failed on the mission field due to inadequate and defective views of the Christian life, i.e., sanctification.

It seems that many missionary volunteers come from Bible colleges and Bible institutes where they are taught that it is possible to live a victorious life in which the fully surrendered believer can enjoy victory over all sin and the complete cessation of struggling with sin. They could then live without sin as long as they allow Christ to live His life through them.

In the context of an isolated or secluded Bible college campus, many students are deceived into thinking that they have "entered into victory." There they are taught that the key to victory is to be fully yielded or surrendered to Christ, viewing themselves as completely passive in His hands, allowing Him to live the Christian life through them.

With sincere enthusiasm, these young men and women offer themselves to be missionaries and are sent as soon as possible to some distant field.

Leaving everything behind them, they cannot help but feel that they are fully surrendered and thus expect to have victory over all besetting sins and to have complete peace within, the struggle with sin being gone. But to their dismay and utter discouragement, they find that their besetting sins were not left back home but followed them to the mission field! They must continually struggle with their sins and can never gain the complete victory over all of them at the same time.

Finding themselves still struggling with sin even though "fully surrendered" and now a missionary, they frantically try to regain the wonderful peace they felt while isolated from the world at the Bible college. So they "yield," "surrender," "present," "know," "let go and let God." In short, they use every formula they know of to gain complete victory and peace.

After meeting defeat at every turn, they then become demoralized, depressed, discouraged, highly introspective, guilty and finally feel that if God had really called them to the mission field, they would be living "the victorious life." Since they are not living this abundant life, they come to the conclusion that they are out of God's will and should quit the mission field and return home.

The strain of expecting and attempting perfection in this life proves too much for some of them and severe mental problems arise. How many missionaries have ulcers and high blood pressure due to the strain caused by the typical Bible school view of the Christian life?

And it should not be assumed that only missionaries can suffer mental and physical damage due to false teaching on sanctification. The same problems are evident in pastors, laymen and even in Seminary and Bible school teachers.

The reason why so many run from one Christian Life conference to the next is that they find it impossible to live the victorious life at home, work or church. The only time they feel they have arisen to the "abundant life" is when they are attending an abundant life conference!

In the light of the above example, we can see how desperately we need clear views of sanctification. *We must be able to believe what we live and live what we believe or serious problems will arise.* For this reason let us begin to clearly set forth the Biblical view of sanctification.

The first task before us is to define the basic meaning of the terms or words used in the Scriptural doctrine of sanctification.

The first mention of the word "sanctify" is found in Genesis 2:3, where we read that God "sanctified" the seventh day. The word "holy" is first found in Exo. 3:5, where Moses is informed that he is standing on "holy ground." In both of these places the words "sanctify" and "holy" refer to what can be called *vocational sanctification.*

In vocational sanctification, a person, object, place or portion of time is set apart for God's purpose and glory. The seventh day was set apart from the other days of the week as a special memorial of the finishing of creation. The ground under Moses feet was "holy" because it was set part from other ground as the place where God's special revelation was given to Moses. The first born was "sanctified," i.e., set apart for God's purpose and glory (Exo. 13:2). The special clothing of the priests were "holy," i.e., set apart to be used only according to divine purpose (Exo. 28:2, 6).

Vocational sanctification is sometimes used in speaking of God's eternal decrees. Jeremiah was "sanctified," i.e., set apart, before he was born (Jer. 1:5). The Apostle Paul was "set apart" from his mother's womb to be a chosen vessel for God's purpose and glory (Gal. 1:15; Acts 9:15).

A Biblical theological survey of the gradual unfolding and deepening concept of sanctification would see vocational sanctification as the basic and starting definition of sanctification.

Nearly all of the early references to sanctification in the Old Testament have in mind the setting apart of something or someone unto special divine purposes.

The New Testament on rare occasions makes reference and usage of vocational sanctification. Peter speaks of the mountain where Jesus was transfigured as being "holy," i.e., set apart (II Pet. 1:18). The writer to the Hebrews speaks of the Old Testament temple as being a "holy place," i.e., the place set apart for God's special presence (Heb. 9:3, 25).

As the concept of sanctification developed, it gradually began to take on a new meaning. This new concept can be called *moral or ethical sanctification.*

When we examine the positive aspect of ethical sanctification, the attention and emphasis is placed on the recreating of sinners once again into the moral image of God (Eph. 4:22-24).

In ethical sanctification we see God bringing justified sinners into conformity with their justification in which there is worked into their life those qualities and characteristics which reflect God's moral character.

Since the Son of God is the perfect image bearer of God (II Cor. 4:4; Col. 1:15), the goal of ethical sanctification is the conforming of elect and justified sinners to Christ's moral character (Rom. 8:29). The qualities, characteristics, and attributes of Christ's moral character which form the pattern of sanctification for all believers can be found in such places as the Beatitudes (Matt. 5:3-16) or the fruit of the Spirit (Gal. 5:22-23). The Apostle Peter exhorts us unto patience and perseverance in the midst of trial and persecution by pointing us to these moral qualities in the life of Christ who is our pattern for holiness.

> For this is thankworthy, if a man for conscience toward God endure grief, suffering wrongfully.
>
> For what glory is it, if, when ye be buffeted for your faults, ye shall take it patiently? But if, when ye do well, and suffer for it, ye take it patiently, this is acceptable with God.
>
> For even hereunto were ye called because Christ also suffered for us, leaving us an example, that ye should follow his steps:
>
> Who did no sin, neither was guile found in his mouth:
>
> Who, when he was reviled, reviled not again; when he suffered, he threatened not; but committed himself to him that judgeth righteously:
>
> Who his own self bare our sins in his own body on the tree, that we, being dead to sins, should live unto righteousness: by whose stripes ye were healed (I Pet. 2:;19-24).

The Apostle Paul in I Corinthians 1:20 goes beyond the statement that Christ Jesus is our pattern in sanctification by stating that *He is our sanctification.*

The righteousness and holiness which is developed in us — which ultimately conforms us to God's moral character — flows out of the person and work of Christ. Without Christ we can neither do nor be anything (John 5:5). The only thing you can call your very own is your sin and rebellion. All the good in you or done by you has as its origin the work of Christ.

That the foundation of the Christian life is the work of Christ has been obscured in our day by an over emphasis on the work of the Holy Spirit in sanctification. What has been forgotten is that the work of the Spirit is to apply what Christ accomplished in His atonement.

In Romans, chapters 6 & 7, the Apostle Paul constantly looks back to the work of Christ as the basis and foundation of sanctification.

In answer to the question, "Shall we continue in sin that grace may abound?" Paul points us to the death, burial, and resurrection of Christ as supplying the power to overcome sin the Christian life. There is no mention of the Holy Spirit.

> What shall we say then? Shall we continue in sin, that grace may abound?
>
> God forbid. How shall we, that are dead to sin, live any longer therein?
>
> Know ye not, that so many of us as were baptized into Jesus Christ were baptized into his death?
>
> Therefore we are buried with him by baptism into death: that like as Christ was raised up from the dead by the glory of the Father, even so we also should walk in newness of life.
>
> For if we have been planted together in the likeness of his death, we shall be also in the likeness of his resurrection:
>
> Knowing this, that our old man is crucified with him, that the body of sin might be destroyed, that henceforth we should not serve sin.
>
> For he that is dead is freed from sin.
>
> Now if we be dead with Christ, we believe that we shall also live with him:
>
> Knowing that Christ being raised from the dead dieth no more; death hath no more dominion over him.
>
> For in that he died, he died unto sin once: but in that he liveth, he liveth unto God.
>
> Likewise reckon ye also yourselves to be dead indeed unto sin, but alive unto God through Jesus Christ our Lord.
>
> Let not sin therefore reign in your mortal body, that ye should obey it in the lusts thereof.

Neither yield ye your members as instruments of unrighteousness unto sin: but yield yourselves unto God, as those that
are alive from the dead, and your members as instruments of
righteousness unto God (Rom. 6:1-13).

The following diagram may be helpful:

Application ———————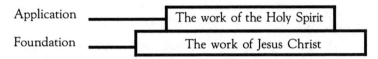

We should never become proud or arrogant over any degree of personal growth in holiness or righteousness. The righteousness which is
slowly and painfully brought into our lives by God in His work of sanctification is not the product of our pious efforts. The source is Christ
alone. We are sanctified only by virtue of our vital union with Him
(I Cor. 1:2).

Let us stress this vital but humbling truth, *we will never have any
righteousness or holiness which we can legitimately call our own. Christ is
our only righteousness and our only sanctification. He is our all in all*

Did you have any righteousness which was your own when you initially turned to God for salvation? No, you came with this attitude,

Nothing in my hand I bring,
Simply to thy cross I cling;
O, Lamb of God, I come.

How do you come to God in prayer *now* that you are a Christian?
Is it not with the same spiritual poverty with which you first came? Yes,
you plead to be dressed in the white robes of Christ's righteousness
because you are deeply conscious of your own personal sinfulness (see
Zech. 3:3-5). He is your sanctification. Outside of His righteousness,
there is nothing but the darkness of sin.

But we are warranted to ask, "How is Christ's righteousness infused
or imparted into our lives?" The answer is to examine the wonderful
work of the Holy Spirit who sanctifies us according to the will of the
Father (I Thess. 4:3) and the intercessory prayers of the Son (John 17:17).

When it comes to the application of the work of Christ to the believer in terms of sanctification, the Scriptures point us to the agency
of the Holy Spirit. Sanctification is said to be "by" or "from" the Spirit.

That I should be the minister of Jesus Christ to the Gentiles,
ministering the gospel of God, that the offering up of the Gen-

tiles might be acceptable, *being sanctified by the Holy Ghost* (Rom. 15:16).

Now the Lord is that Spirit: and where *the Spirit of the Lord is, there is liberty* (II Cor. 3:17).

But we all, with open face beholding as in a glass the glory of the Lord, are changed unto the same image from glory to glory, even as *by the Spirit* of the Lord (II Cor. 3:18).

But we are bound to give thanks always to God for you, brethren beloved of the Lord, because God hath from the beginning chosen you to salvation through *sanctification of the Spirit* and belief of the truth (II Thess. 2:13).

Elect according to the foreknowledge of God the Father, through *sanctification of the Spirit,* unto obedience and sprinkling of the blood of Jesus Christ: Grace unto you, and peace, be multiplied (I Pet. 1:2).

We are absolutely dependent upon the Spirit of God for our sanctification. The following is a brief list of some of the things attributed directly to the work of the Holy Spirit.

Guidance (Matt. 4:1; Acts 11:12; 16:7; Rom. 8:14).
Mortification of sin (Rom. 8:13).
Awareness of God's love (Rom. 5:5).
Assurance (Rom. 8:16).
Effectual prayer (Eph. 6:18; Jude 20).
Comfort (John 14:16).
Disclosure of Christ to the believer (John 15:26; 16:14-15).
Bold witnessing and preaching (Acts 1:8).
Conviction of sin (John 16:8-11).
All gifts (Rom. 12; I Cor. 12).
Hope (Gal. 5:5).
Victory over the works of the flesh (Gal. 5:16).
The fruit of the Spirit (Gal. 5:22-23).
Inner man strengthened (Eph. 3:16).
Unity (Eph. 4:3).

Just from this brief list, it is evident how dependent we are upon the Blessed Spirit for all growth and development in the Christian life.

Seeing that we became a Christian through the convicting and regenerating power of the Holy Spirit, it is no surprise that the Scriptures teach that we must be "perfected," i.e., sanctified by the same Spirit and not by our own pious works.

> O Foolish Galatians, who hath bewitched you, that ye should not obey the truth, before whose eyes Jesus Christ hath been evidently set forth, crucified among you?
>
> This only would I learn of you, Received ye the Spirit by the works of the law, or by the hearing of faith?
>
> Are ye so foolish? having begun in the Spirit, are ye now made perfect by the flesh (Gal. 3:1-3)?

The sanctifying work of the Spirit can be hindered by "quenching" and "grieving" the Spirit.

> And grieve not the Holy Spirit of God, whereby ye are sealed unto the day of redemption (Eph. 4:30).
>
> Quench not the Spirit (I Thess. 5:19).

A consideration of what hinders the Spirit's work of sanctification leads us to examine the negative aspect of ethical sanctification.

Whereas the positive aspect concerned the impartation of certain moral qualities into the life of all believers in order to conform them to the character of Christ who is the image of God, the negative aspect concerns the removal of sin out of the believer. *The positive emphasizes what must be put into the life while the negative emphasizes what must be taken out.*

In the Old Testament, the first development of the concept of sanctification beyond vocational sanctification was the removal of anything in the life which brought about ceremonial defilement or uncleanness (II Chron. 30:13-19). To sanctify the priests or the people began to have the basic meaning of cleansing, washing, or purification.

In the New Testament, the ethical or moral cleansing and purifying aspect of sanctification is clearly referred to in such places as I Cor. 6:9-11; II Cor. 7:1; Eph. 5:26; Titus 2:14; James 4:8-10; I John 1:7, 9; 3:3, etc.

In summary, in vocational sanctification the believer is set apart for divine purposes and glory. In ethical sanctification the believer has Christ's righteousness worked into his moral character and, at the same time, goes through a process of purification in order to deal effectually with remaining sin.

While sanctification is a spiritual process, there are four distinct phases within it.

I. Phase I — The Tyranny of Sin Broken

The first initial step of sanctification takes place in conjunction with regeneration. There is a radical break with the total dominion and tyranny of sin so that the believer now struggles with remaining sin instead of reigning sin.

The Holy Scriptures describe unregenerate sinners as being slaves of and to sin and sin is pictured as their tyrannical master.

> Jesus answered them, Verily, verily, I say unto you, Whosoever committeth sin is the servant of sin (John 8:34).

> But God be thanked, that ye were the servants of sin, but ye have obeyed from the heart that form of doctrine which was delivered you (Rom. 6:17).

> For when ye were the servants of sin, ye were free from righteousness (Rom. 6:20).

> And you hath he quickened, who were dead in trespasses and sins;

> Wherein in time past ye walked according to the course of this world, according to the prince of the power of the air, the spirit that now worketh in the children of disobedience.

> Among whom also we all had our conversation in times past in the lusts of our flesh, fulfilling the desires of the flesh and of the mind; and were by nature the children of wrath, even as others (Eph. 2:1-3).

In the first phase of sanctification, sin is dethroned, the believer dies to sin, the old self is crucified and there is a new principle of holiness implanted in the heart of the believer which will not allow sin to ultimately and permanently regain dominion over the believer.

> For if we have been planted together in the likeness of his death, we shall be also in the likeness of his resurrection:

> knowing this, that our old man is crucified with him, that the body of sin might be destroyed, that henceforth we should not serve sin.

> For he that is dead is freed from sin (Rom. 6:5-7).

> Likewise reckon ye also yourselves to be dead indeed unto sin, but alive unto God through Jesus Christ our Lord (Rom. 6:11).

For sin shall not have dominion over you: for ye are not under the law, but under grace (Rom. 6:14).

Being then made free from sin, ye became the servants of righteousness (Rom. 6:18).

But now being made free from sin, and become servants to God, ye have your fruit unto holiness, and the end everlasting life (Rom. 6:22).

And they that are Christ's have crucified the flesh with the affections and lusts (Gal. 5:24).

That the absolute power of sin has been broken in every believer is used by the Apostle Paul to prove that a person cannot be a real Christian and, at the same time, be completely dominated by sin as a general overall pattern of life.

Know ye not that the unrighteous shall not inherit the kingdom of God? Be not deceived: neither fornicators, nor idolaters, nor adulterers, nor effeminate, nor abusers of themselves with mankind,

Nor thieves, nor covetous, nor drunkards, nor revilers, nor extortioners, shall inherit the kingdom of God.

And such were some of you: but ye are washed, but ye are sanctified, but ye are justified in the name of the Lord Jesus, and by the Spirit of our God (I Cor. 6:9-11).

Now the works of the flesh are manifest, which are these: Adultery, fornication, uncleanness, lasciviousness,

Idolatry, witchcraft, hatred, variance, emulations, wrath, strife, seditions, heresies,

Envyings, murders, drunkenness, revelings, and such like: of the which I tell you before, as I have also told you in time past, that they which do such things shall not inherit the kingdom of God (Gal. 5:19-21).

Paul is not saying that if one commits one of these sins this proves that they are not Christians. Rather, he is stressing that the true believer cannot "practice such things" as a habitual way of life.

David is a good example to illustrate the difference between a regenerate person who sins and an unregenerate who makes a practice of sin, i.e., lives under the dominion of sin as a way of life.

David committed adultery and became ensnared in many other sins such as deceit, hypocrisy and murder. Yet, these sins were not the general pattern of his life. In a short time, his overall pattern of godliness reasserted itself and he repented of his evil ways and, as far as we know, never again fell into such sins. No one can say that he was an adulterous man as an overall picture of his life-style.

David's life is different from the adulterous man who habitually lives an immoral life as his general life-style. If this adulterous man claims to be a Christian, believers are commanded to avoid all social contact with him.

> I wrote unto you in an epistle not to company with fornicators:
>
> Yet not altogether with the fornicators of this world, or with the covetous, or extortioners, or with idolaters; for then must ye needs go out of the world.
>
> But now I have written unto you not to keep company, if any man that is called a brother be a fornicator, or covetous, or an idolater, or a railer, or a drunkard, or an extortioner; with such a one, no, not to eat (I Cor. 5:9-11).

People who profess to be Christians and yet manifest the complete dominion of sin in their lives as a way of life are called "liars" by the Apostle John (I John 2:4) and true believers are warned not to be deceived by their mere profession of faith (I Cor. 6:9; Gal. 6:7).

Although a believer may be overcome by sin at different periods of time, yet the overall general characteristic of his life is a godly walk in pursuit of holiness. Sin can never again ultimately and permanently enslave the believer even though it can and does temporarily regain its old dominion through the devices of Satan and corruption of the heart. Grace will soon reassert itself and dethrone sin.

An understanding of the first phase of sanctification supplies us with a key to understand why sanctification is spoken of in the past, present, and future tenses.

When the Scriptures speak of believers as "having been sanctified" in the past tense as a completed action, this has reference to the first phase of sanctification wherein the tyrannical power of sin has been broken.

Even though the Corinthians were involved in serious sins, yet the Apostles states that they "have been sanctified" (I Cor. 1:2) in the sense that they are no longer dominated by their past sins (I Cor. 6:9-11).

It is a mistake to identify the past tense meaning of sanctification as referring to some sort of "positional sanctification" because: (1) this confuses sanctification with justification and (2) this is in direct violation of the basic meaning of ethical sanctification which is to *make* sinners righteous.

A consideration of the present and future tenses of sanctification leads us to the three other phases.

II. Phase II — Continual Warfare

The second phase of sanctification concerns the present tense process of sanctification in which the believer experiences the positive and negative aspects of ethical sanctification. The believer is progressively conformed to Christ's moral character while, at the same time, remaining sin is progressively dealt with. Thus the New Testament speaks of believers as being sanctified in the sense of a present tense process.

> But we all, with open face beholding as in a glass the glory of the Lord, *are changed into the same image from glory to glory,* even as by the Spirit of the Lord (II Cor. 3:18).

> Having therefore these promises, dearly beloved, *let us cleanse ourselves* from all filthiness of the flesh and spirit, *perfecting holiness* in the fear of God (II Cor. 7:1).

> For *the perfecting of the saints,* for the work of the ministry, *for the edifying* of the body of Christ (Eph. 4:12).

> *Follow* peace with all men, and *holiness,* without which no man shall see the Lord (Heb. 12:14).

> And every man that hath this hope in him *purifieth himself* even as he is pure (I John 3:3).

We are progressively conformed to Christ's character in two ways.

First, the Holy Spirit sovereignly implants and nurtures Christ's righteousness within us. He works in us "the willing and doing of his good pleasure" (Phil. 2:13).

Second, as regenerate believers, we obey the Scriptures under the power and guidance of the Spirit. We make use of those means ordained in God's Word that we might "grow in the grace and knowledge of our Lord and Saviour Jesus Christ" (II Pet. 3:18).

The private means of growth in grace are the meditating, reading, memorizing, and singing of Scripture, worship and praise, praying, fasting, singing of hymns, good works, and witnessing.

The public means of growth in grace are primarily the functions of the assembled church such as the preaching of the Word, giving of offerings, partaking of sacraments, Christian fellowship, the exercising of one's spiritual gifts for the edification of the body, congregational praying and singing.

Remaining sin is dealt with in two ways as well.

First, the Spirit can eradicate or weaken remaining sin or hinder the outbreak of sin according to God's will for the Spirit Himself fights "the flesh" in us.

> For the flesh lusteth against the Spirit, and the Spirit against the flesh: and these are contrary the one to the other; so that ye cannot do the things that ye would (Gal. 5:17).

Since in our "inward man" we "joyfully concur with the law of God," we actively engage in the mortification of our remaining sins through the power of the Spirit.

> Therefore, brethren, we are debtors, not to the flesh, to live after the flesh.
>
> For if ye live after the flesh, ye shall die: but if ye through the Spirit do mortify the deeds of the body, ye shall live.
>
> For as many as are led by the Spirit of God, they are the sons of God (Rom. 8:12-14).

This mortification is done to weaken sin so that it does not regain mastery or dominion over us. Thus the Apostle warns us in Romans 6:12-13.

> Let not sin therefore reign in your mortal body, that ye should obey it in the lusts thereof.
>
> Neither yield ye your members as instruments of unrighteousness unto sin: but yield yourselves unto God, as those that are alive from the dead, and your members as instruments of righteousness unto God.

The Apostle states in II Corinthians 7:1 that "perfecting holiness in the fear of God" has as its focus the cleansing of "ourselves from all defilement of flesh and spirit."

In Phase II our responsibilities are to: (1) strengthen, add to and multiply Christ's moral qualities in our lives (Heb. 12:12-14; II Pet. 1:5-10; II Pet. 1:2-3), (2) to weaken, kill and to attempt all our days to completely subdue our remaining and besetting sins (Rom. 6:12-14; 8:12-14; II Cor. 7:1; Col. 3:1-10).

As the believer engages himself in the pursuit of holiness, he must keep in mind that perfection in this life is impossible (I John 1:8-10). While some sins are eradicated by the Spirit's sovereign work at regeneration and others are eradicated later on, there always remains a continual warfare with sin.

The people who say that they have arrived at the point in their Christian life where there is no longer any struggle with personal sins but within them all is peace either have never been regenerated and do not struggle because they are spiritually dead in their sins or have deceived themselves ;(I John 1:8-10). If the great Apostle Paul could not attain to moral perfection in his life (Phil. 3:12-13) and speaks of his own struggles with sin in such places as Romans 7:14-25; I Corinthians 9:27; II Corinthians 12:7-9, then any believer who claims to have "entered into victory over all sin" must be greatly deceived.

III. **Phase III — Perfected Spirit**

During the second stage or phase of sanctification, the progressive work of perfection and purification is always incomplete but, at death, which is the third phase, the believer's spirit or soul is at once completely perfected and purified. Thus the saints in heaven are described as "the spirits of justified men made perfect" in Hebrews 12:23.

The spirit or soul of the believer enters into the presence of God immediately at death (II Cor. 5:8). Since nothing defiled or unclean can enter heaven (Rev. 21:27), they are rendered perfectly righteous and all their sins are completely eradicated. Now they worship God with complete freedom and abandonment.

This Biblical truth forever refutes the heresy of soul sleep.

IV. **Phase IV — Finalized Victory**

Now that the complete sanctification of soul and spirit has taken place in Phase III, our attention is drawn to the body for it, too, must be completely sanctified (I Thess. 5:23).

When shall the body be completely sanctified? At the Second Coming of Christ when all living believers are transformed and the bodies of dead saints are resurrected.

At the coming of our Lord Jesus Christ (I Thess. 5:23).

For our conversation is in heaven; from whence also we look for the Saviour, the Lord Jesus Christ:

Who shall change our vile body, that it may be fashioned like unto his glorious body, according to the working whereby he is able even to subdue all things unto himself (Phil. 3:20-21).

But some man will say, How are the dead raised up? and with what body do they come? (I Cor. 15:35).

It is sown a natural body; it is raised a spiritual body. There is a natural body, and there is a spiritual body (I Cor. 15:44).

And as we have borne the image of the earthy, we shall also bear the image of the heavenly (I Cor. 15:49).

Behold, I show you a mystery; We shall not all sleep, but we shall all be changed,

In a moment, in the twinkling of an eye, at the last trump: for the trumpet shall sound, and the dead shall be raised incorruptible, and we shall be changed.

For this corruptible must put on incorruption, and this mortal must put on immortality.

So when this corruptible shall have put on incorruption, and this mortal shall have put on immortality, then shall be brought to pass the saying that is written, Death is swallowed up in victory.

O death, where is thy sting? O grave, where is thy victory?

The sting of death is sin; and the strength of sin is the law.

But thanks be to God, which giveth us the victory through our Lord Jesus Christ (I Cor. 15:51-57).

The fourth and final phase of sanctification when elect saints are rendered complete and perfect in the full image of God is the great goal of the history of redemption. It is called in Scripture the glorification of the saints when they are manifested to the world and vindicated in judgment.

> Moreover, whom he did predestinate, them he also called: and whom he called, them he also justified: and whom he justified, them he also glorified (Rom. 8:30).

> But we speak the wisdom of God in a mystery, even the hidden wisdom, which God ordained before the world unto our glory (I Cor. 2:7).

> And that he might make known the riches of his glory on the vessels of mercy, which he had afore prepared unto glory (Rom. 9:23).

The glorification of the saints is connected with the destruction of the old earth and its polluted atmosphere and with the creation of a new earth and a new atmosphere which is free of God's curse on man and on the earth (Gen. 3:17, cf Rom. 8:18-23; II Pet. 3:3-13).

Having completed our brief survey of the four phases or stages of sanctification, we are warranted to ask, are all true believers going to make it to glorification? What assurance do we have that all the elect will be saved? Can any lose their salvation? These questions lead us to our last and concluding chapter in this section.

CHAPTER **17**

Preservation and Perseverance

In our last chapter, we examined the prayer of the Apostle Paul recorded in I Thess. 5:23.

> And the very God of peace sanctify the wholly; and I pray God your whole spirit and soul and body be preserved blameless at the coming of our Lord Jesus Christ.

Given the fact that this prayer was infallibly inspired by the Holy Spirit, we are warranted to ask if Paul had any reason to think that his prayer would be answered. Or, to put it in other words, *on what grounds can we have any confidence in the final and ultimate salvation of all true believers?* Are there any solid Biblical reasons for believing in the total sanctification of all of God's elect?

In verse 24, Paul turns from his prayer unto the basis of his prophetic hope in the ultimate salvation of God's people.

> Faithful is he that calleth you, who also will do it.

The Apostle places the basis of ultimate salvation upon *the covenantal faithfulness of God.* God's faithfulness was displayed when He effectually called us into union with Christ (I Cor. 1:9). And as God's faithfulness *began* our salvation by calling us, His faithfulness guarantees the ultimate *completion* of our salvation. The Apostle says that God "will do it", i.e. He will bring His people to complete sanctification. God's covenantal faithfulness guarantees it.

The Apostle was not establishing a new doctrine but was emphasizing the Biblical doctrine of the preservation of the saints.

That God preserves His people from apostasy and sees it to that all of His elect ultimately enter heaven is the clear teaching of Holy Scripture. Are we not explicitly taught this truth in the following passages?

O love the LORD, all ye his saints: for the LORD *preserveth* the faithful, and plentifully rewardeth the proud doer.

Be of good courage, and he shall strengthen your heart, all ye that hope in the LORD (Psa. 31:23, 24).

The steps of a good man are ordered by the LORD: and he delighteth in his way (Psa. 37:23).

For the LORD loveth judgment, and forsaketh not his saints; they are *preserved* for ever; but the seed of the wicked shall be cut off (Psa. 37:28).

The LORD will *preserve* him, and keep him alive; and he shall be blessed upon the earth: and thou wilt not deliver him unto the will of his enemies (Psa. 41:2).

Ye that love the LORD, hate evil: he *preserveth* the souls of his saints; he delivereth them out of the hand of the wicked (Psa. 97:10).

The LORD *preserveth* the simple: I was brought low, and he helped me (Psa. 116:6).

He will suffer thy foot to be moved: he that *keepeth* thee will not slumber.

Behold, he that *keepeth* Israel shall neither slumber nor sleep.

The LORD is thy *keeper:* the LORD is thy shade upon thy right hand.

The sun shall not smite thee by day, nor the moon by night.

The LORD shall *preserve* thee from all evil: he shall preserve thy soul (Psa. 121:3-7).

Now to him that is of power *to stablish you* according to my gospel, and the preaching of Jesus Christ, according to the revelation of the mystery, which was kept secret since the world began (Rom. 16:25).

For the which cause I also suffer these things: nevertheless I am not ashamed; for I know whom I have believed, and am persuaded that *he is able to keep that which I have commited unto him against that day* (II Tim. 1:12).

And the Lord shall *deliver me* from every evil work, and will *preserve* me unto his heavenly kingdom: to whom be glory for ever and ever. Amen (II Tim. 4:18).

Who are *kept* by the power of God through faith unto salvation ready to be revealed in the last time (I Pet. 1:5).

Jude, the servant of Jesus Christ, and brother of James, to them that are sactified by God the Father, and *preserved* in Jesus Christ, and called (Jude 1).

Now unto him that is able to *keep* you from falling, and to present you faultless before the presence of his glory with exceeding joy (Jude 24).

In addition to the above passages, there are many Biblical arguments which support the doctrine of the final preservation of the saints.

One such argument is that the entire triune God of Father, Son and Holy Spirit is actively involved in securing the ultimate salvation of true believers.

God the Father:

(1) Keeps and guards true believers (I Pet. 1:5; Jude 1, 24).

(2) Completes in them the salvation which He began (Phil. 1:6).

(3) Chastizes His people when they sin against Him (Heb. 12:5-13).

(4) Will not cast them down but lifts them up (Psa. 37:23-25).

(5) Holds true believers safe in His almighty hand (John 10:29).

(6) Gives His people eternal life (John 3:16; I John 5:11-13).

(7) Works in them the willing and doing of His pleasure (Phil. 2:13; Heb. 13:20, 21).

(8) Works all thing together for the good of His elect (Rom. 8:28).

God the Son:

(1) Give eternal life to true believers (John 10:28).

(2) Holds them in His almighty hand and thus they shall never perish (John 10:28).

(3) Secured the ultimate salvation of all those for whom He lived, died, and now intercedes (Heb. 10:14; 7:24-25).

(4) Will not lose one of the elect whom the Father had given Him (John 6:37-40).

(5) Will confirm His people to the end (I Cor. 1:8).

(6) Perserves their spiritual life by virtue of their union with Him (II Cor. 5:17; Rom. 6:9-11).

(7) Prays that the Father will keep, protect, and sanctify all those for whom He died (John 17:6-24).

(8) He is the Finisher as well as the Author of our faith (Heb. 12:2).

God the Holy Spirit:

(1) Savingly seals true believers "unto the day of redemption" (Eph. 1:13, 14; 4:30).

(2) Abides in them forever (John 14:16).

Additional arguments arise from:

(1) The irreversible nature of regeneration for one cannot be "unborn" after being reborn by the Spirit (John 3:1-6).

(2) The finality and irreversible nature of justification. The justified are no longer under condemnation and no one can lay any charge against them (Rom. 8:1, 33).

(3) The unbreakable chain of redemption described in Rom. 8:29, 30 where all those predestinated are eventually glorified.

(4) The indestructable nature of our union with Christ which guarantees that nothing — not even sin — can separate us from His love (Rom. 8:35-39).

(5) True believers can have a full assurance of their eternal salvation (I John 5:11-13). This would be impossible if we could lose our salvation.

(6) If Christ would lose some of the ones whom the Father gave Him, He would fail to accomplish God's will (John 6:32, 39).

(7) John the Apostle explains the apostasy of professing Christians as the falling away of false believers who were never really saved. He states that when someone is truly saved, they will continue in the faith (I John 2:19).

(8) One of the ingredients of the New Covenant is that God would place His Spirit in the hearts of His elect so that they

should never fall away from Him (Jer. 32:38-40; 31:31-34).

(9) Once sin is forgiven, it cannot be imputed back to the person but is remembered no more (Jer. 31:34; Rom. 4:6-8).

(10) It is God's will that not one of the sheep of Christ shall perish (Matt. 18:12-14).

(11) Christ will never cast out or forsake any who come to Him (John 6:37; Heb. 13:5, 6).

(12) Christ secured *eternal* salvation by His death (Heb. 9:12, 15). If a sinner is saved for two years and then is lost, he had only a "two year" salvation. This is hardly eternal or everlasting life.

(13) The eternal security of the believer arises out of the necessity and nature of the atonement. Since the atonement has a definite and particular focus and is executed by God's sovereignty, it naturally follows that all those who are chosen by the Father, purchased by the Son and sealed by the Spirit shall most certainly be preserved by God unto His everlasting Kingdom.

While it is true God preserves His people, we are not to infer from this that we do not have to persevere in holiness. The Scriptures do not teach that the *certainity* of our preservation negates or lessens in any way the *necessity* of our persevering in the faith.

But he that shall endure unto the end, the same shall be saved (Matt. 24:13).

Then said Jesus to those Jews which believed on him, If ye continue in my word, then are ye my disciples indeed (John 8:31).

Moreover, brethren, I declare unto you the gospel which I preached unto you, which also ye have received, and wherein ye stand; By which also ye are saved, if ye keep in memory what I preached unto you, unless ye have believed in vain (I Cor. 15:1-2).

And you, that were sometime alienated and enemies in you mind by wicked works, yet now hath he reconciled in the body of his flesh through death, to present you holy and unblameable and unreproveable in his sight: If ye continue in the faith grounded and settled, and be not moved away from the hope of the gospel, which ye have heard, and which was preached to every creature which is under heaven; whereof I Paul am made a minister (Col. 1:21-23).

Therefore we ought to give the more earnest heed to the things which we heard, lest at any time we should let them slip. For if the word spoken by angels was steadfast, and every transgression and disobedience received a just recompense of reward; How shall we escape, if we neglect so great salvation; which at the first began to be spoken by the Lord, and was confirmed unto us by them that heard him (Heb. 2:1-3).

For we are made partakers of Christ, if we hold the beginning of our confidence steadfast unto the end (Heb. 3:14).

Follow peace with all men, and holiness, without which no man shall see the Lord (Heb. 12:14).

They went out from us, but they were not of us; for if they had been of us, they would no doubt have continued with us: but they went out, that they might be made manifest that they were not all of us (I John 2:19).

The warnings and threats found in the New Testament concerning any professing Christian who falls away from the faith are to be taken at face value because they describe the terrible fate waiting those who follow Judas and Demas. It is not enough to *profess* Christ. You must actually and really *possess* Christ as your personal Lord and Saviour in order to be truly saved.

This brings into focus the difference between the perseverance of the saints and the popular doctrine of "eternal security."

Eternal Security means to many in our day "once saved, always saved, no matter what you do."

On this basis, many individuals have assumed that they are saved merely because they made a decision for Jesus some point in the past. And, despite the fact that their present life and faith are far from Biblical standards, they cling to their supposed salvation-experience.

The only way to defeat the easy-believism and decisionism of our day is to preach the absolute necessity of holiness "without which no man shall see the Lord" (Heb. 12:14).

We must believe and pray knowing that our preservation depends entirely upon God's covenantal faithfulness while, at the same time, striving for and seeking after holiness as if our perseverance depended entirely on our own faithfulness to the Lord.

That the saints do not ultimately fall away from grace or into sin does not mean that Christians don't fall into sin many times in their life time. Abraham lied, David committed adultery and Peter denied the Lord!

As the Westminster Confession of Faith states in Chapter XII, paragraphs I, II, III.

> They, whom God hath accepted in His beloved, effectually called and sanctified by His Spirit, can neither totalay nor finally fall away from the state of grace, but shall certainly persevere therein to the end, and be eternally saved.

> This perseverance of the saints depends not upon their own free will, but upon the immutability of the decree of election, flowing from the free and unchangeable love of God the Father; upon the efficacy of the merit and intercession of Jesus Christ, the abiding of the Spirit, and of the seed of God within them, and the nature of the covenant of grace: from all which ariseth also the certainty and infallibility thereof.

> Nevertheless, they may, through the temptations of Satan and of the world, the prevalency of corruption remaining in them, and the neglect of the means of their preservation, fall into grievous sins; and for, a time, continue therein: whereby they incur God's displeasure, and grieve His Holy Spirit, come to be deprived of some measure of their graces and comforts, have their hearts hardened, and their consciences wounded; hurt and scandalize others, and bring temporal judgments upon themselves.

The relationship between falling into sin and assurance has already been dealt with in chapter 15.

The preservation and perseverance of the saints has been a favorite theme of many great hymns. Meditate on the folowing hymns.

> More secure is no one ever,
>   Than the loved ones of the Saviour;
> Not yon star on high abiding,
>   Nor the bird in homenest hiding.

> God His own doth tend and nourish,
>   In His holy courts they flourish;
> Like a father kind He spares them
>   In His loving arms He bears them.

Neither life nor death can ever,
    From the Lord His children sever;
For His love and deep compassion
    Comforts them in tribulation.

Little flock, to joy then yield thee!
    Jacob's God will ever shield thee;
Rest secure with this Defender,
    At His will all foes surrender.

What He takes or what He gives us,
    Shows the Father's love so precious;
We may trust His purpose wholly —
    'Tis His children's welfare solely.*

Jesus lives, and so shall I.
    Death! thy sting is gone forever!
He who deigned for me to die,
    Lives, the bands of death to sever.
He shall raise me from the dust:
    Jesus is my Hope and Trust.

Jesus lives and reigns supreme;
    And, His kingdom still remaining,
I shall also be with Him,
    Ever-living, ever-reigning.
God has promised: be it must:
    Jesus is my Hope and Trust.

Jesus lives, and by His grace,
    Vict'ry o'er my passions giving,
I will cleanse my heart and ways,
    Ever to His glory living.
Me He raises from the dust.
    Jesus is my Hope and Trust.*

*Hymn: "Jesus Lives"

Jesus lives! I know full well
　　Nought from Him my heart can sever,
Life nor death nor pow'rs of hell,
　　Joy nor grief, henceforth forever.
None of all His saints is lost;
　　Jesus is my Hope and Trust.

Jesus lives and death is now,
　　But my entrance into glory.
Courage, then my soul, for thou
　　Hast a crown of life before thee;
Thou shalt find thy hopes were just;
　　Jesus is the Christian's Trust. Amen.*

*Hymn: "Jesus Lives, and So Do I"

CHAPTER 18

The Question of the Heathen

The subject of the heathen usually arises in the context of witnessing. The unbeliever attempts to escape the Gospel call to repentance and faith by hurling what he thinks is an unanswerable objection to Christianity: "But, what about the heathen? Are you telling me that all those innocent people are going to hell? Even when they didn't have a chance?"

Evidently, to many non-Christians the question of the heathen serves as a challenge to Christianity as well as an escape hatch from the claims of the Gospel on their own conscience. If the heathen can make their way to heaven without believing in Jesus, the unbeliever smugly assumes that he also can make his way to heaven without becoming a Christian. Thus it is not surprising to find many non-Christians totally ignorant concerning the Biblical answer to the heathen question. But it is shocking to discover that many modern professing Christians are just as ignorant. How has this come about?

The Neo-orthodox takeover of the major denominations with their colleges and seminaries has flooded the liberal world with the teaching of universalism. At the same time, some evangelicals have embraced and are propagating a semi-universalism in which any sincere heathen who lives up to the light he has will be saved. They argue that God is too loving to damn those for whom Christ died and who never had a chance. We have talked with students from prominent evangelical colleges and seminaries who do not believe in the historic doctrine of the damnation of all unbelievers including the heathen.

It is only appropriate that in a study of the atonement we should deal with the heathen question. Given the Biblical doctrine of the atonement, we are warranted to ask, "Can the heathen be saved by the work of Christ without hearing of or believing in the person of Christ? Is faith in Jesus Christ always a part of the salvation process or can one skip over faith and repentance and still experience regeneration and obtain justification?" Such questions as these focus our attention on the issue of the eternal destiny of the heathen.

Perhaps the best way to begin our study of the subject is to clarify the question of the heathen.

> Can a sinner be saved from hell even though he does not believe in the true God or in Jesus Christ? Or, upon what grounds can a sinner claim admittance to heaven other than repentance toward God and faith in the Lord Jesus Christ?

The popular "man-in-the-street" answer is that the heathen can be saved from hell even though they do not believe in Jesus Christ. The supposed grounds of the heathen's claim to heaven rests upon these three arguments.

1. If a sinner is sincere in whatever religion he believes in and he lives up to the light he has, it would be unjust for God to condemn him to hell.

2. If a sinner never heard the Gospel, this means that he never had a chance to be saved. Therefore it would be unjust for God to condemn someone who never had a chance.

3. We are condemned if and when we reject Jesus Christ and His Gospel. It is obvious that those who have never heard of the Gospel can not be condemned for rejecting it! Therefore it would be unjust for God to condemn the heathen.

The issue can be further clarified by observing that all unbelievers without exception can be placed into one of the following categories which describe the circumstances of their unbelief.

1. *Ignorance:* The geographic area in which the unbelievers live is so remote that the Gospel message has never penetrated it. The unbelievers have absolutely no opportunity to hear the Gospel even if they wanted to do so.

2. *Neglect:* The Gospel has penetrated the area and is present and available to all but some unbelievers neglect to hear or study it. Thus they are still ignorant of the Gospel and are not saved due to their neglect.

3. *Nominal acquaintance:* The Gospel is vaguely understood but there

is no true saving belief in it. The unbeliever denies or rejects the Gospel and clings to his own pagan ideas and religion.

4. *Nominal acceptance:* The unbeliever professes to accept the Gospel and to believe in Jesus Christ but this profession is false. This is where much of professing Christendom must be placed.

Now, according to the popular conception of the issue the question of the heathen concerns only the first case where sinners are ignorant of the Gospel because there is absolutely no opportunity to hear it. But the Scriptures are very clear that if we neglect, deny or only nominally accept the Gospel, we cannot be saved "for how shall we escape if we neglect so great salvation" (Heb. 2:3).

Another point that should be made is that the proper definition of "heathen" is *any and every unbeliever*. We must not allow people to assume that the word "heathen" refers only to the primitive peoples of the Third World. The unbelievers who live in New York City or London constitute the heathen just as much as a Hindu or an Australian bushman.

One way to bring this truth home to the unbeliever who challenges the Gospel with the heathen question is to respond in the following manner:

Unbeliever:	But, what about the heathen?
Believer:	Well, what about *you*? *You* will not be saved unless *you* believe in Christ.
Unbeliever:	I don't mean *me*. I am referring to the heathen, i.e., those who never heard.
Believer:	Why should *they* concern you? The issue is that *you* are one heathen who has heard the Gospel. Now what are *you* going to do about it? Are you trying to avoid the issue of your sin by bringing up an irrelevant question? The real question is, "What about *your* eternal fate?

The basic and foundational issue in the heathen question is whether or not the Scriptures view ignorance due to neglect or to the absence of the Gospel as constituting sufficient grounds for salvation. And, also, whether or not the lack of faith constitutes unbelief as well as the rejection of faith.

PART I

With these introductory remarks in mind, let us begin our study of this subject by setting forth several opening principles which shall guide us in our study.

Principle I: The Scriptures alone can tell us of the eternal destiny of all those who do not believe in the person and work of Christ as presented in the Biblical Gospel.

We must strive to bring every thought into conformity to the Holy Scriptures. Our faith must be Biblical from beginning to end. For what sayeth the Scriptures?

> To the law and to the testimony: if they speak not according to these, it is because they have no light (Isa. 8:20).

> For all Scripture is given by inspiration of God and is profitable for doctrine (II Tim. 3:16).

Principle II: *We must be careful to avoid the three typical non-Christian approaches to this issue.*

1. The person who is a rationalist thinks that his reason or logic can tell him where the heathen go at death. He usually begins his position by saying,

"I think that. . . ."
"It is only logical that. . . ."
"The only intelligent answer is. . . ."

2. The person who is experience-centered thinks that stories and testimonies which relate human experience will decide the issue. They usually will tell some groundless story which is incapable of verification about some heathen somewhere who supposedly worshipped the true God without actually knowing who or what He really was or who had angels or Jesus appear to him in dreams or visions. They usually begin their position by saying,

"Have you heard the story about. . . ."

3. The person who is a mystic will trust his subjective emotions or feelings to tell him the truth. They usually begin their position by saying,

"I feel that. . . ."

Principle III: *Defend God at all costs.*

Whatever God does is right and just. Do not the Scriptures teach us that "Shall not the Judge of all the earth do right?" (Gen. 18:25). God is not unjust or unloving because He casts the wicked into hell. He is sovereign in His wrath as well as in His grace.

"As it is written, Jacob have I loved, but Esau have I hated. What shall we say then? Is there unrighteousness with God? God forbid. For he saith to Moses, I will have mercy on whom I will have mercy, and I will have compassion on whom I will have compassion. So then it is not of him that willeth, nor of him that runneth, but of God that showeth mercy. For the Scripture saith unto Pharaoh, Even for this same purpose have I raised thee up, that I might show my power in thee, and that my name might be declared throughout all the earth. Therefore hath he mercy on whom he will have mercy, and whom he will he hardeneth. Thou wilt say then unto me. Why doth he yet find fault? For who hath resisted his will? Nay but, O man, who art thou that repliest against God? Shall the thing formed say to him that formed it, Why hast thou made me thus? Hath not the potter power over the clay, of the same lump to make one vessel unto honour, and another unto dishonour? What if God, willing to shew his wrath, and to make his power known, endured with much long-suffering the vessels of wrath fitted to destruction: And that he might make known the riches of his glory on the vessels of mercy, which he had afore prepared unto glory (Rom. 9:13-23).

Some people defend man at all costs even to the degradation of God. "But let God be true and every man a liar" (Rom. 3:4).

Principle IV: *Never tone down a Biblical doctrine because it offends people.*

The Gospel itself is offensive to unbelievers. Should we abandon it because the unregenerate think it foolish?

For the preaching of the cross is to them that perish foolishness; but unto us which are saved it is the power of God. For it is written, I will destroy the wisdom of the wise, and will bring to nothing the understanding of the prudent. Where is the wise? Where is the scribe? Where is the disputer of this world? Hath not God made foolish the wisdom of this world? For after that in the wisdom of God the world by wisdom knew not God, it pleased God by the foolishness of preaching to save them that believe. For the Jews require a sign, and the Greeks seek after wisdom: But we preach Christ crucified, unto the Jews a stumblingblock, and to the Greeks foolishness (I Cor. 1:18-23).

The disciples came to the Lord Jesus and told Him that He had offended the Pharisees. His reaction shows us the proper attitude when the truth offends people.

> Then came his disciples, and said unto him, Knowest thou that the Pharisees were offended, after they heard this saying? But he answered and said, Every plant, which my heavenly Father hath not planted, shall be rooted up. Let them alone: they be blind leaders of the blind. And if the blind lead the blind, both shall fall into the ditch (Matt. 15:12-14).

Principle V: *Take one step at a time.*

There are many issues involved in the heathen question which must be answered before the final answer is given.

Principle VI: *Determine in your spirit to believe whatever God says in His Word for "he that is willing to do the will of God shall know whether or not the doctrine is from God"* (John 7:17).

We must be careful that we approach the heathen issue with an open mind and a humble heart in utter submission to the authority of Scripture.

PART II

With these opening principles completed, we will now set forth the central propositions of our position.

Proposition 1: *All men are lost sinners and in need of salvation.*

This first proposition is so basic to the Christian Gospel that it is impossible to deny its scripturality. Carefully read Romans 1-6, for you will find in this passage a full exposition of the just condemnation of God which rests universally upon all men "for all have sinned; and the wages of sin is death" (Rom. 3:23; 6:23).

Proposition 2: *General Revelation is not sufficient for salvation.*

General revelation is that mute non-verbal witness of the creation that points men to the existence and power of God and to man's own creatureliness and sinnerhood. General revelation confronts all men at all times through the world around them and the voice of their conscience within them (Rom. 1:18-28; 2:14-15).

While general revelation is sufficient to condemn all men because it leaves all mankind "without excuse" (Rom. 1:20), the Scriptures never speak of it as being sufficient to save anyone. In the Bible, salvation is tied to the Gospel and the Gospel comes to us only in God's special revelation, the Holy Scriptures (Rom. 10:17).

It must be further pointed out that the Bible teaches that no sinner has ever perfectly lived up to the light of general revelation. All men suppress and reject the light of creation and worship the creature instead of the Creator (Rom. 1:18, 21-25, 28). Thus there never has been and there never shall be a sinner who lives up to all the light he receives from general revelation (Rom. 3:10-18).

Proposition 3: *The fact of judgment is determined on the basis of the nature of the person in question.*

Because all men are "by nature" sinners, all men are under the wrath of God (Eph. 2:3, cf. Rom. 1:18).

The doctrine of original sin involves the imputation of Adam's sin to all mankind. This imputation is followed by the condemnation of God and the judgment of death (see Psa. 51:5; 58:3; Rom. 5:12-21; I Cor. 15:22).

We sin because we are sinners. What we are by nature determines the fact of judgment. Thus it is wrong to teach that we are lost *if* and *when* we reject Christ. The Gospel is preached to those who are *already* lost and perishing (I Cor. 1:18). You are condemned to hell because of what you are, i.e., a sinner.

The heathen are condemned because of what they are, i.e., their nature. They are sinners. Therefore, they are under God's wrath.

Proposition 4: *The degree of punishment is determined on the basis of the light and life of the person in question.*

Because God is just, there will be degrees of punishment in hell. All sinners in hell will be *perfectly* miserable but not *equally* miserable.

In determining the degree of punishment in hell, our Lord takes into account the words (Matt. 12:26, 37) and works (Matt. 16:27; Rev. 20:11-15; 22:12) of sinners.

Disobedience and unbelief due to ignorance do not deliver one from punishment for ignorance of the Law is no excuse (Lev. 5:17). But sins done in ignorance will not receive as much punishment as sins done consciously in violation of known law.

> And that servant, which *knew* his lord's will, and prepared not himself, neither did according to his will, shall be beaten with *many* stripes. But he that *knew not*, and did commit things

worthy of stripes, shall be beaten with *few* stripes. For unto whomsoever much is given, of him shall be much required: and to whom men have committed much, of him they will ask the more (Luke 12:47-48).

The more you know, the more responsible you are to live up to that light. The greater the responsibility, the greater the punishment.

Certain cities were liable to more divine punishment because they actually saw and heard the Christ and, yet, refused Him.

Verily I say unto you, *It shall be more tolerable* for the land of Sodom and Gomorrah in the day of judgment, than for that city (Matt. 10:15).

Then began he to upbraid the cities wherein most of his mighty works were done, because they repented not: Woe unto thee, Chorazin! woe unto thee, Bethsaida! for if the mighty works, which were done in you, had been done in Tyre and Sidon, they would have repented long ago in sackcloth and ashes. But I say unto you, *It shall be more tolerable* for Tyre and Sidon at the day of judgment, than for you. And thou, Capernaum, which are exalted unto heaven, shalt be brought down to hell: for if the mighty works, which have been done in thee, had been done in Sodom, it would have remained until this day. But I say unto you, *That it shall be more tolerable* for the land of Sodom in the day of judgment, than for thee (Matt. 11:20-24).

The writer of the Hebrews speaks of some unbelievers receiving more punishment than others.

Of *how much sorer punishment*, suppose ye, shall he be thought worthy, who hath trodden under foot the Son of God, and hath counted the blood of the covenant, wherewith it was sanctified, an unholy thing, and hath done despite unto the Spirit of grace? (Heb. 10:29).

The sin of the Pharisees was made greater by their contact with Christ (John 15:22).

While the fact of judgment is determined by what we are, i.e., our nature, the degree of punishment is determined on the basis of the amount of true knowledge we have received and the quality of life that we lived (Rom. 2:3-6).

The following illustration may be helpful to further clarify this point.

Sophie the scrubwoman lived all her life in relative harmlessness. She was kind to all and diligent in her work. But she never received Christ unto salvation because she trusted in her own righteousness.

The infamous Hitler spent his life harming others and working iniquity upon the earth. The evil things he did are known to all.

Now, it came to pass that both Sophie and Hitler died on the same night and both stood before God for judgment (Heb. 9:27).

Since they were both unregenerate sinners, both Sophie and Hitler were condemned to hell. But on the basis of their works, Hitler received greater punishment than Sophie for God rewarded each of them according to their works.

Degrees of punishment reveals that hell is not annihilation but eternal torment. See *Death and the Afterlife* for complete details.

Proposition 5: *The explicit teaching of Scripture is that the only way to escape the wrath of God is to believe in the Lord Jesus Christ.*

Look unto me, and be ye saved, all the ends of the earth; for I am God, and *there is none else* (Isa. 45:22).

He that believeth on the Son hath everlasting life: and *he that believeth not the son shall not see life; but the wrath of God abideth on him* (John 3:36).

I am *the* door: *by me* if any man enter in, he shall be saved, and shall go in and out, and find pasture (John 10:9).

Jesus saith unto him, I am *the way, the truth,* and *the life: no man cometh unto the Father, but by me* (John 14:6).

Neither is there salvation in any other: for there is none other name under heaven given among men, whereby we must be saved (Acts 4:12).

Whom God hath set forth to be a propitiation through faith in his blood, to declare his righteousness for the remission of sins that are past, through the forbearance of God; To declare, I say, at this time his righteousness: that he might be just, and the justifier of him *which believeth in Jesus.* Seeing it is one God, which shall justify the circumcision by faith, and uncircumcision through faith (Rom. 3:25-26, 30).

For other foundation can no man lay than that is laid, which is Jesus Christ (I Cor. 3:11).

> For there is one God, and one mediator between God and men, the man Christ Jesus (I Tim. 2:5).

Proposition 6: *All non-Christian religions are condemned in Scripture because they: (a) are idolatrous-pagan religions are not man's search for God but they are actually man's rejection of God (Rom. 1:18-25) (b) actually give worship to Satan and his demons (I Cor. 10:19-22), and (c) fail to find God through the wisdom of this world (I Cor. 1:18-31).*

The heathen are not worshipping the true God in their pagan religions. We reject the false idea that all religions are just different roads to God. All unbelievers are idolators.

Proposition 7: *The absence of special revelation does not in any way relieve the heathen from perishing.*

The fact that they die physically reveals that God views them as sinners and that they face a Christless eternity in the second death.

> For there is no respect of persons with God. *For as many as have sinned without law shall also perish without law;*
>
> *In the day when God shall judge the secrets of men by Jesus Christ according to my gospel (Rom. 2:11-12, 16).*
>
> *For all* have sinned, and come short of the glory of God (Rom. 3:23).
>
> Wherefore, as by one man sin entered into the world, and death by sin; and so death passed upon *all men*, for that *all* have sinned (Rom. 5:12).
>
> For the wages of sin is death; but the gift of God is eternal life through Jesus Christ our Lord (Rom. 6:23).

Proposition 8: *The Scriptures teach that all unbelievers will be cast into the lake of fire when Jesus returns in glory and power* (see Matt. 25:41, 46; Rev. 21:6).

II Thessalonians 1:8 tells us about the fate of those who do not know God.

> And to you who are troubled rest with us, when the Lord Jesus shall be revealed from heaven with his mighty angels, In flaming fire taking vengeance on *them that know not God, and that*

> *obey not the gospel* of our Lord Jesus Christ: *Who shall be punished with everlasting destruction from the presence of the Lord, and from the glory of his power;* When he shall come to be glorified in his saints, and to be admired in *all them that believe* (because our testimony among you was believed) in that day (II Thess. 1:7-10).

Proposition 9: *Unbelievers must hear or read of the Lord Jesus Christ through a human instrumentality in order to be saved.*

The Gospel does not come to us from angels, visions or dreams. God has committed unto the Church the privilege and responsibility of spreading the Gospel.

> Go *ye* therefore, and teach all nations, baptizing them in the name of the Father, and of the Son, and of the Holy Ghost: Teaching them to observe all things whatsoever I have commanded you: and, lo, I am with you alway, even unto the end of the world. Amen (Matt. 28:19-20).

> And he said unto *them*, Go *ye* into all the world, and preach the gospel to every creature (Mark 16:15).

> For whosoever shall call upon the name of the Lord shall be saved. How then shall they call on him in whom they have not believed? and how shall they believe in him of whom they have not heard? and *how shall they hear without a preacher?* And how shall they preach, except they be sent? as it is written, How beautiful are the feet of them that preach the gospel of peace, and bring glad tidings of good things! But they have not all obeyed the gospel. For Esaias saith, Lord, who hath believed our report? So then *faith cometh by hearing, and hearing by the word of God* (Rom. 10:13-17).

Proposition 10: *God will always send the Gospel by a human instrumentality to those who have been ordained to eternal life.*

Cornelius is a good example of how God will send the Gospel to His elect.

The angel which came to Cornelius did not give him the Gospel for unto angels this ministry was never committed. The angel told Cornelius to send for Peter so that Cornelius would hear the Gospel and be saved.

And he shewed us how he had seen an angel in his house, which stood and said unto him, Send men to Joppa, and call for Simon, whose surname is Peter; *Who shall tell thee words, whereby thou and all thy house shall be saved* (Acts 11:13-14).

Cornelius obeyed the angel and when Peter came and preached the Gospel, then, and not until then, was Cornelius saved (I Cor. 10:44-48).

Cornelius was a moral and God-fearing man (I Cor. 10:1-2). Yet, he was *not* saved until the Gospel came and he placed his faith in Jesus Christ.

It should also be pointed out that God told Paul to continue preaching at Corinth because the elect were in the city (Acts 18:9-10 and II Tim. 2:10).

Proposition 11: *If salvation is possible through ignorance or neglect of the Gospel, then Jesus Christ died in vain, i.e., for nothing.*

His death was necessary and a mockery if salvation can be obtained by any other manner than by believing Him.

I do not frustrate the grace of God: for if righteousness come by the law, then Christ is dead in vain (Gal. 2:21).

Proposition 12: *A survey of the history of redemption reveals that ignorance, neglect and nominal acquaintance or acceptance were never sufficient grounds to deliver anyone from the just wrath of God against sin.*

A. *The Flood:* Man sinned (Gen. 6:1-5, 11-13) and God's judgment came upon him for his sin (Gen. 6:6-7, 13, 17). Only the believer Noah and his family were delivered from God's wrath (Gen. 6:8-10, 14-16, 18-22). Question: Were there any ignorant, sincere and neglectful people in Noah's day? What happened to them? If we asked Noah about the fate of all unbelievers in his day regardless if they were ignorant or neglectful, what would he say? Is the flood a pre-picture of the Judgment Day at the second coming of Jesus Christ? (Matt. 24:37-39; II Pet. 2:5, 9). Since all the heathen (unbelievers) without exception perished under the flood waters of God's wrath, what does this tell us about God's judgment on unbelievers when Christ returns? All unbelievers will perish regardless if they are ignorant or neglectful.

B. *The Tower of Babel:* Man sinned and God's judgment came upon him (Gen. 11). This judgment took two forms. First, human language was diversified. Second, the human race was scattered.

Question: Were there any sincere, ignorant or neglectful people working on the tower? What happened to them? Is it not the case that the two major reasons why some men are ignorant of the Gospel corresponds exactly to God's two judgments, i.e., different languages and mankind scattered over the face of the earth? Thus is not man's ignorance an extension of God's judgment against sin? If so, is it possible to view ignorance as the basis of the heathen's salvation seeing that such ignorance is part of God's judgment against unbelievers?

C. *Sodom and Gomorrah:* Man sinned (Gen. 18:20-21; 19:1-9) and God's judgment came upon him (Gen. 19:10-11; 23-29). Only the believer Lot and his two daughters were delivered from the fire and brimstone.

Question: Were there any sincere, ignorant, and neglectful people living in these cities? What happened to them? Abraham said that "the judge of all the earth shall do right" (Gen. 18:25). What did God do with all the unbelievers in Sodom and Gomorrah? If we asked Abraham and Lot about the eternal fate of all unbelieving sinners, what would they say? Is the destruction of these cities a pre-picture of the coming destruction on the Day of Judgment? (Luke 17:28-30; II Pet. 2:5-9; Jude 7). What significance does this have on the heathen question?

D. *The History of God's People.*

1. *God's Judgment upon Egypt at the time of the Exodus.* Were there any sincere, ignorant, and neglectful Egyptians? Were they saved from the judgment plagues of God? Were only the first born of these who believed God's Word safe from the angel of death or did the angel pass over any houses where the people were sincere, ignorant, or neglectful?

2. *God's Commandment to Israel.* Was idolatry allowed in Israel? What was the penalty for idolatry? (Deut. 18) Was there any difference in the sight of the law whether the idolator was sincere, ignorant, or neglectful? (Lev. 5:17). If sincere or ignorant idol worship saved one from the judgment of God, would this make true worship meaningless because it was not necessary for salvation? How would Moses answer the question of the heathen?

3. *God's Destruction of the Canaanites.* To what fate did God assign the Canaanites? (Josh. 9:24, etc.). Were there any sincere, ignorant or neglectful Canaanites? What happened to them? How would Joshua answer our question?

4. *God's Deliverance of Rahab.* Was Rahab a Canaanite? Why was she delivered while the rest were destroyed? (Josh. 2:8-13). Were the only ones delivered from destruction those who believed in Jehovah? How would Rahab answer our question?

5. *God's View of the Nations.* How did Israel view the idolatrous nations around them (Psa. 9:17)? What happens to those who do not bow to Jehovah (Psa. 2:11-12)?

6. *The Conversion of Ruth (see Ruth).* How, and why, did Ruth join the people of God? Does she not serve to show how Gentiles were saved in Old Testament times? How could they be saved? How would Ruth answer the heathen question?

E. *Jonah and Nineveh (see Jonah).*

Were there any sincere, ignorant, or neglectful people in Nineveh? What fate had God assigned them? Why did the judgment turn away? How would Jonah answer the question of the heathen?

F. *Jesus Christ.*

Did He ever claim to be the only way of salvation? (John 14:6). What did He call false religious leaders? (John 10:8). Did He state that only faith in Him will deliver one from the judgment of God? (John 3:16, 36). How would He answer if we ask Him about the heathen?

G. *The Apostles.*

Did they teach that only faith in Christ saves? (Acts 4:12; 10:43; 16:31; Rom. 5:1; 10:9-13). Did they ever teach that there is no salvation outside of the Gospel? (Rom. 10:14-17). Is Christ the only Mediator between God and man? (I Tim. 2:5). How would they answer the question of the heathen?

H. *Missions.*

Are we commanded to preach the Gospel to all men? (Mark 16:15-16). Why? Do they need it? If the ignorant and sincere can be saved as long as they don't hear the Gospel, do missionaries actually damn more than they save? Would it not be cruel to introduce the Gospel to ignorant people? If men were not already lost and without hope, would missions make any sense?

PART III

Answers to those who think God unjust in condemning the heathen.

I. *How dare anyone accuse God of being unjust in whatever He does!* The Apostle Paul rebukes such a rebellious attitude in Romans 9:11-24.

If the righteous Judge of all the earth has revealed in His Word that all the heathen will be cast into the lake of fire (Rev. 20:15), who is the man that can condemn God?

II. *Sincerity in living up to some of the light one has will only make one a candidate for further light as it did for Cornelius in Acts 10.* But Cornelius had to be saved through the Gospel given by a human messen-

ger (Acts 11:14). Not even the angel could tell Cornelius the Gospel.
Sincerity is not enough.

III. *As sinners, the only thing we deserve is God's eternal wrath in hell.*
The Bible does not teach that God owes us anything or that we even
deserve a chance to be saved. It teaches that we don't in any sense deserve to be saved. Salvation is by GRACE. This means that God does
not owe anyone anything (Rom. 4:1-5). God does not have to save anyone at all. It is all of grace.

IV. *Isn't the real question of the heathen about you, dear unconverted
Reader?* Where will you spend eternity? Flee to Jesus Christ and repent
for the wrath of God is coming upon the earth and who shall stand
in the Day of Judgment without Christ as his advocate?

V. *And what can be said to you, dear Christian?* Does the plight of
the heathen move you at all? Shouldn't their spiritual condition motivate you to be more zealous for missions? The heathen are all around
you. Do you weep for them? Do you witness to them? Oh, may God
stir up His people once again to become a mighty missionary force in
the world today.

Meditate on the following hymns in order to motivate your heart
to pray for the salvation of the heathen.

Send thou, O Lord, to every place
    Swift messengers before thy face,
The heralds of thy wondrous grace,
    Where thou thyself wilt come.

Send men whose eyes have seen the King,
    Men in whose ears his sweet words ring;
Send such thy lost ones home to bring;
    Send them where thou wilt come.

To bring good news to souls in sin;
    The bruised and broken hearts to win;
In ev'ry place to bring them in
    Where thou thyself wilt come.

Gird each one with the Spirit's sword,
    The sword of thine own deathless Word;
And make them conquerors, conquering Lord,
    Where thou thyself wilt come.

Raise up, O Lord the Holy Ghost,
From this broad land a mighty host,
Their war cry, "We will seek the lost
Where thou, O Christ, wilt come. A-Men."*

*Hymn: "Send Thou, O Lord to Every Place"

Speed thy servants, Saviour, speed them;
Thou art Lord of winds and waves;
They were bound, but thou hast freed them;
Now they go to free the slaves:
Be thou with them, 'Tis thine arm alone that saves.
Be thou with them, 'Tis thine arm alone that saves.

Friends, and home, and all for-saking,
Lord, they go at thy command,
As their stay thy promise taking,
While they traverse sea and land:
O be with them; Lead them safely by the hand.
O be with them; Lead them safely by the hand.

When they reach the land of strangers,
And the prospect dark appears,
Nothing seen but toils and dangers,
Nothing felt but doubts and fears,
Be thou with them, Hear their sighs and count their tears.
Be thou with them, Hear their sighs and count their tears.

Where no fruit appears to cheer them,
And they seem to toil in vain,
Then in mercy, Lord, draw near them,
Then their sinking hopes sustain:
Thus supported, Let their zeal revive again.
Thus supported, Let their zeal revive again.

In the midst of opposition let them trust,
O Lord, in thee;
When success attends their mission,
Let thy servants humbler be:
Never leave them Till thy face in Heav'n they see.
Never leave them Till thy face in Heav'n they see. A-Men.*

*Hymn: "Speed Thy Servants, Savior, Speed Them"

CHAPTER 19

Old Testament Salvation

No study of the atonement can be complete without dealing with the issue of Old Testament salvation. This is particularly true in a time when dispensationalism has ensured the hearts of many believers in North American. While there are some aspects of the Darby-Scofield system which are also shared by more orthodox systems, dispensationalism as a whole fails to "rightly divide the Word" at crucial points. This is particularly true in its view of Old Testament salvation.

While modern modified dispensationalists would not teach that there are as many different plans or kinds of salvation as there are dispensations or ages, the original Scofield Bible taught exactly this doctrine. Thus throughout the United States there are many fundamentalists who believe that the Old Testament saints experienced a different salvation than what we experience today. They derived these teachings from several of Scofield's notes.

Examine the following notes found in the Scofield Bible and it will be beyond dispute that the original Scofield Bible taught that *Old Testament saints were saved through obedience to the Law*. We are told that they were not saved by grace through faith as we are today.

1. p. 1002, N.1 on Matt. 6:12, "This is *legal* ground. cf. Eph. 4:32, which is grace. *Under law forgiveness is conditioned upon a like spirit in us;* under grace we are forgiven for Christ's sake, and exhorted to forgive because we have been forgiven."

2. p. 1115, N.1 on John 1:17, "(1) Grace is "the kindness and love of God our Saviour toward man . . . not by works of righteousness which we have done" (Tit. 3:4, 5). It is, therefore, constantly set in con-

trast to law, under which *God demands righteousness from man*, as, under grace, He gives righteousness to man . . . *Law is connected with Moses and works*; grace with Christ and faith . . . *Law demands that blessings be earned*; grace is a free gift. (2) As a dispensation, grace begins with the death and resurrection of Christ. . . . *The point of testing is no longer legal obedience as the conditions of salvation*, but acceptance or rejection of Christ, with good works as a fruit of salvation. . . . "

3. p. 1323, N.1 on I John 3:7, " . . . The righteous man under law *became righteous by doing righteously*; under grace he does righteously because he has been made righteous. . . . "

In the above notes and elsewhere in the Scofield Bible, we are told that Old Testament saints were not saved through faith.

Thus we must conclude that the doctrine of Old Testament salvation is a very important issue to which we must address ourselves. The orthodox position needs to be expounded and defended so that pastors and laymen will know that there is an alternative to dispensational teaching.

With this purpose in mind, we will now state the Biblical position.

> The Old Testament believer experiences and possessed essentially the same salvation which is freely offered to us in the New Testament. There is only one plan of salvation for all sinners of all ages. Different ages or dispensations do not have different kinds of salvation. Salvation is one as to its:

(1) Author: God alone
(2) means of reception: faith alone
(3) basis: Christ alone
(4) character: grace alone
(5) essential content: the same in all ages.

Our Biblical demonstration of the above doctrine will have two parts. In the first section we will set forth certain foundational principles which have direct bearing on our subject. Then, secondly, we will set forth several arguments which support individual parts of our position.

I.   Foundational Principle 1: The Unchanging Character of God

Why was mankind created? Was it not to bear God's image, i.e. to reflect His moral character? We read in Gen. 1:26, 27,

> And God said, Let us make man in our image, after our like-
> ness: and let them have dominion over the fish of the sea, and
> over the fowl of the air, and over the cattle, and over all the
> earth, and over every creeping thing that creepeth upon the earth.

> So God created man in his own image, in the image of God
> created he him; male and female created he them.

But man fell into sin, and his image-bearing capacity and faculties
were distorted and corrupted. He is now called a "child of Satan" because he bears the image of Satan more than he bears the image of
God (John 8:39-47; Eph. 2:1-3).

God in His mercy did not abandon man to His just judgment. Instead, God decreed a plan of salvation which would save man from
the penalty, power, and presence of sin and, at the same time, recreate
him in the image of God (Rom. 8:28-30; Eph. 4:20-32).

Thus we must conclude that man-as-image-bearer was the purpose
of God in creating man and is also the purpose of God in saving man.
*We were created and are saved in order to bear or reflect God's character
in the universe.*

God's purpose in saving man gives us a sure guide in determining the
essential content of salvation, i.e. what salvation will do for and to man.

Is not holiness an attribute to God's character (Isa. 6:3)? It is not
surprising, therefore, to learn that man was originally created in holiness and that God supplies an imputed and imparted holiness in His
plan of salvation for man (Eph. 4:20-24).

Holiness is essential to man's salvation because he cannot be created
in God's image without it. Thus we are told that "without holiness none
shall see the Lord" (Heb. 12:14). Holiness is an essential part of salvation. Without holiness, salvation is impossible. That holiness is essential in salvation because God is holy and man was created and is
saved to bear this aspect of God's character is clear from Lev. 11:44;
I Pet. 1:15, 16.

> For I am the LORD your God: ye shall therefore sanctify your-
> selves, and ye shall be holy; for I am holy: neither shall ye de-
> file yourselves with any manner of creeping thing that creepeth
> upon the earth (Lev. 11:44).

> But as he which hath called you is holy, so be ye holy in all
> manner of conversation; Because it is written, Be ye holy; for
> I am holy (I Pet. 1:15, 16).

We must conclude therefore that God's holiness demands that salvation contain an imputed and imparted holiness for sinners regardless of the age in which they live. *To say that salvation is different in each age is to say that God's character changes.* This is impossible for we are told in Mal. 3:6,

> "I, the LORD, do not change."

Therefore, salvation in the Old Testament as well as in the New Testament *must* supply the needed holiness which will render sinners acceptable in the sight of a holy God.

The same can be said of God's attribute of perfection. Man was created perfect. Through sin, he has lost this perfection. Now, through grace, salvation comes to re-create man in the perfection of God. Thus we read in Matt. 5:48,

> Be ye therefore perfect, even as your Father which is in heaven
> is perfect.

Perfection *must* be a part of salvation regardless of what age in which the sinner lives. Thus glorification awaits *all* the people of God from every age (Rom. 8:28-30). They will *all* be "made like unto Him" when He comes (I John 3:1-2). At the resurrection of the just, *all* the people of God from every age will experience the entire sanctification of body, soul and spirit because no imperfect or unholy creature will be allowed into heaven (I Thess. 5:23, 24; Rev. 21:27). The Old Testament saint must be given perfection as well as holiness if any salvation is to take place at all. The unchangeable character of God demands it.

Just these two Biblical examples are enough to establish the truth that *the unchangable character of God guarantees that salvation will be essentially one throughout all ages.* Indeed, the necessity of holiness and perfection alone can supply us with sufficient reason to see the Old Testament saints regenerated, justified, sanctified, adopted, called, glorified, etc. The entire process of the application of redemption has as its goal, the recreating of man in the image of God. Whatever is needed today to make sinners acceptable in God's sight, has always been and will always be needed.

II.   Foundational Principle 2: The Eternity of the Cross

The relationship between eternity and time is a very difficult subject. But what seems to be clear to nearly every Christian is that time is a creation of God. Time has a beginning and an end because it is bound to created reality. Eternity existed before time and the eternal state will again set in after the day of Judgment. God is transcendent over time and eminent in time at the same time.

Being transcendent above time, God sees all of history from beginning to end as present to His sight. He sees Adam eating the forbidden fruit, the flood, the birth of Christ, the discovery of America, the present situation and future events all at the same time.

Perhaps this diagram will help to understand God's transcendence.

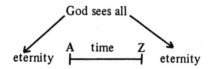

God sees all of time from beginning (A) to end (Z). Everything which we call "past" and "future" is present to Him who sees all. *Thus each incident which happens in time is, at the same time, a fact of eternity.* God does not have to wait until something happens before He can know about it. God's omniscience guarantees that He knows about everything past, present, and future. See *The Battle of the Gods* for a complete statement.

The prophecy is not God's hope that certain things will happen in the future, but instead, prophecy is God telling us what He *knows* will happen because He already views it as accomplished.

This is why prophecy is said to be a "sure word" (II Pet. 1:19). This is why the people of God are said to be "glorified" while this aspect of salvation is yet future and concerns the resurrection of the dead (Rom 8:30). God speaks of our glorification as a fact of eternity while it is yet a future incident in time.

The transcendence of God above or over time guarantees that history will follow God's eternal plan. History is His-story. Time is not unfolding itself according to chance but according to God's eternal purpose.

This is particularly clear in reference to the work of Christ. Christ came to earth at the precise moment God had decreed according to Gal. 4:4, 5,

> But when the fulness of the time was come, God sent forth his Son, made of a woman, made under the law,

To redeem them that were under the law, we might receive the adoption of sons.

The death of Christ is viewed as being planned by God from all eternity in Acts 2:23; 4:27, 28,

Him, being delivered by the determined counsel and foreknowledge of God, ye have taken, and by wicked hands have crucified and slain:

For of a truth against the holy child Jesus, whom thou hast anointed, both Herod, and Pontius Pilate, with the Gentiles, and the people of Israel, were gathered together.

For to do whatsoever the hand and thy counsel determined before to be done.

Thus it is obvious that *the death of Christ is a fact of eternity to God because it is real historical incident in time.*

God has viewed Christ as crucified from all eternity. This is why Peter could speak of salvation as flowing from the blood of a perfect lamb,

But with the precious blood of Christ, as of a lamb without blemish and without spot:

Who verily was *foreordained before the foundation of the world,* but *was manifest in these last times* for you (Pet. 1:19, 20).

In this passage Peter keeps the balance between the eternal and historical aspect of Christ's death. Christ was the Lamb of God before the worlds were created but He was manifested in history to shed His blood for His people.

This truth is further strengthened by Rev. 13:8 where we read,

And all that dwell upon the earth shall worship Him, whose names are not written in the book of life of *the Lamb slain from the foundation of the world.*

We are aware that some commentators have felt uneasy with the phrase "slain from the foundation of the world" and have said that the phrase "from the foundation of the world" should modify the word "written" and not "slain." Thus the verse would read,

" . . . whose names are not written — from the foundation of the world — in the book of life of the Lamb slain."

But there are no real grammatical, textual, contextual or theological reasons to reject the traditional translation. And in the light of Acts 2:23; 4:27, 28; I Pet. 1:19, 20, the principle of the analogy of Scripture would point to the traditional exegesis where Christ is viewed as "the Lamb slain from the foundation of the world."

It was just as easy for the Apostle to speak of our glorification in the past tense, while not yet historically present, as it was to speak of Christ's death as a fact of eternity though recently accomplished in time. In the sight of God, the redemptive work of Christ is a fact of eternity as well as as being a fact of history.

The truth of the transcendent character of the historical work of Christ answers the question: How could Christ's death nearly two thousand years ago save me today? The death of Christ is effectual to save today because God sees Christ dying right now. To Him Christ's death is present. Or, to put it into other words, the effects of Christ death continue on throughout the ages. God applies today what Christ accomplished long ago because God is transcendent.

In the same way, Christ is said to have been "slain from the foundation of the world" (Rev. 13:8).

The verb "slain" is in the perfect passive tense and thus means that His death is viewed as an incident in the past, the results of which are continuing unto the present.

Since the death of Christ is a fact from all eternity because it is a fact of time, the redemptive effects of Christ's work are applied to sinners before Christ came as well as after He came. It is just as easy for God to save an Old Testament saint two thousand years before Christ came as it is to save you or me two thousand years after He came. Perhaps the following diagram will help to illustrate this truth.

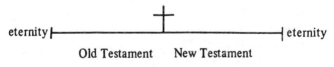

eternity ┣━━━━━━━━━━━━━━━━━━━━━━━━━━━━━┫ eternity

Old Testament   New Testament

space/time history

The benefits of Christ's death are equally applied before and after it was historically accomplished. The Old Testament saints experienced the same salvation as we do today, i.e. the salvation which flowed from the work of Jesus Christ. The Old Testament saints were not saved by their works but by the work of Another. If salvation were possible through obedience to the Law, "Christ died in vain" according to the Apostle Paul in Gal. 2:21. The eternity of the cross guarantees the same salvation in all ages.

III. Foundational Principle 3: The Depravity of Man

It is Biblically accurate to say, "Man has not changed." He is the same as he has always been. His needs are just the same as they were thousands of years ago. This is particularly true of man's sinful nature and needs.

When you consider the Biblical material on total depravity (ex. Rom. 1-3), it is not long before you realize that salvation is constituted in such a way to meet the needs of sinners. Salvation answers the question, "How can a man be just before God" (Job 9:2)?

To say that salvation is not the same in all ages is to say that man's nature and needs have changed from age to age. This is impossible.

Some dispensationalists have said that Old Testament saints were not regenerated or indwelled by the Holy Spirit. But we must say, did not man's fallen nature *require* such works of grace? Could it be that they were not as depraved as we are? That they had inward power to live a godly life by the flesh which we know nothing of, seeing we are dependent upon the Spirit?

Stop and ask yourself, "What do *I* need to be saved and to live a godly life?" Whatever you need, the Old Testament saints needed as well. If you need the new birth, so did they. If you need the indwelling of the Spirit, so did they. The oneness of man's fallen nature guarantees the oneness of salvation in all ages.

IV. Foundation Principle 4: The Unity of the Testaments

We have already shown elsewhere that the Old Testament prefigured the coming of the New Testament. Given just the Old Testament, we are left with:

(1) unexplained ceremonies
(2) unfulfilled prophecies
(3) unsatisfied longings
(4) unfinished destiny.

In the New Testament, the ceremonies are explained, the prophecies fulfilled, the longing satisfied and the destiny of God's people completed.

The people of God are basically one throughout all the ages. Did not the Apostle Paul compare them to one tree in Rom. 11:17? Did he not call Abraham "the father of *all* them that believe" in Rom. 4:11? Are we not all "children of Abraham" by faith (Gal. 3:39)? Is it not the case the Christians are said to be the true "Jews" (Rom. 2:29), the real "circumcision" (Phil. 3:3) and "Israel" (Gal. 6:16)? Do we not constantly find the Church described by Old Testament terminology which was originally applied to Israel (Titus 2:14; I Pet. 2:9, etc.)? Is it not true that the New Covenant was originally given to Israel in Jer. 31:31 but, in the New Testament, it is applied directly to the Church by our Lord (Matt. 26:28) and the Apostles (I Cor. 11:25; Heb. 8:8-13; 10:15-25)? Are not Old Testament "Israel" passages applied to the church (Acts 2:16-36; 15:15-22)?

There is no way to dissolve the unity, continuity and harmony of the Old New Testaments. This unity guarantees the same salvation in all ages because it is always *covenantal* salvation from our covenant God.

Having completed our presentation of these foundational principles, we now turn to a setting forth of particular arguments which also establish our doctrine.

I.   Argument 1: One Author of Salvation: God

No one can really dispute the truth that *God alone is the author of salvation in every age.* Was it not God who first sought out Adam and Eve after their fall into sin (Gen. 3:1-14)? Did He not at that time preach the Gospel to them (Gen. 3:15)? Did not God shed the first blood because of man's sin (Gen. 3:21)? Did not Noah and his family escape destruction because he "found grace in the eyes of the Lord" (Gen. 6:8)? Did not Jonah confess "Salvation is of the Lord" (Jonah 2:9)? Did not John record in John 3:16,

> For God so loved the world, that he gave his only begotten
> Son, that whosoever believeth in him should not perish, but
> have everlasting life.

God alone is the author of salvation regardless of the age. To say that Old Testament saints were saved by their legal obedience to the law is the same as saying that they were the author of their own salvation. No, if a sinner was saved in Old Testament times, it was by the gracious work of God and not by works of righteousness "for by the works of the law shall no flesh be justified" (Gal. 2:16).

II.   Argument 2: Only One Means of Reception: Faith

How did salvation come to the Old Testament saint? Was it earned as Scofield taught? Or, was it received through faith?

In the book of Romans, it is apparent that the Apostle Paul was conscious of the accusation that his gospel was in conflict with the Old

Testament Scripture and the Old Testament view of salvation.

The Pharisees thought that they were saved by their own obedience (Lk. 18:11-14). Thus they complained that Paul's "justification by faith apart from the Law" was unscriptural. They felt that the Gospel was in basic conflict with the Old Testament. It is important to point out at this point that dispensationalism agrees with the Pharisees in their understanding of Old Testament salvation. If Scofield is right, then Paul's gospel is in direct conflict with the Old Testament. Thus Paul was "unscriptural."

Because of the Jewish opposition to the gospel, Paul is carful to quote the Old Testament Scriptures at every point to show that the Gospel is rooted in Old Testament Scripture and experience.

Thus in chapter 1, he begins by mentioning the "gospel of *God*" to emphasize that it is not uniquely Christ's Gospel invented by Him but rather it is God the Father's Gospel as well.

Then he begins his emphasis on the Old Testament basis of the Gospel by saying in verse 2,

> Which He had promised afore by His prophets in the Holy
> Scriptures.

The first two verses of Romans are just a beginning of references to the Old Testament. Indeed, Paul quotes from the Old Testament more times in Romans than in any other of his epistles. Romans is Paul's demonstration that the Gospel was preached "by His prophets in the Holy Scriptures" (Rom. 1:2).

In introducing the Gospel of Christ, Pauls sets forth his position in verse 16,

> For I am not ashamed of the gospel of Christ: for it is the power
> of God unto salvation to every one that believeth; to the Jew
> first, and also to the Greek.

On what grounds does the apostle say that salvation comes to us "by faith" in verse 16? In verse 17, Paul quotes that Old Testament from Hab. 2:4,

> "as it is written, the just shall live by faith."

Thus Paul sees salvation by faith in Hab. 2:4. Old Testament saints were told in this passage by one of God's prophets (verse 2) that the way of salvation was *faith* not works.

After his brief introduction, Paul launches into a full exposition of man's helpless and sinful state by nature. Man is pictured as spiritually unable to do anything for his salvation. It is important to ask, "Does Paul only picture men in his day as being sinners under God's wrath (1:18) or is he speaking of mankind in general, i.e. in every age?

It is obvious that Paul is speaking of fallen human nature regardless of the age because he bases his teaching concerning God's judgment and man's sinfulness on Old Testament passages (Rom. 2:6; 10-18). He concludes that man is so sinful that good works are impossible (3:10-12). He further concludes that works could not save anyone because the Law's function was to reveal sin, not to remove it.

> Now we know that what things soever the law saith, it saith to them who are under the law: that every mouth may be stopped, and all the world may become guilty before God.
>
> Therefore by the deeds of the law there shall no flesh be justified in his sight: for by the law is the knowledge of sin (Rom. 3:19, 20).

Having demonstrated for three chapters that "all have sinned and fallen short of the glory of God" (Rom. 3:23), Paul now turns to the Gospel as the answer to man's needs.

In the Gospel, a righteousness has been provided by the work of Jesus Christ. This righteousness comes to us by faith apart from the works of the law. This is the teaching of the Old Testament as well.

> But now the righteousness of God without the law is manifested, *being witnessed by the law and the prophets;*
>
> *Even the righteousness of God which is by faith of Jesus Christ* unto all and upon all them believe; for there is not difference (Rom. 3:21-22).

This righteousness is the imputed righteousness of justification which comes to us by virtue of the propitiatory sacrifice of Christ.

> Being justified freely by His grace through the redemption that is in Christ Jesus:
>
> Whom God hath set forth to be a propitiation through faith in His blood, to declare His righteousness for the remission of sins that are past, through the forbearance of God;
>
> To declare I say, at this time his righteousness: that he might be just, and the justifier on him which believeth in Jesus (Rom. 3:24-26).

Now Paul begins to prove that justification through faith was experienced by Old Testament saints as well as being taught by such Old Testament prophets as Habakkuk.

His first proof centers on Abraham who represents all the saints who lived *before* the law was given. How was Abraham saved? Paul; tells us in 4:1-5,

> What shall we say then that Abraham our father, as pertaining to the flesh, hath found?
>
> For if Abraham were justified by works, he hath whereof to glory; but not before God.
>
> For what saith the Scripture? *Abraham believed God, and it was counted unto him for righteousness.*
>
> Now to him that worketh is the reward not reckoned of grace, but of debt.
>
> But to him that worketh not, *but believeth on Him that justifieth the ungodly, his faith is counted for righteousness.*

But what about those who lived after the Law? Were they saved by the works of the Law? No, says Paul. David who lived *after* the Law represents all who lived after Moses. David was justified through faith alone. Thus Paul states in 4:6-8,

> Even as David also describeth the blessedness of the man, unto whom God imputeth righteousness without works,
>
> Saying, Blessed are they whose iniquities are forgiven, and whose sins are covered.
>
> Blessed is the man to whom the Lord will not impute sin.

By quoting from the Law (4:1-5), the Writings (4:6-8) and the Prophets (1:17), Paul demonstrates that the entire Old Testament from beginning to end taught the same gospel as he preached, i.e. salvation comes by justification through faith alone. And in case these passages were not enough, Paul even quotes Moses in Rom. 19:5-9 as preaching the Gospel. And he gives the gospel call to come to Christ by quoting Joel 2:32 in Rom. 10:13.

> For whosoever shall call upon the name of the Lord shall be saved.

Since it is clear that Old Testament saints were justified by grace through faith, Paul assumes that they must therefore have the other elements of the application of redemption which he lists in Rom. 8:28-30,

> And we know that all things work together for good to them that love God, to them who are the called according to his purpose.

> For whom he did *foreknow*, he also did *predestinate* to be conformed to the image of his Son, that he might be the firstborn among many brethren.

> Moreover, whom he did predestinate, them he also *called*: and whom he called, them he also *justified*: and whom he justified, them he also *glorified*.

Take Abraham as an example. Was he effectually called? Yes, in Neh. 9:7 and Acts 7:3, 4 we learn that God called Abraham out of idolatry. Was Abraham justified? Yes, in Rom. 4:1-4 we read of his justification. Will Abraham be glorified? Yes, in Matt. 8:11 Jesus pictures Abraham with the glorified saints.

It is an unavoidable conclusion that if Abraham experienced the salvation described in Rom. 8:30, then he likewise experienced what Paul elsewhere includes in the application of redemption: regeneration, adoption, sanctification, preservation, etc.

All the elements of redemption are necessarily connected to one another. Seeing Abraham was justified, this implies regeneration to produce the justifying faith needed (John 3:3, 5) and adoption as the consequence.

We would further point out that a close study of the book of Galatians will reveal the same teaching of the Apostle Paul: *Abraham was saved through believing the Gospel. Old Testament saints were justified by faith apart from the works of the Law.*

> Knowing that a man is not justified by the works of the law, but by the faith of Jesus Christ, even we have believed in Jesus Christ, that we might be justified by the faith of Christ, and not by the works of the law: for by the works of the law shall no flesh be justified (Gal. 2:16).

> Even as Abraham believed God, and it was accounted to him for righteousness.

Knowing ye therefore that they which are of faith, the same
are the children of Abraham.

And the Scripture, foreseeing that God would justify the
heathen through faith, *preached before the gospel unto Abraham*, saying, in thee shall all nations be blessed.

So then they which be of faith are blessed with faithful Abraham.

For as many as are of the works of the law are under the curse:
for it is written, Cursed is every one that continueth not in
all things which are written in the book of the law to do them.

*But that not man if justified by the law in the sight of God, it is
evident: for the just shall live by faith.*

And the law is not of faith; but, The man that doeth them
shall live in them.

Christ hath redeemed us from the curse of the law, being made
a curse for us: for it is written, Cursed in every one that hang-
eth on a tree:

That the blessing of Abraham might come on the Gentiles
through Jesus Christ; that we might receive the promise of the
Spirit through faith (Gal. 3:6-14).

But the Scripture hath concluded all under sin, that the promise of faith of Jesus Christ might be given to them that believe
(Gal. 3:22).

Or again, in Hebrews 11, we are told that the Old Testament saints
lived and died *through faith*. Let us read the story of Moses described
as the triumph in Christ.

By faith Moses, when he was born, was hid three months of
his parents, because they saw he was a proper child; and they
were not afraid of the king's commandment.

By faith Moses, when he was come to years, refused to be called
the son of Pharaoh's daughter;

Choosing rather to suffer affliction with the people of God,
than to enjoy the pleasures of sin for a season;

Esteeming the reproach of Christ greater riches than the trea-sures in Egypt: for he had respect unto the recompense of the reward.

By faith he forsook Egypt, not fearing the wrath of the king: for he endured, as seeing him who is invisible.

Through faith he kept the passover, and the sprinkling of blood, lest he that destroyed the firstborn should touch them.

By faith they passed through the Red sea as by dry land: which the Egyptians assaying to do were drowned (Heb. 11:23-29).

There is one last argument which can be advanced to demonstrate that there has been and now is only one way of salvation: faith alone.

In Romans 3:28, the Apostle concludes his argument which is found verses 21-27 by saying,

Therefore we conclude that a man is justified by faith without the deeds of the law.

Having stated his conclusion, he now deals with every important issue in the early church. This issue can be summarized as follows: Given the radical distinction between Jew and Gentile as manifested in the Old Testament, doesn't this imply that the Jew will have a different way of salvation distinct from a Gentile way of salvation? Doesn't the Jew-Gentile distinction mean two different salvations as well? Maybe the Gentile, who is without the law and covenants, can be saved by faith alone. But the Jew must fulfill Mosaic righteousness as well. The Jew must have works as well as faith. Is this true?

Is he the God of the Jews only? Is he not also of the Gentiles? Yes, of the Gentiles also:

In verse 30, he states that God,

shall justify the circumsion by faith, and uncircumcision through faith.

Justification comes to Jew and Gentile only "by" or "through" faith. This much is clear.

But what we want to point out is *the reason Paul advances to prove there is only one way of salvation: by faith alone.* The reason is given in the first part of verse 30, *seeing that God is one,* he shall justify the circumcision by faith and uncircumcision through faith.

The Apostle argues that there is only one way of salvation which is by faith on the grounds that "God is one." Here we find the Apostle arguing from the unchangable character of God. Because God has only one nature or character which never changes, there can be only one way of salvation for all peoples. *Seeing there is only one God, there can be only one way of salvation.* The only way to say that there has been or is more than one way of salvation is to imply that there are more gods than one. This is impossible.

Was God "one" in the Old Testament as well as in the New? Yes. Is this one God the same God for both Testaments? Yes. Then the way of salvation by faith must be the only way of salvation in both Testaments. The Old Testament saints were saved by faith apart from the works of the law.

At this point it is crucial to emphasize that *the object and character of faith has always been the same throughout all the ages even thou there has been and now are varying degrees of understanding and knowledge in saving faith.*

I. The object of faith has always been the same: The Lord Jesus Christ.

Some have mistakenly thought the faith in the Old Testament had God the Father as its object while faith in the New Testament has the Son of God as its object. But this assumption does not do justice to the Scripture or to the Lord Jesus.

We firmly believe that Jesus Christ has always been the object of saving faith throughout the centuries. Old Testament saints were saved by believing in Him.

1. Did not the Lord Jesus exist from all eternity before His incarnation (John 1:1-18)?

2. Was it not the preincarnate Christ who walked and talked with Adam and Eve in the Garden and preached the Gospel to them (Gen. 3:1-15)?

3. Did not the preincarnate Christ appear in human form to Abraham and promise him a son (Gen. 18:13, 17-33 of John 8:56-58)?

4. Did not the preincarnate Christ appear in human form and wrestle with Jacob and bless him (Gen. 32:24)?

5. Did not Moses meet and believe in the preincarnate Christ (Ex. 3:3-6, 14 of John 8:58; Heb. 11:24-27)?

6. Did not David exhort all to trust in the Son of God (Psa. 2:11, 2)?

7. Is it not true that the Lord Jesus is pictured as the Savior in Psa. 22, the Shepherd in Psa. 23 and the Sovereign in Psa. 24 (John 10)?

8. Is it not true that the Jehovah of the Old Testament in many instances is the Jesus of the New?

9. Are not we explicitly told that Old Testament saints trusted in Christ and received life from Him (I Cor. 10:4)?

10. Did not Abraham hear of Christ in the Gospel message which we heard from Christ (Gal. 3:8, 16)?

11. Did not the Old Testament prophets speak about Christ "by the spirit of Christ which was in them" (I Pet. 1:11)?

12. Did not Agur in Prov. 30:4 reveal that he knew of the Son of God?

13. Does not Heb. 4:2 explicitly state that Israel heard the gospel during the wilderness wanderings but that it did not profit them "not being mixed with faith" (4:2 cf. 3:16-19)?

The Old Testament saints believed in the preincarnate Christ. No one can read such passages as Psa. 2 without coming to this conclusion.

II. The character of faith has always been the same.

Again, some people mistakenly think that Old Testament saints were saved by looking *forward* to the coming of Christ as we are saved by looking *back* to the work of Christ. But again we cannot agree with this notion.

1. Saving faith has as it object the *person* of Christ who accomplished redemption. Faith does *not* have as its sole or chief object the work of Christ. After all, where do we ever read in the Bible "Believe that Christ died for you"? We are told to "believe on the Lord Jesus Christ" (Acts 16:31).

2. We are not saved by looking back to the work of Christ. We are saved by looking up, believing and calling upon His name for salvation (Rom. 10:13). Saving faith is always a personal and immediate closing with Christ or coming to Christ (Matt. 11:28).

We must conclude that Old Testament saints were not saved by looking forward to the work of Christ. They were saved by looking up in present-tense faith fo Jehovah Jesus. Here are a few of the Old Testament. invitations to faith which emphasize this truth.

Look unto me, and be ye saved, all the ends of the earth: for I am God, and there is none else (Isa. 45;22).

Ho, every one that thirsteth, come ye to the waters, and he that hath no money; come ye, buy, and eat; yea, come, buy wine and milk without money and without price (Isa 55:1).

Come now, and let us reason together, saith the LORD: though your sins be as scarlet, they shall be as white as snow; though they be red like crimson, they shall be as wool (Isa. 1:18).

Be wise now therefore, O ye kings: be instructed, ye judges of the earth.

Serve the LORD with fear, and rejoice with trembling.

Kiss the Son, lest he be angry, and ye perish from the way, when his wrath is kindled but a little. Blessed are all they that put their trust in him (Psa. 2:10-12).

Commit thy way unto the LORD; trust also in him; and he shall bring it to pass (Psa. 37:5).

Trust in the LORD with all thine heart; and lean not unto thine own understanding.

In all thy ways acknowledge him, and he shall direct thy paths (Prov. 3:5, 6).

And it shall come to pass, that whosoever shall call on the name of the LORD shall be delivered: for in mount Zion and in Jerusalem shall be deliverance, as the LORD hath said, and in the remnant whom the LORD shall call (Joel 2:32).

3. We must make the distinction between *the quality of faith and the degrees of understanding faith.*

The quality of the faith of Old Testament saints was equal to or, in some cases, greater than the faith of most New Testament believers.

The faith of Old Testament believers was personal, vibrant, strong and triumphant. For this reason the New Testament writers could put forth the Old Testament saints as the Christian's example of triumphant, conquering, and persevering faith (see Heb. 11). Some of the saints were called upon to do great works. They accomplished them through their mighty faith.

But to say that the quality of the faith of Old Testament saints was equal to or greater than faith today is not the same as saying that their faith had the same *content.* They knew so little compared to what we know today. They lived in the shadows of the cross. They did not understand Christ's propitiatory death (I Pet. 1:9-12). Thus their appeal for divine forgiveness was based on God's merciful attributes instead of the blood of Christ (Psa. 51 cf. I John 1:7-2:2). Their faith was simply that God was merciful and He would take care of the sin problem somehow.

An illustration of the difference between the quality of faith and understanding in faith can be drawn from the present conversion experience of sinners. If you, as the reader, have seen saved by God's grace, perhaps you can answer these questions based on your experience.

1. How much do you know today of Christ as compared with what you knew of Him at conversion?

2. Is it not true that you have grown in your understanding?

3. Do you feel that you knew so little of the riches of God in Christ Jesus when at first you believed?

4. But is it not the case with some of you, that while your understanding has increased, the quality of your faith has decreased? Your heart has grown cold even though your knowledge has increased? Do you miss the vitality, zeal, and warmth of your first love? Others of you can humbly confess that the quality of your faith has increased along with your knowledge. To Him alone belongs the glory for this singular mercy.

5. Was this not the case with Old Testament believers? We confess, "How little they knew." But we also urge, "How mightily they believed." In the words of Hebrews 11:32-38,

> And what shall I more say? for the time would fail me to tell of Gideon, and of Barak, and of Samson, and of Jephthah; for David also, and Samuel, and of the prophets:
>
> Who through faith subdued kingdoms, wrought righteousness, obtained promises, stopped the mouths of lions.
>
> Quenched the violence of fire, escaped the edge of the sword, out of weakness were made strong, waxed valiant in fight, turned to flight the armies of the aliens.
>
> Women received their dead raised to life again: and others were tortured, not accepting deliverance; that they might obtain a better resurrection:
>
> And others had trial of cruel mockings and scourgings, yea, moreover of bonds and imprisonment:

They were stoned, they were sawn asunder, were tempted, were slain with the sword: they wandered about in sheepskins and goatskins; being destitute, afflicted, tormented;

Of whom the world was not worthy: they wandered in deserts, and in mountains, and in dens and caves of the earth.

If any doubt remains concerning the quality of the faith of Old Testament saints, we would suggest spending time in the book of Psalms. There you will find Psalms which parallel every experience in the Christian life. Your heart cannot but pray these inspired prayers and praise. You will feel one with the Psalmist in his devotions.

If you read the Psalms regularly or any portion of the Old Testament, you will have to confess, "Oh, that my faith was as strong vital and warm as theirs."

III.   Argument 3: Salvation has only one basis: The work of Jesus Christ.

We have already demonstrated that Old Testament saints were justified through faith apart from the works of the Law. But we must ask, "On what grounds or basis were they justified?"

The Apostle Paul answers this question in Romans 3:24-26,

Being justified freely by his grace through the redemption that is in Christ Jesus:

Whom God hath set forth to be a propitiation through faith in his blood, to declare his righteousness for the remission of sins that are past, through the forbearance of God;

To declare, I say, at this time his righteousness: that he might be just, and the justifier of him which believeth in Jesus.

Justification comes to a sinner by grace. It cannot be earned as Paul pointed this out particularly when discussing Abraham's justification in Romans 4:4, 5,

Now to him that worketh is the reward not reckoned of grace, but of debt.

But to him that worketh not, but believeth on him that justifieth the ungodly, his faith is counted for righteousness.

Elsewhere, the Apostle establishes the truth that grace and works can never be mixed together.

And if by grace, then is it no more of works: otherwise grace
is no more grace. But if it be of works, then is it no more grace:
otherwise work is no more work (Rom. 11:6).

But on what basis is grace given to justify the ungodly? It is on the
basis of "the redemption that is in Christ Jesus" (Rom. 3:24). How and
in what way the work of Christ is imputed to us has already been discussed in the chapter dealing with justification. Therefore, it is sufficient to say that the only way for sinners to be saved in any age is
through the grace which flows out of the saving work of Christ.

IV.   Argument 4: Salvation has essentially one content.

Have we not already virtually proven this proposition? Old Testament saints must necessarily receive and experience essentially the same
salvation which is offered in the Gospel because of:

(1) the unchangeable character of God
(2) the eternity of the cross
(3) the depravity of man
(4) the unity of the Testaments
(5) Salvation has only one: God
(6) There is only one way of salvation: faith
(7) Salvation has only one basis: grace through Christ.

*Seeing there is only one Saviour, and only one way of salvation there can
be but one salvation.* The fact that Paul taught the Old Testament saints
were justified by grace through faith on the basis of Christ's work, is
sufficient grounds to see them receive the rest of the application of salvation.

But we must carefully point out that we said that Old Testament
saints *"essentially"* possessed the same salvation. "Essentially" is not the
same as "Exactly" or "Completely."

The age of the New Covenant is superior to the Old Covenant in
many ways. Read the book of Hebrews where there is a full display
of the superiority of the New Covenant over the Old. Therefore, we
would naturally assume that New Covenant salvation must be superior over Old Covenant salvation. And, indeed, it is.

But, at this point, we must make the distinction between *the experience of salvation itself and the believer's enjoyment of it and assurance
about it.*

Essentially, salvation is the same in all ages. But until Christ came,
there could not be a full enjoyment or assurance of one's full salvation.

The Old Testament saints did not possess the light of the New Testament. Their conscience was never at rest not knowing of the ultimate sacrifice of the Lamb of God.

That this is true is seen in Hebrews 10:1-25 where we read,

For the law having a shadow of good things to come, and not the very image of the things, can never with those sacrifices, which they offered year by year continually, *make the comers thereunto perfect.*

For then would they not have ceased to be offered? because that the worshippers once purged should have *had no more conscience of sins.*

But in those sacrifices *there is a remembrance again made of sins every year.*

For it is not possible that the blood of bulls and of goats should take away sins.

Wherefore, when he cometh into the world, he saith, Sacrifice and offering thou wouldest not, but a body hast thou prepared me:

In burnt offerings and sacrifices for sin thou hast had no pleasure.

Then said I, Lo, I come (in the volume of the book it is written of me) to do thy will, O God.

Above when he said, Sacrifice and offering and burnt offerings and offering for sin thou wouldest not, neither hadst pleasure therein; which are offered by the law;

Then said he, Lo, I come to do thy will, O God. He taketh away the first, that he may establish the second.

By the which will we are sanctified through the offering of the body of Jesus Christ once for all.

And every priest standeth daily ministering and offering oftentimes the same sacrifices, which can never take away sins:

But this man, after he had offered one sacrifice for sins for ever, sat down on the right hand of God;

From henceforth expecting till his enemies be made his footstool.

For by one offering he hath perfected for ever them that are sanctified.

Whereof the Holy Ghost also is a witness to us: for after that he had said before,

This is the covenant that I will make with them after those days, saith the Lord; I will put my laws into their hearts, and in their minds will I write them;

And their sins and iniquities will I remember no more.

Now where remission of these is, there is no more suffering for sin.

Having therefore, brethren, boldness to enter into the holiest by the blood of Jesus,

By a new and living way, which he hath consecrated for us, through the veil, that is to say, his flesh;

And having a high priest over the house of God;

Let us draw near with a true heart *in full assurance of faith, having our hearts sprinkled from an evil conscience,* and our bodies washed with pure water.

Let us hold fast the profession of our faith without wavering; for he is faithful that promised;

And let us consider one another to provoke unto love and to good works:

Not forsaking the assembling of ourselves together, as the manner of some is; but exhorting one another: and so much the more, as ye see the day approaching.

In this passage, we are told that the Old Testament saint did not have a conscience liberated from being smitten by sin because! (1) he did not know of Christ's death and (2) the need for continual animal sacrifices.

But we who live after Christ know that His sacrifice was final and efficacious (vs. 10, 12), and thus a new and living way is opened for us (v. 12) so that we may have boldness to enter into God's presence without fear through the saving work of Christ (v. 19).

Old Testament believers did not have the enjoyment and assurance of salvation which is possible for the New Testament believer. They had essentially the same salvation as we do but they could not understand, enjoy or gain much assurance from it. This is the area where the superiority of New Covenant salvation outshines Old Testament revelation.

In conclusion, salvation is one in author, means, basis, and essential content. In every age sinners have been justified by grace through faith on the basis of Christ's work. In the Old Testament as in the New Testament,

"Salvation is of the Lord."

Objections Answered

Objection 1: The Holy Spirit did not savingly indwell people in the Old Testament. Until Pentecost, the Holy Spirit only came "upon" believers. John said that the Holy Spirit had not be given before Pentecost in John 7:39. If this is true, how could salvation in the Old Testament be the same as in the New?

1. It is *not* true that the Holy Spirit is said to only come "upon" Old Testament believers. If you turn to Gen. 41:38 you find that the Holy Spirit was "in" Joseph. If you compare Num. 27:18 with Deut. 34:9 you will find that the Holy Spirit came "upon" Joshua because the Holy Spirit was "in" him beforehand. Daniel was a man in whom the Holy Spirit indwelt (Dan. 4:8, 9, 18; 15:11, 14; 6:3). The Apostle Peter states plainly in I Pet. 1:11 that the Spirit of Christ was "in" the Old Testament prophets. The Apostle Paul in II Cor. 4:13 clearly quotes Psa. 116:10 as proving that David along with New Testament believers possessed the Holy Spirit. John the Baptist had the filling of the Holy Spirit from a child (Lk. 1:15). Jesus taught that Old Testament believers experienced regeneration by the Holy Spirit for not only does he invite Nicodemus to receive the new birth (John 3:3, 5) but he also tells him that it is Old Testament teaching (John 3:10). In John 14:17 Jesus said that the Holy Spirit already indwelt this disciples. The King James Version reads "shall be in you" but the better Greek reading shows *"is* in you." J.C. Ryle comments, "He is actually in you now, and shall always be in you, and never leave you." In John 20:22, Jesus communicated the Holy Spirit to His disciples. In addition to the above plain statements of Scripture, Rom. 8:9-11 and I Cor. 2:10-16 make the indwelling of the Holy Spirit essential to salvation. No one could be

saved without the indwelling of the Spirit.

2. It is *not* true that Pentecost was the first occasion of the indwelling of the Spirit or that salvation for the disciples began at Pentecost. We must understand the meaning of Pentecost as follows:

A. *The words of Jesus* — (Lk. 24:46-49; Acts 1:8)

Jesus taught that Pentecost would mean *power* for the preaching of the Gospel. Not once is salvation or the indwelling of the Holy Spirit mentioned in connection with Pentecost. The disciples were already saved (Lk. 10:20; John. 15:13, 4, 5; 17:14, etc.)

B. *The account given in Acts* — (Acts 2:1-4)

There is not one word about salvation or the indwelling of the Holy Spirit. The key phrase of Pentecost is found in verse 4 — "filled with the Holy Spirit." The phrase means they were filled with the power of the Holy Spirit and does not mean the indwelling or sealing of the Holy Spirit for salvation. Examine the following passages:

1. The same group of disciples were again "filled with the Holy Spirit" in Acts 4:31.
2. Stephen was a man "filled with the Holy Spirit" and that meant he was filled with spiritual power (Acts 6:5 of 6:8, 7:55, 56).
3. Peter was "filled with the Holy Spirit" for his preaching (Acts 4:8). Throughout Acts there are numerous examples.
4. Paul commands us as Christians "to be filled with the (Holy) Spirit" (Eph. 5:18).
5. A Biblical theological approach would see a gradual unfolding of the concept of being Spirit-filled in order to speak God's word. Notice the connection between "filling" and "speaking" in Num. 11:25; Lk. 1:15; Matt. 3:16; Acts 51:8; 4:8 and Eph. 5:18, 19.

3. John did not in fact say that "the Holy Spirit was not yet *given*, because that Jesus was not yet glorified" because the word "given" is not in the Greek. Thus John was not referring to the normal saving operations of the Spirit in bringing sinners to salvation. But rather, he was referring to the unique and special outpouring of the Spirit of Pentecost. The Holy Spirit was poured out abundantly by Christ as His reward from the Father for His obedience in life and death (Acts 2:32, 33). It is better to read John 7:39,

"The Holy Spirit had not yet *been poured out.*"

Objection 2: The Old Testament saints were under the Old Covenant while we are under the New Covenant. It only stands to reason that they could not have partaken of New Covenant blessings before the New Covenant was instituted.

1. *The New Covenant was revealed in the Old Testament, thus it is not uniquely a New Testament Truth (see Jer. 31:31-34; Ezk. 11:19-21; 36:26, 27).*

2. *The Old Testament believer, by virtue of the eternity of the cross, received New Covenant blessings from God because to God these blessings were secured for them in Christ.*

    A. *Did not the believer in the Old Testament experience regeneration; (see John 3:3, 10; Deut. 10:16 cf. Col. 2:11; Deut. 30:6; Jer. 4:4; Ezk. 18:31, etc.)*

    B. *Did not God write His Law on their hearts (see Psa. 37:31; 40:8; Isa. 57:7)?*

    C. *Did they not receive forgiveness of their sins (see Psa. 32:1, 2, 103:1-14, 10-12, 130:4; Isa. 1:18, 38:17; Micah 7:19, 8:18; etc.)?*

Scofield taught that the sins of Old Testament believers were not really forgiven but that they were only "covered" until Christ died (see N. 1 p. 110 and N. 1 p. 649).

But if "covered" does not mean unconditional and full forgiveness, then we are not yet forgiven because James 5:20 says,

Let him know, that he which converteth a sinner from the error of his way shall save a soul from death and *cover* a multitude of sins.

    D. Did not God preserve His saints in Old Testament times (Psa. 37:23-28)?

    E. Were not the Old Testament saints "in Christ" as we are told that the Spirit of Christ was "in them" and that they received life from Christ (I Pet. 1:11; I Cor. 10:4)?

Was it not by virtue of their union with Christ that they were saved? They were "in Christ" thousands of years before He came just as truly as we were "in Him" thousands of years after He died, even from all eternity.

In summary, Old Testament saints possessed New Covenant blessings by virtue of their union with their Covenant Head, the Lord Jesus Christ. There is no Biblical warrant for the teaching that Old Testament saints were saved by works and that they did not possess the same essential salvation as we do today. They were saved by grace alone through faith alone in Christ alone.

CHAPTER 20

The Love of God

The Apostle Paul prayed that the Ephesian believers would be strengthened in the inner man by the Holy Spirit and that they would experience the reality of the indwelling Christ in order that they, being rooted and grounded in the love of God, might be able to comprehend the breadth, length, height, and depth of the love of Christ which surpasses all finite human knowledge (Eph. 3:14-19). To the degree they came to comprehend and experience the matchless love of Christ, to that degree they would experience the fullness of God in their lives (Eph. 3:19).

The love of God is one of the most dynamic truths of Holy Scripture. As we grow in our understanding of the love of the triune God of Father, Son and Holy Spirit, we should grow in our appreciation of the plan of salvation which flowed from that love. Thus, we should never treat the subject of the love of God in a dry academic manner, but seek to deepen our Christian walk as well as our understanding.

In approaching this subject, there are several principles which should be observed. These principles are given in order to deliver us at the outset of our study from many foolish and unbiblical errors.

Principle 1: *Approach the subject of the love of God with an open mind and a humble heart willing to receive whatever the Bible teaches regardless if it cuts across preconceived ideas* (John 17:7).

Our attitude and manner should express the same kind of teachable spirit as manifested by David in Psalm 119:18, 27, 33, 34, etc.

285

Principle 2: *The extent and objects of God's love are determined by the na-*
ture of the love of God.

Once we arrive at the Biblical characteristics and attributes of the
nature of God's love, then, and only then, can we discern its extent.

With these basic principles in mind, let us begin our study of the
love of God throughout the Scriptures.

    I.   *The Old Testament and the love of God.*

To discover the Old Testament concept of the love of God is not very
difficult. Any believer who owns an exhaustive concordance of the Bible
such as *Strong's Concordance*, can simply look up all the references to
God's love in the Old Testament.

Upon an exhaustive word study of God's love in the Old Testament, the following conclusions are patently clear.

First, in seeking to grasp the nature of God's love in the Old Tes-
tament, it is clear that there are two different kinds or types of love.
It we fail to distinguish between them, then we will fail to grasp the
Old Testament concept of the love of God.

There is a love of God which refers to the bestowal of national, physical, or material blessings and does not refer to any bestowal of salvation (Deut. 7:12-16).

This non-redemptive love is conditional upon man's obedience and
can be rejected by man or withdrawn by God (Hos. 9:15-17).

This non-redemptive love primarily refers to those aspects of the Abrahamic covenant which were material and temporary in nature. Such
things as land, wealth, health, children, etc. (see: Gen 12:1-3; 17:1-4).

In addition to a non-redemptive conditional love of God in the Old
Testament, there is also a redemptive love of God which is concerned
with the bestowal of eternal salvation.

This redemptive love is unconditional, efficacious, and cannot be
rejected or lost (Prov. 3:12; Psa. 1:6; Jer. 31:3; Hos. 14:1-7).

Now, when we turn to consider the objects and extent of God's love
in the Old Testament, we find that the love of God in it's non-
redemptive and redemptive focus had only the covenant people in view.
Not once are we ever told in the Old Testament that God's love extended beyond the covenant community of Israel to the pagan nations
all around.

The non-redemptive love embraced the unbelieving but outwardly
obedient Jew as well as the believing sons of Abraham. But the redemptive love of God is clearly restricted to the elect of God who are

identified as the believing remnant of Israel (Isa. 10:20-22 cf. Rom. 9:23-29).

Those who hold to a universalistic view of God's love have a real problem when they read the Old Testament because there is not a single verse in it which can be used to teach that God's redemptive love has in focus all mankind. One particular verse in the Old Testament abundantly reveals the limited and particular character of God's redemptive love for His elect.

> My son, despise not the chastening of the Lord; neither be weary of his correction: For whom the Lord loveth he correcteth; even as a father the son in whom he delighteth (Prov. 3:11, 12).

The above passage presents a great dilemma for all universalists.

If God loves everyone redemptively, then God looks upon all men as His children and He, accordingly, treats them in a *corrective* way. Thus there cannot be any concept of hell or of *punitive* punishment for the unbeliever.

On the other hand, to see the love of God referred to in Proverbs 3:11, 12 as referring to God's discipline and care of the elect is the only correct interpretation possible. Solomon is using the love of God to make a distinction between the people of God and the wicked.

II.   *The love of God and the New Testament.*

When we turn to examine the love of God in the New Testament, we find that nearly every reference to it has to do with God's redemptive love. This is understandable as the New Covenant concerns spiritual blessings accompanying salvation and does not have in focus the carnal blessings of the Old Covenant (Heb. 8:8-13; 10:15-25).

The redemptive love of God in the New Testament is efficacious, irresistable, and unconditional (Rom. 8:29-30; Eph. 5:25-27; Rev. 1:5).

The objects of God's redemptive love are no longer restricted to the elect in Israel, but now Gentile elect are also included. Salvation now extends to the whole ethnic world of Jew and Gentile (Rom. 9:14-29).

The failure to see the New Testament usage of the word "world" as referring to the inclusion of Gentiles into the Church arises out of a failure to understand or appreciate the Old Testament restriction of God's love to the covenant community.

That the redemptive love of God does not have in focus all mankind, the following considerations will demonstrate.

1. In the New Testament, God's love is consistently placed as the

cause of God's eternal decree of election. Those whom God loves, He elects and predestinates unto salvation. Since God does not elect all mankind unto salvation, it is obvious that He does not redemptively love all mankind.

> For whom he did foreknow, he also did predestinate to be conformed to the image of his son, that he might be the firstborn among many brethren (Rom. 8:29).

> According as he hath chosen us in him before the foundation of the world, that we should be holy and without blame before him in love: Having predestinated us unto the adoption of children by Jesus Christ to himself, according to the good pleasure of his will (Eph. 1:4, 5).

> Knowing, brethren beloved, your election of God (I Thess. 1:4).

> But we are bound to give thanks always to God for you, brethren beloved of the Lord, because God hath from the beginning chosen you to salvation through sanctification of the Spirit and belief of the truth (II Thess. 2:13).

2. God's love not only leads to God's election but it also secures the ultimate salvation of all those chosen unto life eternal.

> I am crucified with Christ: nevertheless I live; yet not I, but Christ liveth in me: and the life which I now live in the flesh I live by the faith of the Son of God, who loved me, and gave himself for me (Gal. 2:20).

> But God, who is rich in mercy, for his great love wherewith he loved us (Eph. 2:4).

> Husbands, love your wives, even as Christ also loved the church, and gave himself for it; That he might sanctify and cleanse it with the washing of water by the word, That he might present it to himself a glorious church, not having spot, or wrinkle, or any such thing; but that it should be holy and without blemish. (Eph. 5:25-27).

> Behold, what manner of love the Father hath bestowed upon us, that we should be called the sons of God: therefore the world knoweth us not, because it knew him not (I Jn. 3:1).

> Beloved, now are we the sons of God, and it doth not yet appear what we shall be: but we know that, when he shall ap-

pear, we shall be like him; for we shall see him as he is (I Jn. 3:2).

Hereby perceive we the love of God, because he laid down his life for us: and we ought to lay down our lives for the brethren (I Jn. 3:16).

We love him, because he first loved us (I Jn. 4:19).

And from Jesus Christ, who is the faithful witness, and the first begotten of the dead, and the prince of the kings of the earth. Unto him that loved us, and washed us from our sins in his own blood (Rev. 1:5).

3. God's redemptive love causes Him to deal with believers as His dear children. He disciplines and corrects them because He loves them. The universalist is faced with the same dilemma which confronted him in the Old Testament. The limited and particular focus of God's redemptive love is obvious in the following passages.

And ye have forgotten the exhortation which speaketh unto you as unto children, My son, despise not thou the chastening of the Lord, nor faint when thou art rebuked of him: For whom the Lord loveth he chasteneth, and scourgeth every son whom he receiveth. If ye endure chastening, God dealeth with you as with sons; for what son is he whom the father chasteneth not? But if ye be without chastisement, whereof all are partakers, then are ye bastards, and not sons. Furthermore we have had fathers of our flesh which corrected us, and we gave them reverence: shall we not much rather be in subjecttion unto the Father of spirits, and live? For they verily for a few days chastened us after their own pleasure; but he for our profit, that we might be partakers of his holiness. Now no chastening for the present seemeth to be joyous, but grievous: nevertheless afterward it yieldeth the peaceable fruit of righteousness unto them which are exercised thereby. Wherefore lift up the hands which hang down, and the feeble knees; and make straight paths for your feet, lest that which is lame be turned out of the way; but let it rather be healed (Heb. 12:5-13).

As many as I love, I rebuke and chasten: be zealous therefore, and repent (Rev. 3:19).

4. The phrases "beloved of God," "beloved of the Lord" or "beloved" are only used of the people of God. If God loved all men with the same redemptive love, we would expect to see the Apostle addressing un-

believers as "beloved of the Lord." But the Apostle never did this because God's redemptive love has in focus only the elect of God.

5. As there was not a single verse in the Old Testament which taught that God's redemptive love was universal, neither do we find such a verse in the New Testament.

We are, of course, aware of the various problem texts which some have used to establish the universalistic doctrine that God loves everyone. If you are concerned over some of these texts, we would refer you back to the principles of approaching problem texts found at the end of the chapter on The Extent of the Atonement.

In order to see how these principles work out in a concrete exegesis of problem texts, the following examples are given.

I.   For God so loved the world, that he gave his only begotten Son, that whosoever believeth in him should not perish, but have everlasting life (John 3:16).

1. What is the nature of the love spoken of in the text? Ans. It has clear reference to redemptive love.

2. According to the rest of the New Testament, who are the objects of God's redemptive love? Ans. The elect or the people of God considered as believers.

3. Given the evidence from the entire New Testament, what would the natural reading of the text tell us? (a) The word "world" must refer to the elect or to the people of God. (b) The word cannot refer to all men for this would contradict the rest of the New Testament in its teaching concerning the nature and objects of redemptive love.

4. Does John use the word "world" elsewhere in his writings? Yes. John uses the word 112 times in his Gospel and Epistles.

5. What is the meaning of the word throughout his writings? There are several different meanings of the word in John's writings.

a.   The entire universe of created reality (John 15:5).
b.   The planet earth (John 21:25).
c.   The general public or a crowd of men (John 7:4, 14:22).
d.   The ethical sense of sinners under the wrath of God and in the control of Satan (I Jn. 5:19).
e.   The ethnic sense of sinners from all ranks and races of mankind, not just Jews but also Gentiles (John 1:29, 4:42 cf. 11:52, 12:32).
f.   The realm of all evil opposition to God (John 7:7; I Jn. 2:15, 16).
g.   The realm of the fallen mankind (John 9:5).

    h.   The body of God's elect (Jn. 1:29, 4:42, 6:33; 51).

6. What is the exact meaning of the word in 3:16?
Clearly not a, b, c, f, or g.
The reference has to do with human beings as seen from the reference to believers in vv. 15,16, 18 and to men in vv. 20, 21.

The emphasis in John 3 is upon men who are in danger of perishing (16), who need eternal life (15, 16), who need to be saved (15, 16, 18), who are condemned (18), who love darkness rather than light (19), who hate the light and refuse to be exposed by it (20). In short, the "world" refers to sinners who are under the wrath of God (3:36). This is clearly indicated (Warfield).

Throughout the writings of John there is an emphasis upon the gentile entrance into salvation. It cannot be doubted but that the "world" which is the object of God's love must be the "world" whose sins have been completely removed by Christ (1:29), and to whom spiritual life has been imparted (6:33, 51), and for whom full propitiation has been completed (I Jn. 2:2). This salvation extends to the Gentile as well as to the Jew. Since Christ was dealing with a Pharisee, He was emphasizing the ethnic universalism of the Gospel. (Turrettin, Owen, Hutchenson, Brown, A. Hodge, Gill, Smeaton, Pink, Lange, Godet, Hendriksen, Henry.)

There is a clear parallel construction between vs. 15-18 and within v. 16 itself which reveals that the equivalent expression for "world" is "all who believe," i.e. all believers.

Examine the following parallel construction within the passage.

A.	B.
v. 15 all who believe	have eternal life
v. 16 the world	
all who believe	may not perish
	have eternal life
v. 17 the world	
the world	should be saved
v. 18 he who believes	is not condemned

As all of column B refers to salvation, so all of column A refers to believers who are the only ones who receive salvation (Calvin, Poole, Flavel).

Conclusion

All of the above interpretations should be viewed as valid for when put together they present a beautiful picture which does full justice to the word "world" in John 3:16. This is the best interpretation possible which is consistent with the New Testament understanding of the nature and objects of God's love and the nature and extent of the death of Christ.

II.   O Jerusalem, Jerusalem, thou that killest the prophets, and stonest them which are sent unto thee, how often would I have gathered thy children together, even as a hen gathereth her chickens under her wings, and ye would not (Matt. 23:37).

1. We correctly quoted the text above because it is quoted wrongly 99% of the time. It does *not* say "How often I would have gathered *you* but *you* would not."

2. What is the larger context? The entire chapter is a unit.

3. Who is speaking? Jesus (v. 1).

4. To whom does Jesus address Himself in this discourse in the temple? In vv. 1-12 Christ is speaking to the disciples and the multitude. In vv. 13-39 Christ is speaking to the Scribes and Pharisees.

5. About whom or what is Christ speaking? The entire discourse concerns the Scribes and Pharisees (vv. 2, 13-16, 25-27, 29).

6. In what capacity does Christ particularly condemn the Scribes and the Pharisees? In their capacity of being the spiritual leaders and guides of the people of Israel (vv. 1, 2, 7, 10, 16, 24).

7. What was Christ's attitude toward the Scribes and the Pharisees? He denounced them (1-12). Then He pronounced upon them a multitude of the curses of God ("woe unto you" 13, 14, 15, 16, 23, 25, 27, 29, 38).

8. What are some of the specific reasons why Jesus cursed the Scribes and Pharisees? (1) They killed the prophets (vv. 31-35). (2) They sought to prevent and to hinder men from entering the kingdom (v. 13).

9. Now that we have seen the larger context, what is the specific context of v. 37? The following questions will tell us.

10. Who is meant by the word "Jerusalem"? Jesus was referring to the Scribes and Pharisees as seen from the following observations.

a.   They are the ones who are being spoken to according to the context and the parallel passage in Lk. 13:31-35.

b.   It is part of the last "woe" begun in verse 29.

c. The designations within v. 29 point to them
    1. They kill the prophets, cf. 31-35.
    2. They prevent men from entering the kingdom, cf. 13.
d. Their condemnation in v. 38 is repeated from 36 and else-
    where applied to them specifically (Matt 21:43-45).
e. The impossibility of the universalistic interpretation. If
    "Jerusalem" refers to all the inhabitants of the city, to whom
    does "thy children" refer?

11. What was the emotional state of Christ when He called the
Scribes and the Pharisees "Jerusalem"? Christ was in a state of righteous anger and He pronounced a curse upon them. There were no
tears and no sobs.

III. And when he was gone forth into the way, there came one
      running and kneeled to him, and asked him, Good Master,
      what shall I do that I may inherit eternal life? And Jesus
      said unto him. Why callest thou me good? There is none
      good but one, that is, God. Thou knowest the command-
      ments, Do not commit adultery, Do not kill, Do not steal,
      Do not bear false witness, Defraud not, Honour thy father
      and mother. And he answered and said unto him, Master,
      all these have I observed from my youth. Then Jesus be-
      holding him loved him, sell whatsoever thou hast, and give
      to the poor, and thou shalt have treasure in heaven: and
      come, take up the cross, and follow me. And he was sad
      at that saying, and went away grieved: for he had great pos-
      session. And Jesus looked round about and saith unto his
      disciples. How hardly shall they that have riches enter into
      the kingdom of God! And the disciples were astonished at
      His words. But Jesus answereth again, and saith unto them,
      Children, how hard is it for them that trust in riches to
      enter into the kingdom of God! It is easier for the camel
      to go through the eye of a needle, than for a rich man to
      enter into the kingdom of God. And they were astonished
      out of measure, saying among themselves, who then can
      be saved? And Jesus looking upon them saith, With men
      it is impossible, but not with God: for with God all things
      are possible" (Mk. 10:17-27).

1. What was the context of Christ's loving the rich young ruler?

   a. The young man ran to Christ which showed his *eagerness.*

b.   He knelt before Christ which showed his *reverence*.
c.   He called Christ, "Good Master" and "Teacher" which showed his *understanding*.
d.   He did these things in public which showed his *boldness*.
e.   He asked the right question which showed his *wisdom*.
f.   He was a keeper of the Law from his youth which showed his *morality*.
g.   Having seen and heard all this, Jesus looks upon him.

2. It was at the point of looking upon this young man that we read, "Jesus felt a love for him." It was not continuous love which Jesus had for him from all eternity. It was a temporary love which came into being upon looking at the man. It was a pleasant positive feeling which was produced in Christ when He observed these virtuous attitudes and actions in the young man. Christ loved His own from the beginning to the end (John 13:1). The love spoken of in this passage clearly began when Jesus looked upon him. And a temporary sorrow replaced this temporary love after the man forsook Christ. Both the context and the construction of the verse points to a temporary love. They cannot be twisted to refer to eternal redemptive love. Yet, even if one is determined to see redemptive love in this verse, then the only conclusion which we can come to and be consistent with the rest of the New Testament is that the young man was eventually saved. There is even an ancient tradition that says that this young man was actually Saul of Tarsus who later became the Apostle Paul.

Conclusion

Oh, the depths of both the wisdom and grace of God! The atonement reveals the mercy of God to helpless sinners. Jesus Christ and His work are the only foundation of acceptance before God.

Once we grasp the richness of God's provision in the saving work of Christ, the attempt to present us to free-civilian, baptism or decessoresm as the ground of salvation will foil. Once we have Christ, our soul-thirst has been quenched and we feel no need of human merit.

Appendix

Calvin and Universal Atonement

Certain Evangelical theologians (such as A.H. Strong and Thiessen) have dogmatically stated that John Calvin believed in universal atonement. They also stated that all orthodox Calvinists are hyper-calvinists (Thiessen, p. 329 and Strong, p. 777). We thus find a situation where they non-Calvinists calls the Calvinists to believe as Calvin believed!

To the Biblically informed Christian, the doctrine of particular redemption rests securely upon the Scriptures and thus he really is not concerned with any man's acceptance or rejection of this precious truth of God's Word.

But for the sake of historical accuracy and theological precision, the question concerning Calvin's belief about the extent of the atonement should be fully answered. It can be clearly demonstrated that Calvin believed in particular redemption and that he did not believe in universal redemption.

I. Argument #1:

No evidence has ever been presented from Calvin's own writings to prove that he believed in universal atonement. Thiessen does not give **one** single reference in all of Calvin's writings to back up his statement. Strong does not give any references either but he presents a spurious composition of his own invention which has been rejected by all Calvin scholars. Others point to Calvin's universal offer of the Gospel and, in ignorance, confuse it with universal atonement. There is not a single sentence in Calvin's writings which either denies limited atonement or promotes universal atonement.

II. Argument #2:

There are definite, clear-cut places in Calvin's writings where he denies universal atonement and teaches particular redemption.

A. In "De vera pariticapatione Christi in coena" Calvin says, "Scire velim quomodo Christi edany impil pro quibut non est crucifixa, et quonodo sanguinem bibant qui exiandis eorun peccatis non est effusus." Tratatus Theologic 1, Opera, tom., p. 731. "(I would like) to know what way can the wicked eat the flesh of Christ which was not crucified for them? And in what way can they drink the blood of Christ which was not shed to expiate their sins?"

The reason why Calvin did not allow unbelievers to the Lord's Table was that it was only for those for whom Christ had died. It was reserved for the elect who manifested themselves in this world by repentance and faith.

B. Calvin taught that all the ones for whom Christ died, died in union with Christ. And as a direct result, they will infallibly receive two blessings: "liberation from death and mortification of the flesh" (Institutes, II, XV-7). This limits Christ's death to those who will be saved, i.e. the elect.

C. Calvin viewed Christ's redemption as being efficacious, i.e. it actually secured the eternal redemption of all those for whom He died (Institutes II XVII).

D. Calvin taught that God loved the elect and planned their holiness and salvation while on the other hand, He hated the reprobate and planned their sin and damnation (Institutes III, XXII-11, XXIII, XXIV-12-17).

E. In the "key" passages where universalists seek to prove their doctrine, Calvin consistently gave the standard Reformed interpretation in which he rejects universal redemption. Check his commentaries and Institutes in the following pages.

1.	I John 2:2	"Whole world" = whole Church.
2.	I Tim. 2:4	"all men" = not all men as individuals but classes such as princes.
3.	John 1:29	"the world" = Gentile as well as Jew.
4.	Ezek. 33:11	"the wicked" = the elect penitent sinners.
5.	II Pet. 3:9	"all" = the elect.

F. In the "key passages where Calvinists prove their doctrines," Calvin gives the Reformed exegisis in his commentaries.

1. John 17:2, 9
2. John 10:8, 10, 11, 26
3. Isa. 53

G. All the great Reformed creeds which flowed from Calvin's Reformation teach the doctrine of particular redemption.

III. Argument #3

Calvin clearly believed in man's depravity, unconditional and particular election, the irresistible work of the Spirit and the final perseverance and preservation of the elect. Universal redemption is inconsistent with these beliefs. Calvin was such a clear thinker that if he held to universal redemption, he would have offered an explanation for his blatant inconsistency. There is no evidence of such an inconsistency or explanation.

IV. Argument #4:

Calvin's contemporaries at Geneva, such as Beza, clearly taught particular redemption. If Calvin believed in universal atonement, his close friends would have known. There is not one single reference in all the literature of his contemporaries that even suggests a suspicion that Calvin was a universalist. He supported Beza's attack on the Lutheran doctrine of universal atonement. This alone is certain evidence as to where Calvin stood.